A GRAMMY® SALUTE
TO MUSIC LEGENDS

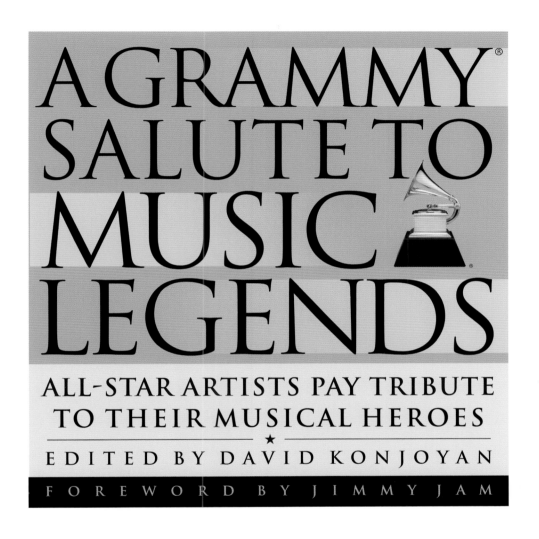

A GRAMMY
SALUTE TO
MUSIC
LEGENDS

ALL-STAR ARTISTS PAY TRIBUTE
TO THEIR MUSICAL HEROES

★

EDITED BY DAVID KONJOYAN

FOREWORD BY JIMMY JAM

HAL LEONARD BOOKS
An Imprint of Hal Leonard LLC

A Grammy salute to music legends

Published in 2017 by Hal Leonard Books
An Imprint of Hal Leonard LLC
7777 West Bluemound Road
Milwaukee, WI 53213

Trade Book Division Editorial Offices
33 Plymouth St., Montclair, NJ 07042

Printed in the United States of America

Book design by John J. Flannery

Library of Congress Cataloging-in-Publication Data

Names: Konjoyan, David, editor.
Title: A Grammy salute to music legends : all-star artists pay tribute to
  their musical heroes / edited by David Konjoyan.
Description: Milwaukee, WI : Hal Leonard Books, 2017.
Identifiers: LCCN 2016037273 | ISBN 9781495045202 (hardcover)
Subjects: LCSH: Grammy Awards.
Classification: LCC ML76.G7 G73 2017 | DDC 780.92/2--dc23
LC record available at https://lccn.loc.gov/2016037273

ISBN: 978-1-4950-4520-2

www.halleonardbooks.com
www.grammy.com

CONTENTS

FOREWORD

JIMMY JAM

In October 2016, my partner Terry Lewis and I were proud to help present the man known as the Godfather of Black Music, our mentor Clarence Avant, with a star on the Hollywood Walk of Fame. As I said at the time, "There would be no Jimmy Jam & Terry Lewis without Clarence Avant."

So who is Clarence Avant? If you don't know, that's one of the important—and I'd add enlightening and entertaining—things you'll learn in this book, and you'll learn it as told by another of his famous mentees, Kenny "Babyface" Edmonds. You'll not only get a deeper appreciation of some of the most groundbreaking artists of the recorded music era, but also a better understanding of how dynamic and interconnected the world of music is. In each essay, a noteworthy musical figure explains how there would be no them without the honoree in question.

Beyond the effect Clarence had on my career, I was also inspired and influenced by so many of the honorees represented here. Like everyone else in the arts, I stand on the shoulders of those who came before me. We all take a little bit of stardust from those stars and use it to fire our imaginations and create new galaxies in a well-established musical universe.

Understanding that each groundbreaking moment in music can create ripples across generations, The Recording Academy focuses a significant portion of its Grammy Awards efforts on the legacies and impact of music's most towering figures through the Special Merit Awards: the Lifetime Achievement Award, Trustees Award, and Technical Grammy Award.

Potential recipients of these awards are brought forward by a committee of experts each year, with 10–12 new honorees ratified by The Academy's Board of Trustees for inclusion in this rarified list.

From 2007–2013, I served as The Recording Academy's Chair and then Chair Emeritus, so I have firsthand knowledge of The Academy's dedication to valuing the essential contributions of music's pioneers. In addition to recognition through these awards, The Academy's efforts include the Grammy Museums in both Los Angeles and Mississippi—where the rich history of music is complemented by technologically advanced interactive exhibits—and education and preservation initiatives such as Living Histories and grant programs that capture the oral histories of legendary music figures and provide funds to preserve and catalog important music collections, respectively.

I've also had the pleasure of participating in many of the annual presentations of these awards, and I'm always moved when I see in the honorees' eyes and hear in their words the appreciation of knowing their legacy has touched so many people.

When I was growing up in Minneapolis—with my musical peers such as Prince, the Time, Morris Day, Jesse Johnson, Alexander O'Neal, and Cynthia Johnson, who would all go on to make a giant impact on music in the '80s and beyond—we were influenced by everything we heard. Early on I listened to pop like America, Seals & Crofts, Chicago, and the Carpenters. When I was 13 I met Terry Lewis, who introduced me to Earth, Wind & Fire; New Birth; and Tower of Power. And in my teens, I was all about Philadelphia International and Kenny Gamble, Leon Huff, and Thom Bell. All the millions of people who have listened to and watched Prince over the years know the debts he owed to James Brown, Jimi Hendrix, Sly Stone, and others.

It's the same for all the writers in this book who show their love and respect for the artists and music industry figures who have impacted their creative lives. It's less "what have you done for me lately," and more "thank you for all you have done for us forever."

A NOTE FROM THE PRESIDENT/CEO OF THE RECORDING ACADEMY

NEIL PORTNOW

For a number of years, I've said that, in many ways, The Recording Academy's Special Merit Awards may be the most heartwarming part of our Grammy Awards process. These awards celebrate a lifetime of achievement, and they generally come at a reflective time in the honorees' lives. At the annual Grammy Week event honoring these recipients, guests have been treated to some of the most genuinely warm, inspiring, and grateful stories and recollections of creative lives well lived.

As truly wonderful as these events have been, in 2016 we had the opportunity to partner with PBS' *Great Performances* to present our Special Merit Awards for the first time on TV with "Grammy Salute to Music Legends." With honorees as wide-ranging as Ruth Brown; John Cage; Celia Cruz; Earth, Wind & Fire; pro audio company EMT; the godfather of stereophonic audio Dr. Harvey Fletcher; Nashville record executive Fred Foster; Herbie Hancock; Jefferson Airplane; Linda Ronstadt; Run DMC; and music archivist Chris Strachwitz, and performers including Lila Downs, Shelby Lynne, Martina McBride, and Naughty by Nature, the show was a remarkable way to highlight the importance of musical legacy and its continuing impact on today's artists.

Whether celebrated at a relatively small, private affair, or in the homes of exponentially more TV viewers, the spirit of *A Grammy Salute to Music Legends* is the spirit of appreciation, generosity, and respect that artists have for one another, as the very personal and reverential artist-written essays in this book make clear.

ACKNOWLEDGMENTS

To all of the Special Merit Awards recipients and tribute writers represented in this book, our great appreciation for your contributions to our culture.

Our deepest thanks to:

Neda Azarfar
Jamie Barnett
Kiana Butler
John Cerullo
Kelly Darr
Renée Fabian
John J. Flannery
Bill Freimuth
Lindsay Gabler
Bill Gibson
Jimmy Jam
Terry Lickona
Margaret R. Marshall
Tim McPhate
Ann Meckelborg
Philip Merrill
Miranda Moore
Amy Pandya
Neil Portnow
Tilman Reitzle
Wes Seeley
Lindsay Wagner
All of the artists' representatives who graciously helped coordinate these tributes
Everyone at The Recording Academy

A GRAMMY® SALUTE
TO MUSIC LEGENDS

INTRODUCTION

David Konjoyan

What becomes a legend most? According to The Recording Academy, which presents the annual Grammy Awards, it's a Special Merit Award. While the Grammys honor the best recordings in a given year, the Special Merit Awards—specifically, the Lifetime Achievement Award, Trustees Award, and Technical Grammy Award—acknowledge a career's worth of contributions to the recording arts. Think of it as a kind of Nobel Prize for music: an acknowledgment of all-time legends by an organization of their peers.

Unlike many such awards, such as the Rock and Roll or Country Music Halls of Fame, The Recording Academy acknowledges all genres as well as executive and technical luminaries, and even less-obvious contributors to the recording arts, such as photographers and comedians.

Perhaps it's fitting that Nikola Tesla, one of the great-grandfathers of radio, said "the sphere of external influence extends to infinite distance." And it's a true cliché of unknown origin that creators and inventors stand on the shoulders of giants.

Through the '50s, '60s, '70s, and even into the '80s, the honorees represented in this book created and expanded blues, classical, country, R&B, rock, rap, and other forms of music The Recording Academy celebrates with its Special Merit Awards.

As with other innovations, whether science-, technology-, or business-related, none happen in a vacuum, and all have deep reverberations. And that's what this book is all about: the sources of those reverberations and the revelations of those who were impacted by them and filtered them into their own groundbreaking work.

In my role at the Grammys, I edit the annual program book that celebrates each awards show and is presented to the artists, musicians, and VIPs in the live audience. The book's purpose is to add context to the awards by providing information on that year's nominees. Its less-stated purpose is to serve as a souvenir of the Grammy telecast. I've seen nominees take several copies home with them at night's end, despite the fact they often don't have personal assistants to tote the books around through the show and several after-parties. In 1999 I held two copies in safekeeping for Elvis Costello so he could visit the men's room unencumbered on the night he won the Best Pop Collaboration with Vocals category for "I Still Have That Other Girl," a song from his project with Burt Bacharach.

One of the highlights of the Grammy program book has always been our Special Merit Awards section. In it, legendary honorees are paid tribute via page-long testimonials by noted artists, musicians, and others who worked with the honorees, grew up as fans, or whose lives and careers were altered by the honorees' gravitational pull. Collected in this book are many of these appreciations, which have been generally seen only by those who attend the Grammy Awards.

Sometimes when "assigning" these, the idea is to create the unexpected, such as having Red Hot Chili Peppers bassist Flea honor jazz giant Charlie Haden, Queen guitarist Brian May swoon over singer/actress Doris Day, or Sen. Patrick Leahy write about his seemingly unlikely relationship with the Grateful Dead. Sometimes it's following the trail of influence: the spirit of empowerment embodied in Melissa Etheridge's salute to Janis Joplin, Ice Cube's homage to Run DMC, or then-teen phenomenon Taylor Swift reflecting on the work of Brenda Lee, a teen star from several generations earlier. And sometimes it's about keying in on the definitive counterpart: Dwight Yoakam on Merle Haggard or Booker T. Jones praising the Memphis Horns.

Just as they do in the studio, all of these artists work differently. Sometimes you reach out to an artist's camp with a request, and three weeks later a fully formed appreciation shows up on your doorstep, like a package you forgot you ordered from Amazon.

Others take a little more hand-holding. This means checking in regularly, offering advice, or providing some guidance—a process not unusual for musicians who routinely collaborate on projects.

Then there are those who take a more active role, not just writing the piece, but editing it as well. While this may sound like a nightmare to the editors out there, it's actually been a rewarding experience.

Dwight Yoakam, who delivered a truly masterful tribute to his local hero, fellow Bakersfield country music great Merle Haggard, got on the phone with me to go over his piece, line by line. It was neither obsessive nor charged with self-doubt. It truly struck me as beautiful caretaking. It seemed to me more an effort to make Merle proud, to treat a king respectfully. Of course, it helped that Dwight was as pleasant as could be.

Later, as that year's Grammys approached, I saw Dwight at the annual Pre-Grammy Gala thrown by Clive Davis and The Recording Academy. I had heard just days before that Merle was reported to have lung cancer. I'm not sure what made me think this was a good idea at a party, but I mentioned the health issue to Dwight. He was unaware, and it was a visible downer. Hopefully he still enjoyed the party, and happily, Merle lived another 10 years.

Patti Smith began her professional career as a journalist, poet, and playwright, so it's no surprise she turned out to be a strong editor. After delivering an engrossing tale of what Jefferson Airplane and San Francisco's Summer of Love meant to her as a young girl developing her passions in life, she and her assistant emailed me to correct name spellings and grammar issues.

Some of the best of these appreciations are those where the spirit of the artist you know on record and in public life shines through in their prose.

Flea penned the most ingeniously rambling love letter to jazz bassist Charlie Haden. He exceeded our stated word count, but such things are easily overlooked when the extra words are assembled so artfully.

I have told colleagues for the last few years that when we asked Kris Kristofferson to write a few paragraphs in honor of Leonard Cohen, he delivered a kind of free-verse poem, which was befitting both artists. I knew that Kris was a uniquely gifted songwriter with a Rhodes Scholar background, and the gem he delivered was proof of his well-rounded talents.

The shortest appreciation we ever received came from Kid Rock, who wrote of the Allman Brothers in some of the simplest prose this side of Hemingway: "If I need to explain to you how great the Allman Brothers are you will never understand anything pertaining to music."

In a few cases we've been lucky to get contributions from greats who have since died.

Venerable Atlantic Records cofounder Ahmet Ertegun wrote fondly in 2001 of his friend and Turkish countryman Arif Mardin, the Atlantic house producer who worked on the classic sides Aretha Franklin cut for the label, was a producer on the highly respected Dusty Springfield Southern soul album *Dusty in Memphis*, and helped the Bee Gees transition from Beatlesque pop rockers to urban blue-eyed soul stars.

In 2007 bassist Charlie Haden paid tribute to jazz innovator Ornette Coleman. Haden was part of Coleman's quartet (along with cornet player Don Cherry and drummer Billy Higgins) that forever altered the course of jazz with 1959's *The Shape of Jazz to Come*, and in his appreciation he provided a sense of how that watershed moment came to be.

That same year, New Orleans' favorite son Allen Toussaint honored his longtime engineer Cosimo Matassa (both sadly have since passed).

In 2009 Dave Brubeck, the man who brought West Coast jazz to the masses, saluted influential label executive and producer George Avakian. (Brubeck would pass in 2012, but Avakian remains a part of the music community at 97.)

These tributes also show how interrelated the performing arts are. The contributors here include Dan Aykroyd (on Booker T. & the MG's), Carol Burnett (on Julie Andrews), and John Lithgow (on Cab Calloway)—all of whom were touched in different ways by those honorees, and all of whom have close musical ties.

Aristotle said, "Man is by nature a political animal," so it's not surprising that even current Sen. Patrick Leahy and Rep. John Conyers Jr. contributed pieces on artists with whom they had an association: the Grateful Dead and Ruth Brown, respectively. Leahy's befriending of the Dead may surprise some, but his recollections of their relationship show sincere respect on both sides. Conyers provided some political clout when Brown spearheaded efforts to regain royalties for artists, in particular for early R&B stars, from labels that had pioneered creative accounting in the music industry.

Though the tributes in this book reflect less than one-third of all the Special Merit Awards recipients through the years (specifically, those since we started commissioning these appreciations roughly 20 years ago), they still reveal the connections between these honorees: how small groups of talented people came together at just the right historic moment, often in very specific geographic locations, to change music history.

Memphis, Tennessee-based Sun Records was arguably the birthplace of rock and roll in the '50s. In the '60s and early '70s, the city became the birthplace of Southern soul, represented by honorees Estelle Axton, the cofounder of Stax Records, Booker T. & the MG's, Al Bell, Willie Mitchell, and the Memphis Horns.

New York's Brill Building was the center of industry titan Don Kirshner's music publishing empire, giving rise to such songwriting stars as Burt Bacharach, Carole King, and Barry Mann and Cynthia Weil. But it also provided a wellspring of songs for such label owners as Scepter Records' Florence Greenberg, who signed Dionne Warwick based on a Brill Building song demo.

The essential role New Orleans played in rock and R&B history is marked by producer/songwriters Dave Bartholomew and Allen Toussaint and engineer Cosimo Matassa—all of whom worked together—as well as with earlier honorees such as Fats Domino.

And San Francisco's fertile Haight-Ashbury was the epicenter of the hippie music culture in the '60s, spawning bands the Grateful Dead and Jefferson Airplane, and drawing Texas transplant Janis Joplin to its embrace of the counterculture and sexual revolution.

One thing I've learned through this process is that artists are generally quick to accept the assignment of praising the artists who influenced them. While most likely deliberate for weeks with agents and managers on tour dates, opening acts, or which studio to record in, they often respond the same day to a request to write about their spiritual mentors. And if you think it's just because it's not as weighty a decision as, say, planning a tour, I don't believe that's the case. Once accepted, many of these artists then take every hour of their allotted time to deliver 350–400 words they deem suitable for the subject. Some have even dropped the assignment, not because it doesn't rate in their busy schedule, but because they're just not coming up with the right words, or they're not "feeling it" in a manner worthy of the subject.

I think many of these artists approach these appreciations much the way they would songwriting. Some are practiced at pounding out a song in a workmanlike fashion, punching in and not leaving until a song is in hand. But others need to follow their muse, to have that lightning strike, finding just the right turn of phrase that sums up their feelings.

However they work, each of these tributes is crafted from the heart and reflects the spirit of what Recording Academy Trustees were ultimately aiming for when they went through a fairly laborious process of imagining and creating them.

The Academy was formally founded in 1958 and staged its first Grammy Awards (a hotel dinner) in 1959, but as early as 1960 The Academy's Board of Trustees, while conducting other business such as trying to get a nascent Grammy Awards show off the ground and literally finding the resources to keep the young organization's lights on, suggested the need for a special award to honor a person who had made an "overwhelming" contribution to the industry.

The next year, at the official Trustees meeting on October 7–8, 1961, at the Beverly Hilton Hotel, a resolution was passed "that the National Awards Committee make recommendations to the Trustees as to what various . . . Merit Awards are to be recommended for approval this year."

However, at the next Trustees meeting, taking place October 13–14, 1962, it was noted no action on the award had been taken, and the apparently unanswered question was posed as to whether the Trustees wanted to appoint one or more members to look into it further.

At that meeting, Trustee Michael Kapp (who came from a royal family of the industry—his brother Jack had run the American arm of Decca Records, and brother David launched Kapp Records) suggested special awards be given to pioneers of the industry.

The first actual action on a special award came in 1963. Bob Yorke, an RCA Records vice president, made the recommendation to present a Golden Achievement Award to Bing Crosby on the Grammy show (at the time, a taped network special sponsored by Timex). It was later resolved that the Golden Achievement Award would from that point forward be called the Bing Crosby Award. As a result, 1963 saw Crosby receive the first-ever Recording Academy Special Merit Award.

Even after the adoption of the Crosby Award, throughout the '60s several other special awards were suggested but never ratified, including Best New Country and Western Artist,

Most Promising New Classical Recording Artist, and Best Composition by a Contemporary Classical Composer, among others.

But by 1968, only five Crosby Award recipients had been honored. The Academy's Trustees had deliberately set the bar high for ratifying an honoree—a three-quarter vote—and were beginning to come to terms with the fact that approving honorees was a steeper hurdle than they may have intended.

Trustee Stan Cornyn, the influential Warner Bros. Records creative services guru, stated at the annual meeting in 1969 that special awards were a major function of The Academy, as they represented the one avenue Trustees had to select people who did not fit into the Awards categories but deserved recognition.

Still finding their collective footing regarding awards of special merit, the Trustees sparked a bit of controversy in 1971 when it was determined the Bing Crosby Award would go to Elvis Presley. A&M Records cofounder Jerry Moss wrote a letter to then–Academy National President Wesley H. Rose suggesting that giving the Crosby award to rock and roll artists such as Presley was inappropriate. This followed an open letter from producer Phil Spector to the *Los Angeles Times* calling the award equivalent to giving the Kate Smith Award to Bob Dylan.

It was moved at that year's Trustees meeting to dispose of the Bing Crosby Award. Ultimately, the few recipients of the award would be folded into the roster of the Lifetime Achievement Award, which was yet to be created.

The remainder of the decade would see more wrestling with the appropriate ratification vote and the names and purpose of the awards to be presented. By the end of the '70s, only the following awards had been formalized:

Trustees Awards
1967: John Culshaw/Georg Solti
1968: Krzysztof Penderecki, Duke Ellington/Billy Strayhorn
1970: Dr. Robert Moog
1971: John Hammond, Chris Albertson, Larry Hiller
(the above awarded for specific records or works)
1971: Paul Weston
1972: The Beatles
1977: Thomas A. Edison
1977: Leopold Stokowski
1979: Goddard Lieberson, Frank Sinatra

Bing Crosby Award
1963: Bing Crosby (as Golden Achievement Award)
1965: Frank Sinatra
1966: Duke Ellington
1967: Ella Fitzgerald
1968: Irving Berlin
1971: Elvis Presley
1972: Mahalia Jackson, Louis Armstrong

That's 21 honorees over a period of 20 years since the very first mention of a special award in 1960, with some pretty large lapses in between, including a four-year period between 1972–1977 with no Trustees Awards and two multiyear blank spaces for the Bing Crosby Award between 1962–1965 and 1968–1971.

Nevertheless, it seems clear from the record that The Academy wanted to present more awards, and in 1982 The Academy's Special Merit Awards would enter their contemporary age.

The Bing Crosby Award became The Recording Academy Lifetime Achievement Award, and was designated as strictly for performers. Then, in 1983, the Trustees determined that the Trustees Award would be presented for nonperforming contributions, to complement the Lifetime Achievement Award.

For the first time, candidates were put forward for vote at the Trustees meeting. The recommendations were:

Lifetime Achievement Award
Jointly to Charlie Parker, Thelonious Monk, and Dizzy Gillespie (though it was ultimately moved to present only to Charlie Parker)
Chuck Berry
Al Jolson
Arturo Toscanini
Antal Doráti
Sarah Vaughan

Trustees Award
Béla Bartok
Peter Goldmark & Associates (from CBS Labs, which helped develop microgroove recording technology)
Chuck Berry, Charlie Parker, Arturo Toscanini, Sarah Vaughan, and Béla Bartok would ultimately be ratified, marking the beginning of multiple annual honorees.

Today, The Academy awards five Special Merit Awards that go beyond the scope of the annual Grammy Awards: the Lifetime Achievement Award, the Trustees Award, and the Technical Grammy Award (whose recipients are represented in this book), as well as the Music Educator Award, and, presented on occasion, the Grammy Legend Award. Through 2016, there have been a total of 351 recipients across all the awards. Not counting those who have received multiple awards, that's nearly 350 of the most essential musical figures of the recorded music era.

For anyone looking for a starting place in understanding and appreciating the artists, producers, songwriters, and innovators who created the music by which we love, cry, celebrate, and dance, and share as our universal language, look no further than these lists (available on page 187).

And as you explore the tributes contained in this book, consider the words of William Shakespeare: "If music be the food of love, play on." Or, in Little Richard's translation, "Wop bop a loo bop a lop bom bom!"

THE ALLMAN BROTHERS BAND

LIFETIME ACHIEVEMENT AWARD, 2012

WirelImage.com

When Duane Allman convinced soul singer Wilson Pickett to record the Beatles' "Hey Jude" during a 1969 session at Muscle Shoals' Fame Studios, to which Allman added an incendiary guitar solo coda, many argue the foundation for southern rock had been laid.

When the Allman Brothers Band (guitarist Duane, keyboardist/vocalist Gregg Allman, guitarist/vocalist Dickey Betts, bassist Berry Oakley, and drummers Butch Trucks and Jaimoe) formed later in 1969, the brothers brought their love of southern R&B and soul to their mix of rock and blues. Former Otis Redding manager Phil Walden, who had persuaded Duane to form a band, signed the Allmans to his new Capricorn label, and a new sound, emanating from a rootsy label that understood its authenticity, was born.

The band never had a huge chart presence with their singles, though songs such as "Melissa" and "Midnight Rider" would become rock standards, and "Ramblin' Man" hit No. 2 on the *Billboard* Hot 100. Their Grammy Hall of Fame–inducted live album *At Fillmore East* captured a band that brought jazz-level interplay and interpretation to the jam-band aesthetic.

The remarkable artistic heights the band scaled in a short period ended just as quickly. Duane was killed in a motorcycle accident in 1971, and Oakley died after a motorcycle crash a year later. The band has carried on through the decades with Gregg leading the fight, and has featured excellent additional players such as guitarists Warren Haynes and Derek Trucks (Butch's nephew).

Even though their most essential work was created over the course of less than a half-decade, the Allmans would influence countless musicians, and not just those who would go on to form southern rock acts such as Lynyrd Skynyrd, the Marshall Tucker Band, and Little Feat.

My friend Jackie Avery called me and said, "Duane wanted to know if you'd play in his band." I said, "Man, I'm going to New York to be a jazz musician and starve to death." And he said, "Well Jai, before you go to New York and starve to death, why don't you go through Alabama and talk to Duane and maybe play with him a couple of days." I thought about it, maybe 15 seconds. Then I remember a little light bulb went off in my head. A friend of mine named Charles Otis, when I was 16 years old, told me, "If you want to make some money, go play with them white boys."

—Jaimoe, acceptance speech, 2012

THE ALLMAN BROTHERS BAND
Tribute by Kid Rock
February 12, 2012

If I need to explain to you how great the Allman Brothers are you will never understand anything pertaining to music. And I love Dickey Betts.

God bless the Allman Brothers Band.

(Five-time Grammy nominee Kid Rock joined the Allman Brothers Band onstage at one of their 40th anniversary concerts at New York's Beacon Theatre in 2009.)

Tribute by Kenny Wayne Shepherd

Every time I hear an Allman Brothers Band song I can't help but stop what I'm doing and listen. Their music is impossible to ignore, and is the thread that holds the fabric of southern rock together. Being from the South myself, I grew up listening to these guys, and they seem to have created the soundtrack to my childhood. As a result, the music of the Allman Brothers has played an instrumental role in influencing who I am as an artist and how my music is written and performed. I'm certain I am only one of many musicians who will so readily admit this.

The Allman Brothers Band were formed in Jacksonville, Florida, in 1969 by brothers Duane and Gregg Allman. Many have called the band the principal architects of southern rock. By incorporating elements of blues, jazz, and country music, they created a signature sound that is immediately identifiable to all generations of music lovers. Songs such as "Ramblin' Man," "Midnight Rider," "Melissa," "Whipping Post," "Jessica," "One Way Out," and "Statesboro Blues" have solidified the Allman Brothers' place in music history.

The band has continued to reinvent themselves by adding some of the best players in the industry with each incarnation while maintaining their signature sound. The list of members reads like a *Who's Who* of southern rock and jam-band royalty: Duane and Greg Allman, Dickey Betts, Berry Oakley, Butch Trucks, Jai Johanny "Jaimoe" Johanson, Chuck Leavell, Lamar Williams, Johnny Neel, Marc Quiñones, Allen Woody, Warren Haynes, Jimmy Herring, Oteil Burbridge, and Derek Trucks, among others.

Having produced 11 gold and four platinum albums from 1971–2004, being inducted into the Rock and Roll Hall of Fame in 1995, and with four of their guitarists voted as members of *Rolling Stone*'s 100 Greatest Guitarists of All Time list, the Allman Brothers Band have serious pedigree.

I have been blessed to share the stage with this incredible band, and have gotten to know several members personally. They are top-notch musicians and top-notch people. It's my honor to pay tribute to one of the greatest rock and roll bands of all time, and to thank them for changing the face of music forever, and for the better.

(Kenny Wayne Shepherd is a five-time Grammy nominee.)

JULIE ANDREWS
LIFETIME ACHIEVEMENT AWARD, 2011

WireImage.com

Can you really say anything negative about Mary Poppins? Probably not and get away with it. Surely social media shaming would follow. But acknowledging Julie Andrews' star-making turns in *Mary Poppins* (1964) and *The Sound of Music* (1965)—and her persona in those films as a decorous Englishwoman who just happened to be gifted with a stunning singing voice—is to also point out the stereotyping she had to overcome to create a varied and ongoing stage, film, and singing career.

Those two films, which established Andrews in the minds of millions of moviegoers and music listeners, came just as turbulence was beginning to buffet a society wrestling with Vietnam and a burgeoning counterculture. No spoonful of sugar could cure the changing of the times, and Andrews would soon find herself somewhat out of favor, despite the fact that she had starred in the longest-running Broadway musical at that time (*My Fair Lady*), had one of the top-grossing films of all time (*The Sound of Music*), and sold millions of soundtrack and original cast albums. (The original cast albums for *Camelot*, *Mary Poppins*, and *My Fair Lady* and the soundtrack to *The Sound of Music* have all been inducted into the Grammy Hall of Fame.)

As a result, Andrews' second career act began early, but she won new fans and established a legacy beyond her high-profile early accomplishments. In 1969, Andrews married filmmaker Blake Edwards, whom she met while shooting his *Darling Lili*. After a somewhat dry period during the '70s, Andrews' union with Edwards would bear more than marital fruit when she starred in his hits *S.O.B.* and *Victor Victoria* in the early '80s. (The latter brought her third Oscar nomination.)

Ultimately, all this would lead to further TV specials and recordings, and her position as a revered and refined leading lady of entertainment, even if you do still think of her primarily as the singer of "Supercalifragilisticexpialidocious" and "My Favorite Things."

The sounds of music have been my life from my early days as a child in English musicals to the present, and they have created opportunities beyond my wildest imaginings. Playing in this sandbox has brought me so much joy and hopefully to others as well.
                                        —Julie Andrews, acceptance speech, 2011

JULIE ANDREWS
Tribute by Carol Burnett
February 13, 2011

Julie and I met for the first time in 1960, when mutual friends of ours brought Julie to see me in an off-Broadway show I was doing, *Once upon a Mattress*. She had already done *My Fair Lady*, and I was pretty much in awe. After the show that night, we all went to a restaurant where we had Chinese and those poor guys who were with us didn't have a prayer. Julie and I never stopped yapping. It was as if I had found my long-lost twin, and some evil being had stolen her at birth and stuck her over there, somewhere in England. That evening kicked off what was to be (so far) a 50-year relationship . . . professional, and best of all . . . personal.

We did our first television special in 1962. We began calling each other "Chum." During our rehearsal breaks, we talked about the men in our lives and our careers and our futures.

In the '70s, we did another special, and during our rehearsal breaks we talked about our husbands, our children, and schools.

Then we got together for yet another special in the '80s, and during those rehearsal breaks we talked about hot flashes, hormones, and *vit*-amins.

If we ever do another one, we'll most likely be delving into the mysteries of Metamucil.

Julie won a Grammy in 1964 for her work in the classic *Mary Poppins* (for which she also won a best actress Oscar), and she has won three Tony Awards and has received a Life Achievement Award from the Screen Actors Guild. She has earned her renown as a singer, an actress, and one of the greatest all-around entertainers with whom I've had the pleasure of working. In addition to *Mary Poppins*, her classic works include *The Sound of Music* and *Victor Victoria*, both of which she made her own on film and on Broadway.

This Lifetime Achievement Award is so very much deserved. Julie has constantly given us her all. And her all is awe-inspiring. Her talent is unsurpassed. She's a consummate actress, and her voice is a gift from the gods. She is a great "Dame" in every good sense of the word.

Congratulations, Chum.

(Entertainer Carol Burnett won an Emmy Award in 1963 for her performance in *Julie and Carol at Carnegie Hall*. Her hit variety show, *The Carol Burnett Show*, ran from 1967–1978. She has earned two Grammy nominations in the Best Spoken Word category.)

GEORGE AVAKIAN

TRUSTEES AWARD, 2009

George Avakian may be the most important music industry executive you've never heard of, especially for those who appreciate the vinyl LP and its renaissance in the last half-decade or so.

Avakian was a producer and A&R representative with Columbia Records starting in the '40s. He signed and produced jazz greats Miles Davis, Louis Armstrong, Dave Brubeck, and Erroll Garner, among others. Early on in his tenure, he was a major proponent of the vinyl LP, which had been developed by his label. Avakian saw the advantages of the better sound quality and longer playing time over 78 rpm discs, and he produced the first 10-inch disc that Columbia released, as well as its first 12-inch long player.

In 1959 Avakian moved to Warner Bros. Records in Los Angeles, a fledging offshoot of the film company. He was put in charge of the pop division with a mandate to build a roster of contemporary acts. His first signings included the Everly Brothers and a young comedian named Bob Newhart, who would win the Album of the Year Grammy for 1960 with the Avakian-produced *The Button-Down Mind of Bob Newhart*.

Avakian was offered the presidency at Warner Bros. Records, but turned it down to stay in music production and out of Los Angeles. A former Recording Academy chairman/president, he received *Down Beat* magazine's Lifetime Achievement Award in 2000 and the National Endowment for the Arts A.B. Spellman Jazz Advocacy Award, which is the nation's highest honor in jazz, among other awards recognizing his vast contributions to American music.

Live long enough, stay out of jail, and you'll never know what will happen.
—George Avakian, acceptance speech, 2009

WireImage.com

GEORGE AVAKIAN
Tribute by Dave Brubeck
February 8, 2009

George Avakian came into my life at a crucial moment. We met while I was working at the Black Hawk in San Francisco in the '50s. My partners at Fantasy, the record company that had issued my original trio recordings and the first Dave Brubeck Quartet albums, had decided to dissolve our partnership. I felt somewhat adrift, uncertain about the future, because I had always thought in terms of Fantasy being my home label. So when George Avakian came into the Black Hawk several nights in a row to hear the group, and then began to talk to me about signing with Columbia Records, I listened carefully.

We had many conversations about the future of recording, new technology, and the growing interest in modern jazz. In these long philosophical exchanges I found in George a sympathetic ear, and decided that if he were my A&R man at Columbia I would be assured the freedom to pursue my own vision as I had hoped to do on my own label. He made me realize that many of the ideas I'd talked about and that had been rejected by other producers—such as melding jazz with symphonic work and chamber ensembles—he considered seriously. As I recall, one of George's impressive selling points to me was the fact that he was married to Anahid Ajemian, a violinist with a fine reputation in performing contemporary music in New York (along with her pianist sister Maro, who lived in the Bay Area).

A few years before George Avakian came into my life, my wife Iola had started contacting colleges about Brubeck concerts. Two of the last recordings I had made for Fantasy were *Jazz at Oberlin* and *Jazz at the College of the Pacific*. At that time the Quartet was playing engagements in jazz clubs such as Birdland in New York, the Blue Note in Chicago, Storyville in Boston, and on "off" nights we would sometimes play concerts in college venues. Because we were getting more and more concert engagements, George decided to capitalize on this new idea and, rather than go into the studio, he decided our first LP on Columbia Records should be *Jazz Goes to College*, compiled from tapes of live campus radio broadcasts. The success of our first concert album was beyond George's or my wildest hope. It is a prime example of George supporting a new idea and developing it to reach a greater audience.

While at Columbia, George introduced me to then–company president Goddard Lieberson, who, like George, put his trust in the artists and was open to their ideas. I feel that George set the stage for my own expansion and growth as an artist on the Columbia label. He has carried that respect and trust in the artist into whatever role he has played in the recording industry. That is why I am grateful for his early confidence, guidance, and contribution to my own career, and his lifelong devotion to jazz and the recording industry.

(Jazz great Dave Brubeck earned a Lifetime Achievement Award from The Recording Academy in 1996. Two of Brubeck's recordings, including his classic 1959 album *Time Out*, have been inducted into the Grammy Hall of Fame.)

CLARENCE AVANT

TRUSTEES AWARD, 2008

Wirelmage.com

One of the earliest and most important African-American businessmen and dealmakers in music, Clarence Avant has played a major role in starting black-owned and –run businesses and helping to develop a number of essential artists over his career.

Avant began his career out of high school working as a lounge manager, where he met R&B singer Little Willie John, who was impressed with Avant and asked him to be his tour manager. More management clients would follow as Avant demonstrated keen business smarts. In 1967 Avant brokered the first joint venture between an African-American artist and a major record label, MGM, when he helped create Venture Records with former Motown songwriter William "Mickey" Stevenson. He also helped engineer the sale of Stax Records to Gulf & Western in 1968.

In 1969 Avant would launch his own label, Sussex Records, signing and developing notable acts such as Bill Withers (who would win the Best Rhythm & Blues Song Grammy for 1971 for "Ain't No Sunshine"), Dennis Coffey, and Detroit-based soft rock group Gallery, all of whom had major hits.

In 1976 Avant founded Tabu Records, signings artists such as the S.O.S. Band and Kool & the Gang. He also helped launch the songwriting and producing careers of Jimmy Jam and Terry Lewis at the label. They would go on to major success, including Janet Jackson's most important records.

Avant ultimately became an experienced and trusted consultant and mentor—in particular to up-and-coming black executive talent such as former Motown president and CEO Jheryl Busby—carving out a unique career expanding the music business opportunities for many African-Americans.

CLARENCE AVANT
Tribute by Kenny "Babyface" Edmonds
February 10, 2008

When I think of Clarence Avant, I think of a few specific words. He's a mentor; Clarence can be very blunt, but he will always be straight with you, and that's the best feedback you can get from someone. He's a connector; he helps you connect the dots in your life and your business, and things you may not fully understand, they're roads he's already traveled down. And he's a blessing; it's very hard to find that kind of person who's so giving to so many different people.

Clarence Avant has been a success in the music business. He started Sussex and Tabu Records, was chairman of Motown Records, became the first African-American to serve on the international management board for Polygram, and is president of his own publishing companies, Avant Garde and Interior Music Corp. But his own success in business is only part of his story. One of his greatest legacies is his dedication to providing opportunities to others.

I first met Clarence with L.A. Reid when we were just starting out. We heard he worked with Jimmy Jam and Terry Lewis, and we were Jimmy and Terry junkies. We wanted to be them. Clarence had no idea who we were, but he gave us a few ideas and helped us with some bad business deals we were in. We knew he was the person who would help steer us down the right path in this industry.

What we learned about Clarence is what so many others he's helped know. If Clarence sees someone being taken advantage of, whether he's stepping on toes or not, he'll do what he believes is right. That's how he became the godfather to a lot of people.

Throughout our careers we went to him: When we did our first record deal, and when we started LaFace. But it wasn't just about music that Clarence would share his wisdom. The first time I ever met a president was at Clarence's house. He'd tell me, "Don't put your time just into music, get involved in the world." Watching him has influenced my participation in the world around me.

Clarence's impact on the industry, on the world, is immeasurable. He's a rarity. You won't find another person with Clarence's gig. There's no one like him. I don't know who the next one will be. I don't know that there *will* be a next one.

(Kenny "Babyface" Edmonds has written and produced for artists ranging from Whitney Houston to Eric Clapton. He launched LaFace Records in 1989 with partner Antonio "L.A." Reid. He's won 11 Grammy Awards, including three consecutive Producer of the Year awards from 1995–1997.)

ESTELLE AXTON

TRUSTEES AWARD, 2007

From the '70s on, many complained about the corporatization of the music business, and even a style of slickly produced music called corporate rock. But there was at least one instance where former bankers helped create one of the most fertile music environments in the country.

In the late '50s, bank employee Jim Stewart began Satellite Records in Memphis, Tennessee. In 1959, his elder sister and, yes, bank employee Estelle Axton mortgaged her house to help fund the label, which was set up to record country and rockabilly artists. Before long, after a name change to Stax (taking the first two letters of their respective surnames), the label moved to a black neighborhood and soon became a meeting ground for a racially mixed group of musicians who created a gritty soul sound that would rival Motown's hit factory in the '60s.

If you think Axton just provided some seed money, you'd be wrong. In fact, she took a leading role in vetting and developing the artists signed to the label, and that was an impressive bit of A&R work. Among those who made Stax home were house band Booker T. & the MG's, Rufus Thomas, Otis Redding, the Staple Singers, Isaac Hayes, Sam & Dave, and many others. Among the executives who cut their teeth at the label were Chips Moman and Al Bell. They would all come to respectfully call Axton "Lady A."

Originally, Stax was distributed through Atlantic Records, and the labels enjoyed phenomenal success into the early '70s. A later distribution deal with CBS would prove less advantageous, and Stax was forced into bankruptcy in the mid-'70s. But in its prime, Stax churned out hit after hit and put Southern soul on the map, nurtured by a mother figure beloved by her artists.

Charlie Gillett Collection/Redferns/Getty Images

ESTELLE AXTON
Tribute by Isaac Hayes and David Porter
February 11, 2007

Estelle Axton was so highly respected around Stax, we called her "Lady A." That's all you had to say. She was a tremendously positive spirit at a time in this country when whites and blacks, certainly in the South, were not gravitating to each other in that kind of open way. She was almost like a mother to us.

In 1957 Estelle Axton's brother Jim Stewart formed Satellite Records. In 1958 she mortgaged her home to build an updated studio and planted the seed for what would become the legendary home of southern soul music.

But her real gift was her ability to embrace and mentor aspiring young musicians. She encouraged us, played records for us, and told us to study the records. She would say, "You've got to have something as good as these records." She did this not just with us, but with others, like Booker T. Jones, William Bell, and Homer Banks. She was a tremendous visionary in recognizing the African-American talent around her. And she had a real appreciation for the potential we had. She was a mentor to every young kid that came in there interested in the music business.

There was an amazing transition that was happening at that time—going from the great Chuck Berry/Fats Domino-type records to a more soulful kind of record—and this lady was really at the forefront in recognizing the potential, encouraging young kids, and then making sure the door to the studio was open. Clearly, her contribution was essential. To us, she was what some would consider Clive Davis to be to the industry today: She saw raw talent and knew what buttons to push to inspire the talent.

The spirit at Stax was one of helping and sharing to make the best records, and we think that spirit came about because that was Estelle's spirit. Most of what was ultimately heard from Stax Records came out because of the beauty of this lady, recognizing and nurturing the talent, sharing information, and making sure the door was open. Any recognition for her is long overdue.

(Isaac Hayes and David Porter were the top songwriting/producing team at Stax Records. Among their many hits were Sam & Dave's "Soul Man," Lou Rawls' "Your Good Thing (Is About to End)," and the Fabulous Thunderbirds' "Wrap It Up (I'll Take It)." They were inducted into the Songwriters Hall of Fame in 2005.)

BURT BACHARACH

LIFETIME ACHIEVEMENT AWARD, 2008

One of the great American composers of the pop and rock era, Burt Bacharach is also among the few honored with both a Recording Academy Trustees Award (along with his songwriting partner Hal David) and a Lifetime Achievement Award. He was among the rare cadre of songwriters who became a recording artist, performer, and personality in his own right. Sure, a marriage to actress Angie Dickinson helped, but Bacharach's legacy as an icon to artists ranging from Elvis Costello to Noel Gallagher, and his continuing writing and performing, have endured well into his 80s.

Bacharach started his songwriting career in earnest in the Brill Building in New York, the music factory that served up a conveyor belt of hit songs by writers that included Carole King, Neil Diamond, Barry Mann and Cynthia Weil, Laura Nyro, Phil Spector, and many others. But while scoring hits for his and David's songs in the early '60s, the team also stumbled upon their muse, a demo singer named Dionne Warwick. The three would enjoy a huge string of hits, including "Don't Make Me Over," "Walk on By," and "Alfie" (all in the Grammy Hall of Fame), as well as "Anyone Who Had a Heart," "I Say A Little Prayer," and many others.

At the same time, Bacharach enjoyed hits with others through the years: "What the World Needs Now Is Love" (Jackie DeShannon), "This Guy's in Love with You" (Herb Alpert), "The Look of Love" (Dusty Springfield), "(They Long to Be) Close to You" (Carpenters), "Arthur's Theme (Best That You Can Do)" (Christopher Cross). And these are just the tip of the Bacharachberg.

At the same time, he was making his own records, hosting his own TV specials, and appearing regularly on the TV talk show circuit. His incredible influence would ultimately be reflected in unexpected places. His likeness would appear, like a boyhood bedroom poster, on the cover of Oasis' *Definitely Maybe*. He recorded an album with Elvis Costello (*Painted From Memory*) that resulted in a Grammy for "I Still Have That Other Girl." And he appeared in Mike Myers' *Austin Powers* series. All of which took him from songwriter to pop culture touchstone.

BURT BACHARACH
Tribute by Jackie DeShannon
February 10, 2008

Burt Bacharach is a true American original. His songs encompass gospel, rock, classical, jazz, folk, bossa nova, R&B, and Broadway. When you listen to Burt's melodies, you realize he is someone blessed with a unique gift—the power of writing extraordinary music. His compositions take you to that special place in your heart where you feel your deepest emotions.

I admired Burt's talents long before I had the opportunity to work with him. I was recording for Liberty Records in 1965 when I got the news he and his writing partner, Hal David, would be producing my next recording date. I was so excited, as I knew this would be something quite special.

While we were rehearsing and listening to the songs for the first session, one tune stood out from all the rest. I knew immediately from the moment I first heard it that "What the World Needs Now Is Love" and I belonged together. The chorus has this wonderful gospel feeling. I felt at home because I grew up singing in church in Kentucky. The verse has an amazingly lyrical and haunting melody. Along with Hal's beautiful words, we created a magical record that has truly stood the test of time. I will always cherish that wonderful collaboration we achieved at Bell Sound Studios in New York.

With his compelling chord changes and unusual time signatures, Burt's arranging skills provide the icing on the cake. He knows all the instruments and textures needed to bring his work to full flower. He's an immaculate, painstaking craftsman in the studio and on the stage. Over the years, I've also had the extreme pleasure of witnessing Bacharach the master in concert, conducting the orchestra and performing the songs he's so carefully constructed. It's an incredible experience. He will take you on a musical journey that you will never forget. His genius is apparent to all who listen and enjoy.

(Jackie DeShannon won the Song of the Year Grammy for 1981 for "Bette Davis Eyes." Her recording of "What the World Needs Now Is Love" was inducted into the Grammy Hall of Fame in 2008.)

DAVE BARTHOLOMEW

 TRUSTEES AWARD, 2012

While simplified versions of the birth of rock and roll begin and end with Elvis Presley, songwriter/bandleader Dave Bartholomew is one of the many essential figures in rock's more detailed story.

Arguably, his biggest single credential in that regard is his work with fellow New Orleanian Fats Domino. Domino's first single, "The Fat Man," cowritten and produced by Bartholomew, is among the handful of records cited as the first rock and roll recording. If that's not argument enough though, Bartholomew's own late '40s band, Dave Bartholomew and the Dew Droppers, were called a model for early rock and roll bands by music writer Robert Palmer.

Bartholomew's recording career began in earnest when he was hired by Imperial Records founder Lew Chudd as the label's A&R head. His hits at the label included a string of records he cowrote and produced for Domino, including "Ain't It a Shame," "Blue Monday," and "I'm Walkin'." He also produced the hits "Blueberry Hill" and "Walking to New Orleans."

Bartholomew worked with other artists at the label as well, including Smiley Lewis, for whom he wrote and produced "I Hear You Knocking" and "One Night," which became oft-recorded and major hits for other artists. He also did work at other labels, including King, where he wrote and recorded the original version of "My Ding-a-Ling," which Chuck Berry made into a giant novelty hit in 1972.

"Ain't It a Shame," "The Fat Man," and "Blueberry Hill" have been inducted into the Grammy Hall of Fame, and Bartholomew himself was put in the Rock and Roll Hall of Fame and Songwriters Hall of Fame, acknowledging a powerful behind-the-scenes figure of the rock era.

> *Everyone knows about what he's done in music . . . but I'd like to say one thing that most people don't know. If you can take all the hits he's written, all the hits he's produced, multiply that times 1000, that's the type of father he is.*
> —Ron Bartholomew, son, acceptance speech, 2012

DAVE BARTHOLOMEW
Tribute by Dr. John

February 12, 2012

Guys like Dave Bartholomew come along once in a lifetime. Dave gave breaks to so many fantastic artists, from Fats Domino and Smiley Lewis to Johnny Fuller, Pee Wee Crayton, and Snooks Eaglin, and great musicians like Papa Yellow "Tuts" Washington, Allen Toussaint, Huey Smith, James Booker, and Edward Franks. The list of musicians who played in his band and who he opened doors for is endless.

He is the bluesiest, jazziest guy; a man always on top of his game who could pull off big-band hits and small group sessions. Dave is also the most consummate bizness cat I ever met. He always threw everybody out the studio when his sessions wuz going on. He is a trumpet player, songwriter, record producer, big-band leader, bizness man, as well as kindhearted.

For all of his responsibilities, he can keep it all together in times of confusion. No matter what, Dave kept it all rollin', a consummate bandleader. He kept a great band with the best players of the time. He was always ahead of the pack and this racket. He was stone bizness, but he did the best with what he had to deal with. He did so much work at Cosimo Matassa's studio and he got the most from all the musicians he used. He worked for Lew Chudd for many years at Imperial Records 'til Lou sold the label. Together, they found and recorded some of the greatest music to come out of New Orleans. They say Dave wrote more than 4000 songs, and he probably arranged thousands more. In 1991 he was inducted into the Rock and Roll Hall of Fame. He's also in the Songwriters Hall of Fame and the Louisiana Music Hall of Fame. He was swing and big band and R&B and rock and roll. Dave never stopped bein' the Dave who played bebop à la blues à la Dave ballads à la Dave totally original. That's Dave Bartholomew.

You touched people all around this world with music, the magic of yo horn, yo productions, and yo genius for putting things togetha.

(Dr. John, aka Mac Rebennack, is a six-time Grammy winner, including Best Contemporary Blues Album for 2008's *City That Care Forgot*, his ode to post–Hurricane Katrina New Orleans. He was inducted into the Rock and Roll Hall of Fame in 2011.)

THE BEATLES

LIFETIME ACHIEVEMENT AWARD, 2014

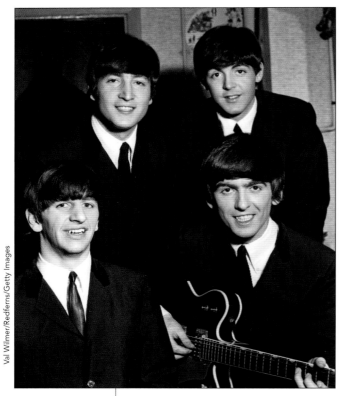

Val Wilmer/Redferns/Getty Images

Very little more need be said about the consequence of the Beatles, probably even for a 10-year-old who may be picking up this book. But just in case, here's a quick synopsis:

The Beatles—George Harrison, John Lennon, Paul McCartney, and Ringo Starr—came from Liverpool, England, in the early '60s. They altered or created everything we know about rock. They influenced everyone. They were more popular than Jesus.

But there is a Grammy-specific curiosity worth noting. Many might wonder why the Beatles received a Lifetime Achievement Award in 2014. Where was The Recording Academy's collective head, waiting so long to honor rock's most important band?

In fact, the Beatles had received a Trustees Award in 1972, when that award was still being fully defined and was often presented to performers. This created a seeming omission of the Beatles from the Lifetime list. No doubt part of the reason for this award was to fill that gap. But it's also fitting that the Beatles are among a handful of honorees to be recognized for a Lifetime Achievement Award as performers and a Trustees Award as nonperformers, given their role as songwriters and the influence they ultimately had on the use of the recording studio as an artistic instrument.

I met George, Paul, and John. And we became this band that did really, really well . . . and made some incredible music.

—Ringo Starr, acceptance speech, 2014

THE BEATLES
Tribute by Danger Mouse
January 26, 2014

I didn't grow up on the Beatles. In fact, by the time I got to college I couldn't have named one Beatles song if you put a gun to my head. Honestly. I listened to '80s pop when I was young, and mostly to hip-hop in middle/high school. My parents were exclusively '60s/'70s soul/R&B listeners, so I was oblivious. My tastes expanded a bit when I was in college, but the Beatles were always this huge group that I just thought couldn't be all that interesting if they were so popular. Any pictures I remembered had them all dressed alike and smiling a lot. I like darker, melancholy music in general, so I was skeptical. However, as I got more into music, and even started making music, I started to hear more and more about how the Beatles had been a huge influence on much of the music I was discovering. I had some research to do.

I bought the albums, read books, and watched any documentaries I could find. What an unreal story. They were immediately a worldwide sensation by their early 20s. They wrote their own material when that was all but unheard of, worked their asses off touring the world playing hit after hit. Girls and boys alike went crazy for them. Every year, from their first records in 1963, they got bigger and bigger and more influential in both music and popular culture.

However, the thing that really spoke to me was when at the peak of their career—with anything and everything a band at that time could have possibly wanted—they made a change. In 1966 the Beatles stopped playing live. The decision was one that allowed them to make music that wouldn't have to be replicated at a concert. This would open up all kinds of opportunities for them to try different recording techniques and experiment in the studio in ways no one making popular music had ever really done. They pioneered things like guitar distortion, overdubbing vocals, multitrack recording, tape loops, and countless other recording techniques that are now standards today . . . even sampling. All of these things had influenced much of the music I'd loved growing up, and now it was making me really look at creating music as an art form.

In a five-year span the Beatles released *Rubber Soul*, *Revolver*, *Sgt. Pepper's Lonely Hearts Club Band*, *Magical Mystery Tour*, *The Beatles* (the White Album), *Abbey Road*, and *Let It Be*—arguably the greatest span of consecutive albums put together by anyone to date. They tried to push boundaries musically and challenge what's accepted of people in their popular position. Here was a band who had achieved the ultimate fame and fortune and instead of basking in more adoration, they veered away from millions of screaming girls to do something more challenging and meaningful to them. Of course, they didn't really lose much of the fame and fortune after all, but that's not the point. The point was that sometimes it's not what you have, but what you choose to do with what you have that can change the world, and inspire other people to do the same.

(Danger Mouse is a five-time Grammy winner, including wins for Producer of the Year and as a member of Gnarls Barkley. In 2004 he released *The Grey Album*, a project combining vocal performances from Jay Z's *The Black Album* with samples from the Beatles' *White Album*.)

BEE GEES

LIFETIME ACHIEVEMENT AWARD, 2015

Michael Ochs Archives/Getty Images

For anyone who still thinks of the Bee Gees as silk-suit disco stars, it's time, finally, to think again. Sure, the group crafted some of that era's finest dance music, whether it was partnering with producer Arif Mardin for the white-funk workout "Jive Talkin'" or helming the genre's defining album, the *Saturday Night Fever* soundtrack, the Album of the Year Grammy winner for 1978 and truly a cultural phenomenon. In fact, the impact of *Fever* was so great it branded Barry, Robin, and Maurice Gibb as something they weren't: a disco group. It overshadowed the fact that in many ways, the Bee Gees were no less pop chameleons than David Bowie.

The British-born and Australian-raised brothers began their career making Beatles-influenced, ornate chamber pop, scoring chart hits such as the soulful "To Love Somebody," the vaguely psychedelic "Lonely Days," and the stunning self-shaming ballad "I Started a Joke." But it was telling that "To Love Somebody," their first hit, was written by the brothers for Otis Redding. They always had blue-eyed souls. But not so much that they couldn't write a good country tune, whether it was "Come On Over," covered by Olivia Newton-John, or "Islands in the Stream," which Kenny Rogers and Dolly Parton took to No. 1 on the country *and* pop charts.

As producers and writers, they impacted a countless variety of artists: Rogers, Parton, Newton-John, Frankie Valli, Dionne Warwick, Tavares, Yvonne Elliman, Barbra Streisand, Diana Ross, and Tina Turner. As an influence, they impacted many more.

We had a lot of cliffs to climb. You have to have as many stiffs as you have hits. We got that record. We'd have a huge hit and then we'd have a huge flop. And we'd go, "OK, let's try again." And we always tried again.

—Barry Gibb, acceptance speech, 2015

BEE GEES
Tribute by Russ Titelman
February 8, 2015

When I think about the Bee Gees just as songwriters, it makes me think of Irving Berlin. Like him, Barry, Robin, and Maurice Gibb cranked out beautifully crafted, unusual, complicated, melodic popular songs one after another, hit after hit. They wrote story songs such as "I've Gotta Get a Message to You" and "New York Mining Disaster 1941;" dark, brooding ballads such as "Holiday," "How Can You Mend a Broken Heart," and "How Deep Is Your Love;" and such pop masterpieces as "To Love Somebody" and "Run to Me." Then, after a decade of writing and performing these miraculous three-minute movies, they came up with "Jive Talkin'" and "Stayin' Alive," which ushered in the disco era and changed music forever. They also wrote hits for other artists, including "Islands in the Stream" for Kenny Rogers and Dolly Parton, and "Guilty" and "Woman in Love" for Barbra Streisand.

I always thought that what constituted a great record was this: You had never heard anything like it before or after. So it was not only the songs but the unique sound they created. With their tight harmonies; Robin's sweet, soulful lead vocals; Barry's signature falsetto; and rockin' instrumental tracks, you knew it was the Bee Gees from the first notes you heard.

In 1997 I was welcomed into the Bee Gees family when Barry called and asked me to produce three tracks on their upcoming *Still Waters* album. I had the time of my life and we made great music. They were professional, creative, generous, and so very funny!

One incident comes to mind. We were working on "Alone," which became the first single off the album, and I thought we needed something different at the end so I suggested a vocal counterpoint section like the end of the Beach Boys' "God Only Knows." They liked the idea so the three of them went upstairs to work on it and in five or 10 minutes came back with a fully formed ending. They immediately went into the studio and laid down the parts. The whole thing took about a half hour. I was completely blown away.

While they were singing I looked over at John Merchant, their engineer, and with a big smile on my face said, "It's the Bee Gees!"

Barry, Robin, and Maurice, your work has been an inspiration to us all. Thank you.

(A three-time Grammy-winning producer, Russ Titelman has worked with artists such as Eric Clapton, George Harrison, Chaka Khan, Cyndi Lauper, Randy Newman, James Taylor, and Steve Winwood, among others. He served as the coproducer for the Bee Gees' 1997 album *Still Waters*, which featured the hit "Alone.")

AL BELL

TRUSTEES AWARD, 2011

Wireimage.com

In the heyday of the music business, the highest compliment you could pay an executive was to say he was a real record man. This meant that the executive was committed to the artists *and* the music, not just the bottom line. Al Bell was all of that, and maybe a bit more.

Bell started his career as a radio DJ and ultimately became a station manager in his Little Rock, Arkansas, hometown. The experience clearly taught him a lot about music and hit records. He was hired in 1965 by Memphis' Stax Records for a job that was no doubt familiar territory for him: promoting records to radio stations. He proved to be an indispensable asset, helping to break acts such as Isaac Hayes, Otis Redding, Sam & Dave, and the Staple Singers.

But while promotion men were seen mostly as the sales people of the industry, Bell parlayed his role into far deeper involvement with the artists and label. He would become the executive vice president of Stax and ultimately a co-owner, and he would play more than a business role in the music the label was releasing. Bell produced many of Stax's releases as the label moved toward the '70s, including *Hot Buttered Soul*, the 1969 album that established songwriter Isaac Hayes as a major force in evolving the sound of soul music, and he wrote the Staple Singers' triumphant anti-racism hit "I'll Take You There," which made No. 1 on the *Billboard* Hot 100 in 1972.

Though a bad distribution deal would undermine Bell's growing ambitions for Stax in the mid-'70s, he'd go on to form his own independent marketing company and label, hitting with Tag Team's No. 2 hit "Whoomp! (There it Is)" in 1993, and putting an exclamation mark on a remarkable career.

AL BELL
Tribute by Huey Lewis
February 13, 2011

Al Bell might be the person most responsible for my musical taste.

Growing up in the San Francisco Bay Area in the '60s, with folk music and early psychedelic music as a backdrop, my constant radio companion was soul station KDIA in Oakland. Not the obvious choice for a suburban white kid, but then, my dad was a jazz drummer and my mom loved psychedelic stuff, and I needed something of my own. KDIA was the sister station of the famous WDIA in Memphis. Needless to say, both stations played a healthy dose of Stax records, which were either promoted, commissioned, produced, or written by Al Bell.

Alvertis Isbell was old school before the term. Soul music came from the church, and Al knew the church. As a young man he worked for Dr. Martin Luther King Jr. at the Southern Christian Leadership Conference, and when he speaks, the similarity is striking. He came to Stax from radio where he was a DJ, both in Little Rock, Arkansas, and Washington, D.C. He started as a promotion man. Incredibly hardworking and dynamic, he became a co-owner in Stax and grew the company into the second-largest black-owned business of the '70s. He was incredibly ambitious, famously releasing 27 albums and 30 singles in one month. He was "hands-on," producing and even writing hits for the label, including "I'll Take You There" for the Staple Singers. In 1972 he produced Wattstax, the all-Stax concert at the Los Angeles Coliseum, and the Golden Globe-nominated film about the event. It's been said "he put Memphis on the map," an incredible statement when you consider the vast musical history of the town.

The demise of Stax Records in the mid-'70s was complicated and messy and resulted in Al retreating from the business for several years. But Al Bell is a fighter and he did not give up. With the help of Berry Gordy Jr. he rebuilt his career, first as president of Motown Records and then with his own label, Bellmark Records. And now as chairman of the Memphis Music Foundation, Al Bell is back in Memphis, doing what he's always been doing . . . promoting Memphis music.

In his 70s, he seems newly invigorated. He's still a workaholic (his friends say he works 24 hours a day, breaking only at midnight to eat his wife's fried chicken), and still as passionate as ever. When I saw him in 2010, it was at the Stax Museum of American Soul Music in Memphis at a playback party for our then-new record, *Soulsville*, which is a tribute to Memphis soul music. He was dressed immaculately, as usual, in a suit and monogrammed shirt, with his tie perfectly matching his pocket square and his cuff links shining. He was complimentary of the album, and especially the song selection, but then I knew we'd have the same taste.

(Huey Lewis and the News won the 1985 Grammy for Best Music Video, Long Form for *Huey Lewis & the News: The Heart of Rock 'n' Roll*. That same year the group received a Record of the Year nomination for "The Power of Love.")

MARILYN AND ALAN BERGMAN

♫ TRUSTEES AWARD, 2013

WireImage.com

It's not a common occurrence in the rock era that lyric-exclusive songwriters have built hall of fame-level careers. They exist to be sure: Burt Bacharach's partner Hal David, Elton John lyricist Bernie Taupin, Brill Building writers such as Cynthia Weil and Gerry Goffin.

In that rarified stratum reside Marilyn and Alan Bergman. The pair have turned their personal partnership into one of the top songwriting marriages as well. They won a Song of the Year Grammy for "The Way We Were" for 1974 as well as the Grammy for Album of Best Original Score Written for a Motion Picture or a Television Special that same year. They won Oscars for "The Windmills of Your Mind" from *The Thomas Crown Affair* (1968), "The Way We Were" (1973), and *Yentl* (1983). They've also won four Emmys, putting them a Tony Award away from an EGOT.

Their list of noteworthy songs also includes "Nice 'n' Easy," "You Don't Bring Me Flowers," and lyrics to the Arthur Lyman exotica classic "Yellow Bird."

Their words are poetic in the best sense, bringing brilliantly crafted emotion to their songs, as in the images of confusion seemingly effortlessly strung together in "Windmills:"

> Round,
> Like a circle in a spiral
> Like a wheel within a wheel
> Never ending or beginning
> On an ever-spinning reel
> Like a snowball down a mountain
> Or a carnival balloon
> Like a carousel that's turning
> Running rings around the moon
> Like a clock whose hands are sweeping
> Past the minutes of its face
> And the world is like an apple
> Whirling silently in space
> Like the circles that you find
> In the windmills of your mind

They were inducted into the Songwriters Hall of Fame in 1980, but they've also given back to the songwriting community. Marilyn served as president and chairman of the board of the performing rights organization ASCAP for 15 years and Alan serves as a member of the Library of Congress National Film Preservation Board, among other board service. All of which is fitting perhaps for a couple in their seventh decade of songwriting.

To do something you love to do—and we do love to write songs—with somebody you love, you really have the world around you and comforting you, making it all wonderful.
    —Alan Bergman, acceptance speech, 2013

MARILYN AND ALAN BERGMAN
Tribute by Cynthia Weil and Barry Mann
February 10, 2013

Those who have attempted either would say the two most difficult things to accomplish in life are a successful partnership and a successful marriage. Combine both endeavors and the odds against you rise appreciably, but this year we proudly honor two people who have beaten those very odds and excelled gloriously at both undertakings. The fact that they both write the lyrics and have to debate titles, rhymes, and concepts boggles the mind. They have managed to create the soundtrack to our lives in film, theater, and TV, and on the radio, and the fact that they have done this without bloodshed speaks volumes to their personal strength, angelic nature, and extraordinary talent.

Wrap your head around some of these achievements. In film they've won Oscars for "The Way We Were" (which also won two Grammys), "The Windmills of Your Mind" (from *The Thomas Crown Affair*) and the score for *Yentl*. On TV we can only say "And Then There's Maude" and the theme to *In the Heat of the Night*: How different yet how right on can two TV themes be? (They also won four Emmys.)

Then there's the stage and their wonderful work for the musical *Ballroom*, both touching and literate, in other words very "Bergmanesque." And now for radio: "That Face," "What Are You Doing the Rest of Your Life?," "Nice 'n' Easy," "How Do You Keep the Music Playing" . . . how do they do it?

Inquiring couples who also write want to know. How do they continue to produce work that is timeless and outstanding and continue to create with an enthusiasm that never diminishes? The truth is they are so special and so perfect, we'd like to slap them around a little, but then, they are so gracious, kind, and elegant that we want to sing their praises and worship at their computer. We are all so lucky to have known them and their work, and to know them personally is a treat all its own.

There are no two people more deserving of the Trustees Award and we salute them with respect, love, and admiration.

(Wife-and-husband team Cynthia Weil and Barry Mann are two of the greatest songwriters to emerge from New York's Brill Building. They've won two Grammys, including Song of the Year for 1987 for "Somewhere Out There." The recording of their song "On Broadway" was inducted into the Grammy Hall of Fame in 2013.)

BLIND BOYS OF ALABAMA

LIFETIME ACHIEVEMENT AWARD, 2009

Wirelmage.com

Few artists west of Tony Bennett can argue they've enjoyed their greatest success six and seven decades into their career, but the Blind Boys of Alabama are such a rare case. Having formed in the '30s, the Boys would win their first of five Grammy Awards for 2001, with such original members as founder Clarence Fountain, George Scott, and Jimmy Carter still active in the group.

Formed at the Alabama School for the Negro Deaf and Blind in Alabama as the Happy Land Jubilee Singers, the group—all but one of whom were blind—scratched together a subsistence living singing throughout the South in the '30s and '40s. They began recording in the late '40s for a series of small labels, enjoying a number of gospel hits. In the '60s they became involved with Dr. Martin Luther King Jr. and the civil rights movement, and their hard gospel singing style would influence artists who crossed over from gospel to pop such as Marvin Gaye.

But it was a starring role in the '80s musical *The Gospel at Colonus* that brought them to the attention of a wider audience. The renewed attention led to bookings and ultimately high profile U.S. and European tours in the '90s. In the early 2000s they would tour and record with Peter Gabriel, record a joint album with Ben Harper in 2004 (*There Will be a Light*), and win gospel Grammy Awards for 2002, 2003, 2004, and 2008. They were inducted into the Gospel Music Hall of Fame in 2003. It's a latter-day success story that's hard to turn a blind eye to.

I had to pinch myself to see if I was dreaming today. So I did, and it hurt. So it must be real.
—Jimmy Carter, acceptance speech, 2009

BLIND BOYS OF ALABAMA
Tribute by Ben Harper
February 8, 2009

Close your eyes for a few moments, and with them closed imagine the mid-1930s—the Great Depression, the dust bowl, silent movies, and deep-rooted segregation with no end in sight. Envision with closed eyes a town called Talladega, Alabama, home to a school named the Alabama School for the Negro Deaf and Blind—a school where weaving baskets and caning chairs were considered the highest possible vocations. This was the birthplace of the greatest gospel tradition in American music history. This was the birthplace of the Blind Boys of Alabama.

From the invention of radio, television, and record players, to the invention of the Internet, through world wars and cold wars, from FDR to Barack Obama, and now well into their eighth decade of touring, writing, and recording, the Blind Boys have not only faithfully remained, endured, and persevered, they have evolved, thrived, and flourished as the premier purveyors of gospel music the world over.

When you hear the Blind Boys singing it is as instantly recognizable as it is original, inhabiting a place in the soul no other sound can. Having the opportunity to write, sing, record, and tour with the Blind Boys of Alabama has been the highest musical privilege in my lifetime. I still sit in humble disbelief when I hear my voice singing with theirs. The memories of our time and friendship are as sacred as the sound that comes from their voices.

From the famed Capitol Studios to the Apollo Theater in Harlem—where I had, respectively, the great privilege of recording and performing with them—from the floor of the United Nations to the White House, the Blind Boys of Alabama have triumphantly carried soul gospel music into the 21st century, producing a timeless body of work that will inspire generations to come.

(Ben Harper and the Blind Boys of Alabama performed together on Harper's Grammy-winning album, 2004's *There Will be a Light*.)

BOOKER T. & THE MG'S

Rick Diamond/WireImage for The Recording Academy/Getty Images

For those who have wondered why all those great '60s Stax Records recordings from Otis Redding, Sam & Dave, Carla Thomas, Isaac Hayes, and others seemed to have a familiar, earthy soulfulness, the answer was Booker T. & the MG's. The house band at Stax Records, the MG's were the magic sauce that was the finishing touch on a recipe of great songs, inspiring artists and a special place and time in history.

Booker T. & the MG's—keyboardist Booker T. Jones, guitarist Steve Cropper, drummer Al Jackson Jr., and bassists Donald "Duck" Dunn and Lewie Steinberg—encapsulated everything the Stax ethic stood for: an undeniably rock-steady groove (it's been said their rhythm section originated Southern soul), amazing taste and creativity in their playing, and a colorblind mixed-race makeup. They can be heard on records ranging from Otis Redding's "(Sittin' on) The Dock of the Bay" (which Cropper cowrote) to Sam & Dave's "Soul Man," Rufus Thomas' "Walkin' the Dog," and Eddie Floyd's "Knock on Wood," among dozens of other hits.

Unlike other groups that regularly backed artists out of a single location—Motown's Funk Brothers, Fame Studio's Swampers, Los Angeles' Wrecking Crew—the MG's were also hit artists in their own right, scoring Top 20 instrumentals with the instantly recognizable "Green Onions," "Time is Tight," and "Soul-Limbo," among others. These hits, most often written by the band and picked up as TV show or advertising themes, made the MG's one of the top instrumental acts of the era, as well-loved by fans as they were by the singers they backed with one of soul music's most unforgettable sounds.

Jim Stewart said, "You know we can't put out a record with one side. We have to have a second side for it." He said, "You guys have anything?" We came up with this thing Al Jackson ended up calling "Green Onions." That started the whole thing. Fast-forward to the backseat of a limo in Monterey, California, about six years later with the sound of motorcycles all around. I looked out the window and I was expecting to see police cars out there but it was Hells Angels escorting us to the Monterey Pop Festival.
—Booker T. Jones, acceptance speech, 2007

BOOKER T. & THE MG'S
Tribute by Dan Aykroyd
February 11, 2007

As the creators of their own unique soul sound and as the house band on countless hit records that defined the sound of the South in the '60s and '70s at Stax Records, Booker T. & the MG's—guitarist Steve Cropper, bassist Donald "Duck" Dunn, drummer Al Jackson Jr., organist Booker T. Jones and original bassist Lewie Steinberg—have become giants of American music.

The Great African-American Songbook has yielded numerous pieces of music for all the times in our lives. Songs that we will associate always with specific places, people, and events. The most powerful is that sure touch on our nation's pulse, the ubiquitous classic "Green Onions." This giant composition never fails to stir rhythm in our blood, whether we hear it played on a pirated download, in TV and radio commercials, or live onstage by both imitators and its originators. It got a generation through its war and forever became the official theme for U.S. motorheads when George Lucas laid it into the *American Graffiti* soundtrack with complete emotional effectiveness.

Booker T. Jones' deep burbling organ, the drive of Duck Dunn's stone solid bassbone with Steve Cropper's guitar-funk crying throughout make this urban soul march a vibrant anthem, which like all great music transcends geographical borders.

This song is the flagship of the Stax-Volt movement. Like any classic it doesn't age. It sounds better and wholly contemporary with every listening. Serious, bad, tough, and exciting. Booker T. & the MG's' "Green Onions" is a song for a time, for all times, for all peoples, for all places—one for our planet to share until the end of existence.

(Academy Award- and Grammy-nominated actor/writer Dan Aykroyd cowrote and starred in the 1980 film *The Blues Brothers*, which prominently featured MG's members Steve Cropper and Donald "Duck" Dunn.)

DAVID BOWIE

 ## LIFETIME ACHIEVEMENT AWARD, 2006

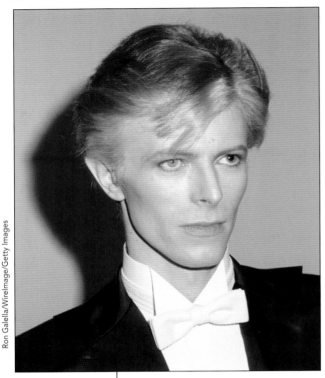

Ron Galella/WireImage/Getty Images

"Tomorrow belongs to those who can hear it coming," David Bowie once said. It's perhaps the best self-description of an artist who always seemed to have his hands on the planchette of the Ouija board. Bowie's ever-shifting styles and characters weren't so much an effort to confound as they were peeks into a future that Bowie imagined. His perceptive notions of glam rock, electronic music, punk, fashion, and even gender identity would prove influential on an astoundingly varied list of artists.

Though it may seem Bowie sprang fully formed as the orange-haired alien singer of "Space Oddity," he had formative years just as other artists. In the '60s, Bowie migrated from mod to traditional song stylist to mime (he formed his own mime company). It was in a sort of hazy singer/ songwriter guise that Bowie hit on "Space Oddity" and launched his music career in earnest. But he showed early on that he was a restless searcher, trying on new styles of music and new personas with which to deliver them.

So came the otherworldly glam rocker Ziggy Stardust, the conflicted Aladdin Sane, the avant dark-eyed soul singer the Thin White Duke. And with each of them a dive into new musical territory that would ultimately help give rise to entire musical movements, from new wave and the new romantics to goth and electronica.

Lady Gaga energetically paid tribute to Bowie on the 58th Grammy Awards in 2016 (he had died just a month prior to the show), but in truth, countless acts could have done the honor. Few artists in the rock era have had the widespread impact of even one of Bowie's incarnations.

DAVID BOWIE
Tribute by Win Butler
February 8, 2006

How can a song that someone created in 1977 in a studio in Berlin travel through the air into a suburban bedroom in 1997 in Houston, Texas, and make all of the "current" music playing on the radio sound old-fashioned? The first time I heard "Heroes" I didn't know who had written it or when, but I knew it filled me with a feeling of mystery and possibility . . . his music showed me shapes that I had no language to describe. As I discovered his records, I always felt like Bowie respected me as a listener enough not to spell everything out, to leave some room for shadows. Growing up when I did it seemed beyond belief that anything as individual and beautiful and hard to pin down as the music of David Bowie could have been pop music!

How could you ever hope to imitate David Bowie? Write songs that are equal parts George Orwell and Elvis, help pioneer electronics in rock music, and define what is possible in a stage show . . . oh, and have a completely unique voice and always manage to look like you're from the future (even when you are only wearing a suit in a film from 30 years ago). It has been so inspiring to meet an artist who has been creating such important work for so long and is still hungry for knowledge and new experiences and new sounds. I can't think of another artist who could be receiving a Lifetime Achievement Award when the best song he ever wrote could be on his next album.

(Win Butler is the cofounder of Arcade Fire, who won the Album of the Year Grammy for 2010 for *The Suburbs*. David Bowie contributed vocals to the title track of Arcade Fire's 2013 album *Reflektor* and performed live with the band at Fashion Rocks in New York in 2005.)

OWEN BRADLEY

TRUSTEES AWARD, 2006

Michael Ochs Archives/Getty Images

Owen Bradley did more to shape the nascent Nashville music scene in the '50s and '60s than perhaps any other individual, including the stars for which he helped create many of the era's most lasting recordings, such as Kitty Wells, Patsy Cline, Brenda Lee, and Loretta Lynn.

Bradley was a radio station music director and musician who began working at Decca Records in 1947 and, as an assistant, started learning the ropes about producing records. Before long, he was producing records himself, and in 1961, he opened a recording studio with his brother Harold, one of the area's top session guitarists. The studio, a house with an attached Quonset hut that contained the recording facility, became the first music establishment on what would become Nashville's Music Row. Bradley became vice president of Decca's Nashville division.

While he was more than capable of producing hard country, bluegrass, and honky-tonk, Bradley, along with his contemporary Chet Atkins, became best known for what would be called mundanely "the Nashville Sound" and more colorfully, "countrypolitan." It was a more urban, pop-oriented brand of country with smooth strings and backing vocals. It revolutionized country music and to this day continues to reverberate on the country charts.

The vast number of artists he worked with made some of country's most enduring music, whether it was Loretta Lynn's "Coal Miner's Daughter," Brenda Lee's "I'm Sorry," Patsy Cline's "Walkin' After Midnight," or records by Webb Pierce and Conway Twitty. Later, fans who grew up with his music, such as k.d. lang, would lure him out of semi-retirement to work his magic. Many of the records he helped create have won Grammys or have been inducted into the Grammy Hall of Fame.

OWEN BRADLEY
Tribute by k.d. lang
February 8, 2006

In 1955, Owen Bradley built the first music business structure (a Quonset hut recording studio) on what would become Music Row in Nashville. He was a hit songwriter, a talented keyboardist, a successful bandleader, a radio star, and as a producer he was one of the architects of the famed "Nashville Sound."

He loved hillbilly music and he loved jazz, and out of those two passions he invented "countrypolitan," the sound that crossed Patsy Cline, among others, over into stardom. He created a sound that kept the integrity of each artist, as his greatest strength was his love for singers and the song. He respected the instincts of singers, and he worked with many great artists—including Kitty Wells, Patsy Cline, Brenda Lee, and Loretta Lynn— not to change their basic essence, but to enhance it, to expand on their sound without losing their core.

I went to Nashville to work with Owen, who produced my album *Shadowland* in 1987, with the intent of making a countrypolitan record, with respect for Patsy and Loretta. Owen was very gentle, with a great laugh, and he loved to listen to music together, and loved to eat frozen grapes. Most of all he loved his boat; he always wore his captain's hat, even in the studio, and somehow I hope he's still on his boat, out on the big lake.

(k.d. lang has won four Grammy Awards and was honored in October 2005 with the National Arts Centre Award in her native Canada.)

RUTH BROWN

 ## LIFETIME ACHIEVEMENT AWARD, 2016

Giles Petard/Redferns/Getty Images

Known as the woman who built Ahmet Ertegun's Atlantic Records thanks to her many early hits that helped put the label on the music map, Ruth Brown had two distinct careers—first as the definitive R&B singer of the '50s, and later as a theater star, actor, NPR radio host, and freedom fighter for artists' rights. Her influence was wide-ranging, not just on female singers who would follow her lead as a strong early voice in R&B and rock and roll, but on artists such as rock icon Little Richard, whose style is an admitted echo of the squeals Brown emits on classic recordings such as "(Mama) He Treats Your Daughter Mean."

Brown was a classic church-trained singer who turned her testifying for the Lord to singing the blues. Her career was almost derailed by a serious car accident en route to New York to sign her Atlantic recording contract. But fate wasn't to be unkind, at least at that point. She went on to score dozens of R&B and rock hits.

But by the early '60s, her career was winding down. She spent the next decade-plus toiling at nine-to-five jobs, a surprising turn of events that would inform her activism for the payment of royalties to R&B's early artists, efforts that would help lead to the formation of the Rhythm & Blues Foundation. By the mid-'70s, a career renaissance was underway with a starring role in John Water's *Hairspray* and a Grammy- and Tony-winning role in the Broadway show *Black and Blue*.

The Recording Academy's Lifetime Achievement Award complements her 1993 induction into the Rock and Roll Hall of Fame.

I was privileged enough to serve many years as my mother Ruth Brown's manager. And I, as well as my brother Ron and our attorney Howell, were allowed to take part in many honors my mother received. I can say very confidently that this award, being presented to her by the Grammys today, would be as meaningful, if not more to her, than any award she ever received. I just wish she could have been here personally to accept it.

—Earl Swanson, son, acceptance speech, 2016

RUTH BROWN
Tribute by Rep. John Conyers Jr.
February 15, 2016

Ruth Brown was born Ruth Weston in January 1928, and passed away on November 17, 2006, and in between built one of the great rhythm and blues careers of all time.

Born in Portsmouth, Virginia, to a choir director, she was a pure talent with a voice that could simultaneously convey sorrow, joy, pain, and hope. She never learned to read music because as she put it, "I woke up one morning and I could sing." She began performing early, at just four years old, at the local Emmanuel African Methodist Episcopal Church where her father directed the choir.

Known as Miss Rhythm, her bold performances on classics like "So Long," "Teardrops from My Eyes," and "(Mama) He Treats Your Daughter Mean" brought her widespread acclaim in the 1940s and 1950s. But somewhere along the way, she fell on hard times, the victim of industry practices that took advantage of African-American artists. But like the tone of her songs, her story is one that moves beyond heartache and toward triumph.

The woman who had helped build Atlantic Records may not have been able to afford a telephone at one point, but her voice was not going to be silenced.

She became an activist for artists' rights, helping to change industry practices and recover royalties for artists who were wrongfully denied the fruits of their genius. She was a tireless advocate for copyright reform, a driving force behind the Rhythm & Blues Foundation, and an example to other artists in her later years when her powerful voice once again returned her to stardom—winning a Grammy for Best Jazz Vocal Performance, Female for *Blues on Broadway* as well as a Tony Award for her part in *Black and Blue* in 1989.

As a member of both the Congressional Black Caucus and the House Judiciary Committee, I worked with Ruth to enact copyright reform and to promote and preserve rhythm and blues music. I was so affected by her personal story, perseverance, and empathy for her fellow R&B artists, that I sponsored a resolution in 2006 in the House of Representatives honoring her great legacy.

An indomitable spirit, a brilliant singer, and good and decent person, Miss Rhythm made tremendous contributions to our world. Today, we acknowledge these important contributions and remember how fortunate we all are to have been moved by Ruth Brown's voice.

(John Conyers Jr. is currently serving his 27th term as a Democratic representative for Southeast Michigan and is the ranking member of the House Committee on the Judiciary. In 2001 he received the Grammys on the Hill Award from The Recording Academy.)

JOHN CAGE

TRUSTEES AWARD, 2016

Lots of artists experiment. In one way or another, virtually all of the honorees represented in this book took the chance of moving in a direction that had either never been considered, or was thought "wrong." But few experimented with the same sense of purpose as composer John Cage.

Born in Los Angeles in 1912, Cage's formative years found him experimenting already, specifically with finding the best outlet for his creative pursuits, no doubt influenced by his inventor father. Traveling through Europe and delving into architecture, poetry, painting, and other fields, Cage finally returned to the United States and focused on music.

It was his teacher Arnold Schoenberg who would later call Cage a genius inventor, not a composer, a description Cage adopted.

Among his many innovations was the prepared piano, which gained recognition through Cage's *Sonatas and Interludes for Prepared Piano*. The recording was given an almost cartoon-music texture by placing objects on or between the strings of the piano. In 1952 Cage introduced "4' 33"," a piece in which the musical performers assemble but don't play, with the atmospheric sounds of the musicians and audience designed to be the music. The piece, among others, led to Cage being credited as an early influence on performance art before the term had been coined. He was also a pioneer in creating works based on chance (informed by his reading of the *I Ching*), found sounds, and electronic devices.

All this would make Cage a bit of a confounding presence in his day, but a major influence. In his prime, his work would exert some pull on experimental composers such as Karlheinz Stockhausen and Philip Glass. Later, he would impact a number of rock acts that gravitated to the rebellious nature in the sense of chance and noise in his work. Frank Zappa, Sonic Youth, and Stereolab (who named a song after Cage) have spoken of their affection. EDM artist Aphex Twin adopted the prepared piano. And Radiohead vocalist Thom Yorke has called Cage a hero.

As his biographer Ken Silverman once put it, "Turn over any rock and there's John Cage."
—Laura Kuhn, director of the John Cage Trust, acceptance speech, 2016

JOHN CAGE
Tribute by Thurston Moore
February 15, 2016

Like his father, John Cage was an inventor, a moniker he preferred to that of composer, and one bestowed upon him by his music composition and theory teacher Arnold Schoenberg. It was Schoenberg, who had slight regard for his student as composer but considerable feelings for him as genius, to whom Cage had promised to devote his life to music.

This promise of devotion to creative light and discipline is concurrent to Cage's profound attraction to Buddhist philosophy. It is what defines him as the most significant pioneer in 20th century experimental music.

When Cage introduced the notion of nonhierarchical interdisciplinary performance in 1952 at Black Mountain College, he not only created the first audacious "happening" event but also the liberation of the artist to employ his or her most organic means of "play" within the discipline of the score.

This unification of both academic and wild creativity is—alongside the writing ideologies of Jack Kerouac, Diane di Prima, et al.; abstract expressionist visual art of Franz Kline, Lee Krasner, et al.; modern dance of Cage's life partner Merce Cunningham, bebop jazz of Thelonious Monk, and the avant-garde jazz of Sun Ra and later John Coltrane—the true template for all that is radical and challenging in music and art today.

John Cage, September 5, 1912–August 12, 1992, is an influence nonpareil for perpetual generations of music and language, inadvertently creating a blueprint for the spirit of rock and roll, a reflection of nature and the human condition in both rebelliousness and meditation, a music that moves where the spirit takes it.

(Thurston Moore is a cofounder of indie rock pioneers Sonic Youth. Their 1999 album, *SYR 4: Goodbye 20th Century*, featured a cover of John Cage's "Six.")

CAB CALLOWAY

LIFETIME ACHIEVEMENT AWARD, 2008

Gilles Petard/Redferns/Getty Images

Cab Calloway was a one-man cultural force. He was a star bandleader, recording artist, stage performer, songwriter, and personality as well as a veritable arbiter of what was hip. Calloway's biggest hit, "Minnie the Moocher" (Grammy Hall of Fame, 1999), was as defining a signature as any artist has ever created, yet his career lasted decades beyond it and he is remembered and celebrated for many other achievements.

After several years of performing club circuits in the Midwest, Calloway would migrate to New York, and in 1930, he and his orchestra performed as a temporary replacement for Duke Ellington's band at the Cotton Club. They were so popular, Calloway's group quickly became the co-house band with Ellington's. Calloway's band was talented to be sure—musicians such as Dizzy Gillespie, Chu Berry, and Doc Cheatham passed through it—but the band also stood out thanks to the zoot-suited, energetic personality of Calloway himself, who would sing, dance, and entertain as much as lead the band.

Calloway hit with "Minnie" in 1931, and soon became known as the "Hi-De-Ho Man" thanks to the song's infectious chorus. Through the '30s and much of the '40s, Calloway was as hot as any entertainer: The Cotton Club was the hip "it" spot in New York, he began making film appearances, his dancing included a flowing step noted as a precursor to Michael Jackson's moonwalk, and he even wrote (or inspired, depending on the source) a book, *Hepster's Dictionary: Language of Jive*, positioning him as the definitive source in what was trending culturally.

After the big band craze died down, Calloway went on to star on Broadway, including a revival of "Porgy and Bess" in the role of Sportin' Life, which some have said was modeled after him. He continued performing almost up to his death in 1994, appearing in *The Blues Brothers* in 1980 and in the Janet Jackson video "Alright" in 1990, among other later turns.

> *Cab Calloway was a man of firsts . . . KRS-One considers Cab the first MC for using call-and-response in his song "Minnie the Moocher." He pioneered the foundation for America's next true art form, hip-hop.*
> Cabella Calloway Langsam, daughter, acceptance speech, 2008

CAB CALLOWAY
Tribute by John Lithgow
February 10, 2008

Cab Calloway was an American original. All through the middle decades of the 20th century, he entertained millions with his exuberant, jazzy energy. He was a kind of clown prince of the big band era, all fun and flash, scat, and dance. Everybody knew his music. His signature song, "Minnie the Moocher," put the three syllables "hi de ho" into our national vocabulary, and Calloway himself was the "Hi-De-Ho Man."

Calloway's father was a Rochester, New York, lawyer, his mother a school teacher and church organist. They disapproved of jazz and wanted Cab to finish college and study law. A dutiful son, he tried not one but two schools. But it was never meant to be. One night he happened to meet Louis Armstrong in Chicago, and that was that. Before you could say "scat," Calloway was performing with his orchestra at the Cotton Club. And the next 40 years were the stuff of legend.

I remember Calloway from my childhood. Of all the jazz that my folks listened to, his was the music that spoke most directly to us kids, with its rollicking rhythms and squealing solos, Cab's mischievous voice, his corny rhymes, and his zany call-and-response. It was no wonder that he became the most familiar voice on the soundtrack of Betty Boop cartoons. Betty turned "Minnie the Moocher" into a huge hit for kids. No one seemed to notice or even care that the song was all about smoking dope in a Chinatown opium den (or, as Cab put it, "kicking the gong around").

A few years ago, when I was casting about for great old novelty songs to fill up my first CD for children, I came across Calloway's classic, "Everybody Eats When They Come to My House." There it was, that irascible voice from my earliest memories:

"Have a banana, Hannah!

Try the salami, Tommy!

Give with the gravy, Davey!

Everybody eats when they come to my house!"

What better way to welcome children to the rhythm, the joy, the irresistible fun of music? It is the first cut on the first recording I ever did for kids.

By miraculous good fortune, I was doing a play in Washington, D.C., in the early '70s when Calloway happened to be appearing in the theatre next door. He was playing "Vernon Hines," the second-banana comic role in *Pajama Game*. The show was no great shakes, and Calloway himself was clearly past his manic prime. But you could still see the impish grin on his face, the lively spring in his gait, the devilish glint in his eye. Lucky me. I got to see Cab Calloway in the flesh: one of the great, happy spirits of our musical history.

(A Tony Award winner and Oscar nominee, actor John Lithgow has received four Grammy nominations, including three for his children's album recordings.)

ROSEMARY CLOONEY

 ## LIFETIME ACHIEVEMENT AWARD, 2002

Paramount Pictures/Getty Images

Today, Rosemary Clooney may be best known as actor George Clooney's aunt. While it's a nice celebrity association, it sells Rosemary criminally short of her own impressive achievements. Before Elvis Presley changed the world as we knew it, Clooney was one of the most popular singers of her day. Among her signature songs were "Come On-a My House" (her first big hit, and though she disliked it, it made her a star), "Half as Much," "Hey There," and "This Ole House."

Like many of her contemporaries, such as Doris Day and Patti Page, she was a smooth, pitch-perfect vocalist who could swing a jazz vocal and sweetly croon a ballad.

She had a star turn in 1954's *White Christmas* with Bing Crosby, Danny Kaye, and Vera-Ellen. Though it would prove to be her only major film role, it was the year's top-grossing movie, topping its next closest rival, *The Caine Mutiny*, by more than 30 percent in box office receipts.

Most of her peak work predated the Grammy Awards, but her 1954 single "Hey There" was inducted into the Grammy Hall of Fame in 1999. In the '90s, Clooney enjoyed a renaissance, releasing a series of well-received albums on the Concord Jazz label and reveling in the acknowledgment of a younger generation of women singers who recognized the impression she made on the music world.

Rosie is one of the greatest women I've ever known in my life, and such a talent.
—Keely Smith, Grammy-winning jazz vocalist
and friend, acceptance speech, 2002

ROSEMARY CLOONEY
Tribute by Diana Krall
February 27, 2002

The first Rosemary Clooney record I bought, when I was about 14 years old, was *Everything's Coming Up Rosie*—her first album for Concord in 1977. That was her "comeback" record, but Rosemary Clooney had always been a part of my life. Every Christmas my family watched *White Christmas* (we still do). My father would play "Count Your Blessings" on the piano. And Rosemary was heard in our home more than just on Christmas Eve.

As a jazz piano player, I was drawn to Rosemary's recordings because I love the way she sings—her singing influenced my playing. I would play along with her records, trying to capture the same feel. She is true to the melody, yet makes it uniquely hers.

And she knows how to tell a story—both ours and her own. When Rosemary sings a song, you know she knows what she's talking about—every lyric she sings, you know she's lived. The best piece of advice she ever gave me was, "Just sing the damn song, honey, it's all right there!"

Rosemary began singing with her sister Betty in Cincinnati, entering amateur contests. They then sang in a band led by Tony Pastor. Rosemary went solo, joining Columbia Records in 1950, and began a string of hits that included "You're Just in Love," "Half As Much," and "Hey There," running up a total of 13 Top 40 hits in the early '50s alone.

Now, several comebacks into her stellar career, Rosemary has developed an even greater understanding of her voice and the unique and powerfully effective way she approaches a song.

Rosemary Clooney is one of the most important interpreters of American popular song, and she has collaborated with some of the finest arrangers, musicians, and singers of our time, including Guy Mitchell, Marlene Dietrich, the Benny Goodman Sextet, and Duke Ellington. This is not only because of her great talent, but because of who she is—generous, smart, funny, indomitable; devoted to her family and dedicated to her music; mother and mentor, girl singer and road warrior. Rosemary is always herself—she's too honest not to be, whether onstage or off. Congratulations my dear Rosemary, you are a blessing to us all.

(Diana Krall won the Best Jazz Vocal Performance Grammy for 1999 for her album *When I Look in Your Eyes* and Best Jazz Vocal Album for 2002 for *Live in Paris*.)

LEONARD COHEN

LIFETIME ACHIEVEMENT AWARD, 2010

WireImage.com

For someone who was really a poet and novelist, Leonard Cohen did pretty well in music. Songs of his such as "Suzanne," "Bird on a Wire," and "Hallelujah," despite never having true hit recordings made of them, have become standards of a sort, widely enjoyed in many different cover versions.

In truth, Cohen learned guitar at age 13 and in his high school years played country songs in cafes in his native Canada. But while in college and during the early years of his career, he concentrated on literature, publishing an acclaimed book of poetry (*Let Us Compare Mythologies*, 1956), and an equally acclaimed novel (*Beautiful Losers*, 1966).

Cohen turned to songwriting as an extension of his poetry, and gained attention through a cover of "Suzanne" by Judy Collins. He released his own *Songs of Leonard Cohen* in 1967 to critical raves. His deeply melancholy songs, sung in his uniquely dour monotone, struck a chord, particularly with the college crowd. As such, he became perhaps the unlikeliest of rock stars, invited to play festivals like the Isle of Wight, where his performance awed the crowd despite its standing in stark contrast to the acts that preceded him, including Jethro Tull and Jimi Hendrix.

In 1987 Grammy-winning singer Jennifer Warnes released the well-respected *Famous Blue Raincoat: The Songs of Leonard Cohen*, which set the stage for one of Cohen's finest albums the next year, *I'm Your Man*.

Since then, Cohen's debut album has been inducted into the Grammy Hall of Fame, and he became a pillar for singer/songwriters who move against the prevailing pop wisdom of their era.

I want to thank The Academy for allowing me to be part of this distinguished company—this notable band as we make our way towards the finish line that some of us have already crossed.

—Leonard Cohen, acceptance speech, 2010

LEONARD COHEN
Tribute by Kris Kristofferson
January 31, 2010

The studio where I worked was dark, everybody gone, and producer Bob Johnston, who I knew from his great work there with my two biggest heroes—Bob Dylan and Johnny Cash—had something he wanted me to hear.

"Listen to this," he said.

It was a low, powerful voice carving out the words like a chisel in stone.

Like a bird on a wire.

Like a drunk in a midnight choir.

I have tried in my way to be free.

"That's my epitaph," I said.

It sounded like the voice of God. Still does. A kind, curious, superior intellect with a holy sense of humor. I got to see him in action a short time thereafter when he pulled a semi-miracle at the 1970 Isle of Wight Festival—the last of the Woodstock-like festivals. The summer of love had become an audience of enemies, half a million pissed-off people, like skinheads, and pink panthers, Algerians, etc., and the hills full of people who thought they deserved a free concert and would eventually tear down the walls. Everybody was mad about something, and they all took it out on the performers. They didn't like anyone, from Jimi Hendrix to Tiny Tim. Jimi kept trying for an extra hour or so, God bless him, but it wasn't happening. And the violence was increasing.

By the time they got around to Leonard—after two a.m.—they were burning the concession stands. And a truck. He left his trailer and walked onstage in his pajamas and a raincoat. He took 20 minutes to tune up. I figured they would kill him. I really felt sorry for him. It was so noisy I knew they would never hear how good he is. And then it happened. I've never seen anything like it. It was as if everyone quit breathing. You could hear a pin drop. They loved him. They still didn't like the rest of us, but they really loved him. I told Zal Yanovsky I'd like that kind of background music for my songs, referring to the tasty work of Bob Johnston and the boys and Jennifer Warnes.

"Boss," Zal said, "Leonard is an angst poet. You're an alcoholic."

My daughter says he's a pirate/poet. I think he'd like that.

His life and his art are a beautiful love song. Unlike any other. He's one of a kind.

(A three-time Grammy winner, Kris Kristofferson's songs, including "Me and Bobby McGee," "For the Good Times," and "Sunday Morning Coming Down," helped redefine Nashville songwriting. He was honored with a Recording Academy Lifetime Achievement Award in 2014.)

ORNETTE COLEMAN

LIFETIME ACHIEVEMENT AWARD, 2007

In 1959, from almost out of nowhere, Ornette Coleman changed the shape of jazz to come. Literally. Coleman and his quartet—Don Cherry on cornet, Charlie Haden on bass, and Billy Higgins on drums—eschewed traditional notions of chordal improvisation with the stunning album *The Shape of Jazz to Come* (Grammy Hall of Fame, 2015), at once winning admirers who saw a brave new jazz explorer and detractors who feared a musical anarchist. He followed *Shape* with the release of the album *Free Jazz*, a term he's credited with having coined, and the summation of his pursuit of music without boundaries.

Over time, the admirers have proved more prescient. Coleman's music, as well as his constantly inquisitive nature, has impressed a wide variety of acolytes, from those who found a kindred spirit in their own jazz pursuits—such as Cherry and Haden—to followers such as Pat Metheny and fellow music adventurers Jerry Garcia, Lou Reed, and others.

Coleman was born and raised in Texas and played in several local groups, but from the beginning was an unorthodox player. He caught on with Paul Bley's band and traveled with them to Los Angeles, where he relocated. He worked as an elevator operator while looking for empathetic musicians who understood what many heard as an out-of-tune player. Ultimately hooking up with Cherry, Haden, and Higgins, Coleman's release of *Shape* came as a bolt of lightning, which some found enlightening and others shocking.

He would continue making unorthodox moves throughout his career, "retiring" from music in his prime to learn violin, creating music that would come to be called free funk, and working with unlikely musicians such as Garcia, ultimately becoming a revered jazz icon before his death in 2015.

I believe music itself is eternal in relationship to sound.
—Ornette Coleman, acceptance speech, 2007

ORNETTE COLEMAN
Tribute by Charlie Haden
February 11, 2007

In 1957 I'd just arrived in Los Angeles from Missouri and was playing with Paul Bley at the Hillcrest Club. On my off nights I'd sometimes go to a club called the Hague where Gerry Mulligan and Chet Baker used to play. One night an alto player came in and asked if he could sit in. He opened his case and took out a white plastic alto. As soon as he started to play the whole room lit up for me. I couldn't believe how beautiful and brilliant it was. I knew I wanted to play music with him.

I subsequently met Ornette, who invited me to come over to his house and play. We got in his little Studebaker and went to his studio apartment, with music everywhere. He chose a piece of music and said to me, "Let's play this . . . I've written down some changes underneath the melody, but when I start to improvise," he said, "just follow me because I'm going to create a new chord structure." I thought to myself, "Man, this is how I've been wanting to play!" We played for three days, stopping only to eat.

We started rehearsing with Don Cherry and Billy Higgins. The four of us were all at the right place at the right time feeling the same way about music, and the Ornette Coleman Quartet was born. Before long, Nesuhi Ertegun from Atlantic Records signed us and we recorded *The Shape of Jazz to Come*.

The great thing about Ornette was that he loved Charlie Parker and could play in that style when he wanted to. But he wanted to play what he was hearing and go in his own direction, playing his own vocabulary, his own melodies—which were very unique. The tunes he was composing were innovative, with unusual intervals, different interludes, endings, motifs, codas, and introductions.

He's still inventing and searching. He's one of the few innovators in music today.

He continues to bring new music to the world. I hope he keeps doing it forever. The inimitable Ornette Coleman!

(Charlie Haden played bass as an integral part of Ornette Coleman's groundbreaking quartet starting in the late 1950s. He received three Grammy Awards and The Recording Academy Lifetime Achievement Award. He died July 11, 2014.)

LIFETIME ACHIEVEMENT AWARD, 2016

Lee Celano/AFP/Getty Images

In her lengthy career, singer Celia Cruz came a long way from winning cakes in singing contests in her native Cuba to becoming the Queen of Salsa throughout the world, known as much for her music as her signature looks and charisma.

She dressed the music in resplendent, colorful dresses and a constant, wide smile that reflected the effervescence of both her personality and salsa music. She appeared at the Latin Grammy Awards in 2002 with towering blue-and-white hair.

In 1950 Cruz got her first big break when she joined La Sonora Matancera, one of Latin music's top bands. She toured with them for 15 years, establishing her credentials. She began a solo career with a string of duet albums with Tito Puente. Though Cruz would eventually become the Queen of Salsa and Puente the King of Latin Music, these early recordings were not massive successes, but they led to her signing with Vaya Records, and a successful duet album with Johnny Pacheco, who co-owned sister imprint Fania Records. She would begin a long association with the Fania All Stars, and her fame would hit a pinnacle with her appearance in the 1992 film *The Mambo Kings*, at the age of 67.

By the time of her death in 2003, the four-time Latin Grammy and three-time Grammy Award winner was so beloved, an estimated 75,000 fans came to pay their respects as she lay in state in Miami's Freedom Tower.

In explaining how she ultimately met her father's dream that she become a teacher, Cruz also summed up the lasting value of her music: "I have fulfilled my father's wish to be a teacher as, through my music, I teach generations of people about my culture and the happiness that is found in just living life."

CELIA CRUZ
Tribute by Marc Anthony
February 15, 2016

I remember listening to Celia Cruz's music blasting out of the windows in my neighborhood in East Harlem, New York, long before I started doing music professionally. By that time she was one of the greatest living legends of our time.

My first interaction with Celia as a salsa singer was when I recorded my first album, *Otra Nota*. We were part of the same record label. From the moment we met, she welcomed me with open arms and became my professional godmother, always supportive and so protective of me.

I'll never forget the first time I was able to share the stage with her. I was so nervous! At that time I did not have a lot of experience performing on the big stages of the world, and yet there I was next to her and in the company of all of these great musicians. That night she embraced me in a very special way—the way only those who had the good fortune of being close to her presence could experience.

Her mastery of voice and song and her powerful transformation onstage were some of her many qualities. She possessed a voice like no other and an undeniable way of conducting herself in front of her audience and her fellow musicians. A lady in a male-dominated world, who handled her career with consistency, discipline, and admirable class.

She was so into details. Not even her intense work schedule and touring demands around the world would let her forget her friends and family's birthdays, and her Christmas cards with her personal touch were a yearly event. We all wondered how in the world this woman, with so many responsibilities as a worldwide performer and wife, found the time to pause and devote personal attention to so many of us. And indeed she did. She also had a great sense of humor.

Celia took her responsibility on the stage very seriously. It was amazing to see her sitting backstage quietly and serenely before it was her time to go on. From the instant that orchestra played the first chord she became this gigantic presence. She never, ever disappointed her audience.

Her legacy is so vast there is not enough space on this page, but the fact remains that her contribution to music will continue to have an impact worldwide for generations to come.

(A two-time Grammy winner and five-time Latin Grammy winner, Marc Anthony cohosted 2003's ¡Celia Cruz: Azúcar!, an all-star tribute to Cruz. He was honored as the 2016 Latin Recording Academy Person of the Year.)

TOM DOWD

TRUSTEES AWARD, 2002

Michael Ochs Archives/Getty Images

They say pop music isn't rocket science. Maybe, but Tom Dowd is proof it doesn't hurt to have a rocket scientist—or at least someone who for a time pursued a degree in nuclear physics—on your side. Dowd was a house engineer/producer at Atlantic from the label's early years, but his path to music was unique.

Even as he was learning piano, tuba, and bass, Dowd was also employed in the physics lab at Columbia University. At 18, he was drafted into the military. He soon found himself working on the Manhattan Project, the secret effort to develop the atomic bomb. Impressive, but Dowd was about to embark on his most explosive work.

At Atlantic he recorded what would become historic sides by Ray Charles, the Drifters, Ruth Brown, and others, as well as jazz greats such as John Coltrane and Ornette Coleman. His innovations included convincing fellow Atlantic executive Jerry Wexler to install a multitrack recording system in the label's studio, making Atlantic the first label to record using multiple tracks. He also helped pioneer stereo sound and the use of linear faders rather than knobs.

But as it turns out, this was all child's play. Dowd went on to produce Derek & the Dominos' *Layla and Other Assorted Love Songs*, arguably Eric Clapton's best album. Maybe Duane Allman's best album too. As Clapton points out, Dowd, who nearly became a full-time scientist, was the alchemist who helped the guitarist channel his romantic angst and addictive binges into some of his most honest and passionate music ever.

Dowd did the same with so many great artists, from the Allman Brothers and the Rascals to Booker T. & the MG's and Otis Redding. His contributions to the music of the rock era can't be overestimated.

> *I was never a good enough musician to make a living being a musician. I was a scientist; I was trained as a physicist. But I didn't have the patience to put in 10 more years to become a Nobel Prize winner, OK? [The audience roars in laughter.] I have had one good time the last 55 years putting together my scientific knowledge [and] my musical background.*
>
> —Tom Dowd, acceptance speech, 2002

CELIA CRUZ
Tribute by Marc Anthony
February 15, 2016

I remember listening to Celia Cruz's music blasting out of the windows in my neighborhood in East Harlem, New York, long before I started doing music professionally. By that time she was one of the greatest living legends of our time.

My first interaction with Celia as a salsa singer was when I recorded my first album, *Otra Nota*. We were part of the same record label. From the moment we met, she welcomed me with open arms and became my professional godmother, always supportive and so protective of me.

I'll never forget the first time I was able to share the stage with her. I was so nervous! At that time I did not have a lot of experience performing on the big stages of the world, and yet there I was next to her and in the company of all of these great musicians. That night she embraced me in a very special way—the way only those who had the good fortune of being close to her presence could experience.

Her mastery of voice and song and her powerful transformation onstage were some of her many qualities. She possessed a voice like no other and an undeniable way of conducting herself in front of her audience and her fellow musicians. A lady in a male-dominated world, who handled her career with consistency, discipline, and admirable class.

She was so into details. Not even her intense work schedule and touring demands around the world would let her forget her friends and family's birthdays, and her Christmas cards with her personal touch were a yearly event. We all wondered how in the world this woman, with so many responsibilities as a worldwide performer and wife, found the time to pause and devote personal attention to so many of us. And indeed she did. She also had a great sense of humor.

Celia took her responsibility on the stage very seriously. It was amazing to see her sitting backstage quietly and serenely before it was her time to go on. From the instant that orchestra played the first chord she became this gigantic presence. She never, ever disappointed her audience.

Her legacy is so vast there is not enough space on this page, but the fact remains that her contribution to music will continue to have an impact worldwide for generations to come.

(A two-time Grammy winner and five-time Latin Grammy winner, Marc Anthony cohosted 2003's ¡Celia Cruz: Azúcar!, an all-star tribute to Cruz. He was honored as the 2016 Latin Recording Academy Person of the Year.)

LIFETIME ACHIEVEMENT AWARD, 2008

Today singer/actress Doris Day is no doubt best remembered for her '50s romantic comedies such as *Pillow Talk* with Rock Hudson and *Teacher's Pet* alongside Clark Gable, from TV's *The Doris Day Show*, which ran from 1968–1973, or as the singer of her signature hit "Que Sera, Sera (Whatever Will Be, Will Be)." And while those efforts made her a household name, these selective memories skim the surface of a dauntingly talented singer and actress.

Day originally trained to be a dancer, but when an accident left her with an injured leg, she listened to, and began singing along with, big bands and Ella Fitzgerald on the radio during her recuperation. She earned a featured spot singing on a local Cincinnati radio station after an amateur showcase. Shortly after, she auditioned for bandleader Bob Crosby and won a spot in his band. A few months later, she was with Les Brown's band. She was only 17, but her voice had an emotional resonance and dexterity of someone wise well beyond those years. During World War II, she cut "Sentimental Journey" (Grammy Hall of Fame, 1998) with Brown's band. The song became a huge hit, especially with soldiers serving overseas. But it's also testament to a singer with a flawless voice and skilled jazz phrasing. She rightfully became one of the big band era's biggest singing stars.

She would also prove herself a serious actress in films such as *Storm Warning* (1951) and Alfred Hitchcock's *The Man Who Knew Too Much* (1956). In the '50s and '60s her recordings would move toward the pop of "Que Sera Sera" and "Secret Love" (both also in the Grammy Hall of Fame), but her singing would be no less accomplished and her warm persona no less inviting.

DORIS DAY
Tribute by Brian May

February 10, 2008

I spend a lot of time watching old movies out of the corner of my eye, because my dear wife is devoted to the vintage Hollywood genre—Fred Astaire, James Mason, James Cagney. I follow them all, by proxy. And I often wonder what some of the singers in these films would have sounded like with the benefit of Pro Tools to fix the little inaccuracies.

But when the divine Doris Day comes on, there is suddenly no need for tricks—and as a perfectionist I go into a kind of trance. I melt. You know, it is simply unbelievable how accurate she is. I think one day someone will be able to prove that she had the best pitch of any female singer in history. But she is way beyond accurate; every note is found, approached by various routes according to context, hit with a million different inflections, caressed, adored, and allowed to gently fall to the Earth. She is technically unmatched, adorable, mind-blowingly expressive, and probably the best interpreter of a song I ever heard.

The scope of Doris Day's career is amazing. Beginning life in an Ohio suburb as Doris Kappelhoff in 1924, she was, at a young age, on her way to a professional dance career when injury curtailed that dream. Lucky for us, perhaps. She turned to singing, and, as vocalist for the bands of Bob Crosby and Les Brown, she soon became one of the finest big band singers of the era. And in her first film, *Romance on the High Seas*, she proved herself a legitimate actress too. In the '50s and '60s, through films with Rock Hudson, Jimmy Stewart, and others, she became a star, and then an icon, and in the '60s and '70s became both all over again on TV with *The Doris Day Show*.

My own music, rock music with Queen and beyond, might seem to belong to a very different genre, but the threads of music are all tied up together—we are all in the same river, we all try to speak from the heart, and the divine Doris Day speaks to me as clearly as to all the millions of fans she has inspired and influenced over the years. She might just be the most wonderful chanteuse in history. I just hope she knows how much she is still loved and respected.

Doris Rocks!

(Four-time Grammy nominee Brian May is guitarist for the band Queen, of "Bohemian Rhapsody," "We Will Rock You," and "We Are the Champions" fame. Queen was inducted into the Rock and Roll Hall of Fame in 2001.)

TOM DOWD

TRUSTEES AWARD, 2002

They say pop music isn't rocket science. Maybe, but Tom Dowd is proof it doesn't hurt to have a rocket scientist—or at least someone who for a time pursued a degree in nuclear physics—on your side. Dowd was a house engineer/producer at Atlantic from the label's early years, but his path to music was unique.

Even as he was learning piano, tuba, and bass, Dowd was also employed in the physics lab at Columbia University. At 18, he was drafted into the military. He soon found himself working on the Manhattan Project, the secret effort to develop the atomic bomb. Impressive, but Dowd was about to embark on his most explosive work.

At Atlantic he recorded what would become historic sides by Ray Charles, the Drifters, Ruth Brown, and others, as well as jazz greats such as John Coltrane and Ornette Coleman. His innovations included convincing fellow Atlantic executive Jerry Wexler to install a multitrack recording system in the label's studio, making Atlantic the first label to record using multiple tracks. He also helped pioneer stereo sound and the use of linear faders rather than knobs.

But as it turns out, this was all child's play. Dowd went on to produce Derek & the Dominos' *Layla and Other Assorted Love Songs*, arguably Eric Clapton's best album. Maybe Duane Allman's best album too. As Clapton points out, Dowd, who nearly became a full-time scientist, was the alchemist who helped the guitarist channel his romantic angst and addictive binges into some of his most honest and passionate music ever.

Dowd did the same with so many great artists, from the Allman Brothers and the Rascals to Booker T. & the MG's and Otis Redding. His contributions to the music of the rock era can't be overestimated.

> *I was never a good enough musician to make a living being a musician. I was a scientist; I was trained as a physicist. But I didn't have the patience to put in 10 more years to become a Nobel Prize winner, OK? [The audience roars in laughter.] I have had one good time the last 55 years putting together my scientific knowledge [and] my musical background.*
>
> —Tom Dowd, acceptance speech, 2002

TOM DOWD
Tribute by Eric Clapton
February 27, 2002

I first met producer/engineer Tom Dowd at Atlantic studios in New York, after Cream had signed with Ahmet Ertegun to ATCO Records in 1967. We were set to make our first serious album, having already made one with Robert Stigwood—which to be honest, was more like a home video, although very much made from the heart. But now we were going to be swimming in the big waters, with very big fish.

On our first day there we met Otis Redding, who just dropped by for a chat with Tom and Ahmet. I couldn't believe it. My mouth would go dry every time someone walked through the door of that place; it was like a musician's heaven. (Incidentally, we finished that album, *Disraeli Gears*, in one weekend.)

It was during that period, and again and again in later years, that Tom tried to impress upon me the concept that, no matter how alternative or specialized we believed our music to be, there was no way to hide behind that. Once it was released as a record, then we were in the marketplace along with everyone else, including our heroes, and we would be judged, ultimately, on nothing but our merits. It was a hard lesson to learn, but one of great value for me in the years to come.

All through the '60s, '70s, and '80s, I worked with Tom again and again on album after album, including *461 Ocean Boulevard*, *One in Every Crowd*, *E.C. Was Here*, *Money and Cigarettes*, and most significantly, *Layla and Other Assorted Love Songs*. For better or worse, the strength of that latter album rested almost entirely on Tom's faith in me. I had no finished songs, no real concept or idea of where I was going, nothing but an abstract burning passion for live, spontaneous music. On top of everything else, I refused to make the record under my own name, and was developing a powerful drink and drug problem—not a great position for any record producer to be placed in, but Tom pulled it off. He saw the potential and exercised the most incredible patience in getting through the obstacles that I would constantly place in front of him. It's little wonder that I eventually came to look on him as a father figure.

It was through this development of our relationship that I gradually began to learn who I was and what my skills were. Tom gave so much time to me, teaching me to recognize my individuality, to value myself, yet at the same time pushing me forward, encouraging me to try new methods and techniques. I owe him more than I can ever repay.

So far, I have written only of my own experience with Tom, and that is only a tiny piece of the picture. He has worked with everyone I can think of, at least everyone that I like, and has probably given to each of those artists at least as much as he gave to me, and perhaps, sometimes even more. It is almost inconceivable that one man could give so much love, and yet I know he does, and has, over and over again.

There is a tribe of musicians, spread all over the world, who have been fostered and nurtured by Tom Dowd. We know who we are, and we are proud of who we are, but most of all, we are proud of him. I am honored and privileged to be one of them.

(Guitarist Eric Clapton has won 17 Grammy Awards.)

EARTH, WIND & FIRE

LIFETIME ACHIEVEMENT AWARD, 2016

Michael Ochs Archives/Getty Images

Earth, Wind & Fire founder Maurice White created perhaps the most successful R&B/funk band of the '70s and '80s. That he did it while incorporating African instrumentation and a hard-to-define spirituality into the music was pretty astounding for the time. Whether or not fans were clear what a serpentine fire or a ship fantasii were, they grooved to the songs as if the message were as simple and clear as "Boogie Wonderland."

And for a good reason: The songs do indeed boogie. EW&F are a tight, horn-driven funk band borne in the spirit of James Brown's Famous Flames but infused with a melodic pop sensibility and uplifting message. Combined with an invigorating stage show, the band became an irresistible force, reportedly the first African-American act to sell out Madison Square Garden.

Among their six Grammy wins were awards for classic EW&F workouts "Shining Star" and "Boogie Wonderland," and also for the ballad "After the Love Has Gone," cowritten by David Foster. The group has netted 17 total nominations.

As the era of civil rights protest songs and early-'70s blaxploitation cautionary tales such as Curtis Mayfield's "Superfly" drifted toward the hedonistic disco epoch, EW&F may have been the perfect bridge. Espousing spiritual love and the ethereal majesty of the universe in sexually charged funk rhythms may have been just as timely as it ultimately proved to be timeless.

EARTH, WIND & FIRE
Tribute by Big Boi
February 15, 2016

Earth, Wind & Fire were established by Maurice White in Chicago in 1969 with the vision of spirituality and universal love. From their 1971 self-titled debut album and classics such as 1975's *That's the Way of the World* and 1976's *Spirit* to 2013's *Now, Then & Forever*, they have helped bridge the gap between the music tastes of all ethnicities.

With songs like "Shining Star," "September," "Reasons," and "Let's Groove," Earth, Wind & Fire moved the music world one song at a time. This funky talented group is not only considered one of the best in the R&B genre, but they incorporated elements of jazz, pop, disco, soul, and even rock into their timeless music, selling more than 90 million albums worldwide. Along the way, the gifted group became the first African-American act to sell out Madison Square Garden.

Maurice White, Verdine White, Philip Bailey, Ralph Johnson, Larry Dunn, Johnny Graham, Al McKay, Fred White, and Andrew Woolfolk collaborated to create this rich, eclectic sound, with a plethora of instruments and the goal of uniting all in peace and harmony.

As we all know, this universally appreciated group has received numerous accolades for their relentless leadership in music, and I am honored to celebrate their Lifetime Achievement Award.

(As one-half of the six-time Grammy-winning duo OutKast, Big Boi performed the group's chart-topping hit "The Way You Move" with Earth, Wind & Fire at the 46th Grammy Awards in 2004. The following year he was featured on "This Is How I Feel," a track included on Earth, Wind & Fire's album *Illumination*.)

DAVID "HONEYBOY" EDWARDS

LIFETIME ACHIEVEMENT AWARD, 2010

As the title of the 2007 Grammy-winning album *Last of the Great Mississippi Bluesmen: Live in Dallas*—featuring David "Honeyboy" Edwards, Robert Lockwood Jr., Pinetop Perkins, and Henry Townsend—suggests, when Edwards died in 2011 at the age of 96, he reportedly was the last blues player who lived and played with the likes of Charley Patton and Robert Johnson.

But for the bulk of his career, and arguably its most essential years, he was a seldom-recorded itinerant musician in the South, moving from town to town playing on the streets for nickels and dimes while encountering the likes of blues greats such as Johnson, Patton, and Tommy Johnson, from whom Edwards says he learned much about playing guitar. He was said to be present when Robert Johnson took the drink that was poisoned by a jealous husband. He was recorded in 1942 by folklorist Alan Lomax for the Library of Congress, but didn't record commercially until 1951, and even then he didn't create a vast body of recordings.

Nevertheless, he was widely revered by latter day rock and blues guitarists and blues aficionados. Artists such as Mick Fleetwood recruited Edwards to play with Fleetwood Mac in 1969, and Rolling Stone Keith Richards made a pilgrimage to a small Connecticut club in 2004 to check out a true original of the Delta blues. "Honeyboy" was inducted into the Blues Foundation's Blues Hall of Fame in 1996 and was recognized with the National Endowment for the Arts National Heritage Fellowship Award in 2002.

DAVID "HONEYBOY" EDWARDS
Tribute by Mick Fleetwood
January 31, 2010

David "Honeyboy" Edwards came into this world on June 28, 1915, in Shaw, Mississippi. He ultimately climbed to the top of the blues scene and now, at 94 years young, still tours regularly and globally. Honeyboy is one of the last of the original Delta bluesmen. He has no pretense, no ruse. He is what he is in the most beautiful and pure way—a bluesman who defines bluesmen.

After years of hearing about Honeyboy from producer Mike Vernon, I finally got to play with him in 1969 while the original Fleetwood Mac was recording the album *Blues Jam in Chicago*. Honeyboy is featured on three tracks on that album, and recording with him is a memory I will always treasure.

Honeyboy Edwards was a major player in defining the Delta blues sound. Moving to Chicago in the mid-'50s, Honeyboy played small clubs and street corners with the likes of Floyd Jones, Johnny Temple, and Kansas City Red. In 1972 Honeyboy met harmonica player Michael Frank, and the two soon became fast friends. In 1976 they hit the North Side blues scene as the Honeyboy Edwards Blues Band.

Honeyboy's musical path has led him to collaborations, concerts, and recordings with almost every major blues legend, including Robert Johnson, Charley Patton, Sonny Boy Williamson, Howlin' Wolf, Lightnin' Hopkins, Little Walter, Magic Sam, Muddy Waters, and scores of other greats.

In 1996 Honeyboy was inducted into the Blues Hall of Fame. In 2007 he was honored with a Grammy (along with other artists on the album *Last of the Great Mississippi Delta Bluesmen: Live in Dallas*) in the Best Traditional Blues Album category. That same year, while touring Europe with my band, the Mick Fleetwood Blues Band, I was honored to have Honeyboy on the bill. He brought the house down and I remember standing in the wings waiting to go on while Honeyboy took his bows during a long standing ovation.

David "Honeyboy" Edwards has spent his life playing and singing the blues. He's touched millions of hearts and souls, guiding his fans through the medicine he simply calls "the blues." And tomorrow, Honeyboy will get up, grab his guitar, and play another club somewhere. Through this prestigious award, and his decades of recordings and live performances, David "Honeyboy" Edward's legacy will continue on forever.

(Mick Fleetwood won the Album of the Year Grammy for 1977 with Fleetwood Mac for the album *Rumours*.)

CLARENCE "LEO" FENDER

Courtesy of G&L Musical Instruments

There were a number of key ingredients in the stew that became rock and roll: the blues, boogie-woogie, western swing, country music, and arguably a certain Tupelo, Mississippi–born former truck driver who brought them all together in a studio in Memphis, Tennessee.

Certainly somewhere in there fits the solid-body electric guitar, as amplified instruments allowed for the transition away from big bands. And as players began experimenting with distortion and other sounds and techniques, the electric guitar was essential in rock and roll's evolution.

Leo Fender's instruments, introduced in the early '50s, remain among the cornerstones for thousands of musicians. In 1951 Fender introduced what would become the Telecaster (though it started life as the Esquire and then Broadcaster). In late 1953, using techniques common to the technology industry today—iteration based on user feedback from the Telecaster—Fender issued the Stratocaster. The Tele and Strat continue today as two of the most popular electric guitars on the market. Among the players who have strongly favored one or the other are Jeff Beck, Eric Clapton, David Gilmour, Buddy Guy, Jimi Hendrix, Mark Knopfler, Stevie Ray Vaughan, and Bruce Springsteen, among hundreds of others.

Fender was well regarded for his creation of other instruments as well, including the Jazz Bass guitar, the Jaguar and Jazzmaster guitars, and the Twin Reverb amplifier. Due to poor health, in 1965 Fender sold the company to CBS. He died in 1991 after having suffered from Parkinson's disease for many years. But every time a legend or a novice picks up a Tele or a Strat is a reminder of the prescient designs of Leo Fender.

Leo never kept one guitar of all the ones he made because he said, "The next one I make is going to be so much better. Why do I want to keep something that's inferior?"
—Phyllis Fender, wife, acceptance speech, 2009

CLARENCE "LEO" FENDER
Tribute by Eric Johnson
February 8, 2009

When I was 11 years old, I started playing guitar, largely because I was drawn to the attractive mystique of the 1960s. It was a new era—a new movement in art and creativity. Right in the heartbeat of the action was Fender Musical Instruments, a company that was moving and shaking, stirring and fueling a whole new momentum for rock music and other genres.

There was a genius, like a majestic puppeteer, who helped orchestrate this original wave of beauty. The man behind the magic was Clarence "Leo" Fender. It is difficult to put into perspective the accomplishments of this one man. There was no available trail before he blazed it. Despite the fact that he had only vintage radios to reference, the amplifiers that he designed and built in the 1950s and 1960s, such as the Fender Twin Amp and Fender Twin Reverb, are still considered the benchmark of tone and are widely viewed as the best-sounding amplifiers even now, some 50 years later. It's hard to improve upon great work that was done right the first time around!

And the guitars . . . Leo's contribution is an elegant centerpiece that not only references the music, but also our world, our culture, and our modern age. There is not a corner of the earth that hasn't been touched or inspired by his inventions. Many of the sounds in music we know today are the direct efforts of Leo Fender. He designed original and aesthetically stunning instruments. Timeless in their artful beauty, the Stratocaster and the Telecaster still hold, even after 50 years, their coveted positions as some of the very best instruments ever made.

Mr. Fender thrived on "Fender Firsts," which were unprecedented innovations and groundbreaking technologies such as the synchronized tremolo and intonating bridge introduced in 1954. He constantly improved and updated his offerings each year, dreaming endlessly of new products to inspire the next budding artist. He was forever stirred by the love of his craft, not for money or for fame. Leo gladly lost revenue on some models in order to provide them to select musicians who were inspired and moved by these particular creations.

Clearly, Leo Fender was not an ordinary man. He was an instrument himself, expressing through his being the light of intuition. Someone once spoke of him as being "in a state of grace" when he designed and invented his musical gems. There is no doubt that Mr. Fender's legacy will resound for many ages to come. Like a fine sculptor, he crafted and shaped countless works of beauty during his lifetime, keeping his attention and his hands close to these treasures to ensure their quality. In doing so, he shaped and inspired millions of lives. I will always have strong and deep gratitude for this man, and I feel blessed to be one of those lives.

(An eight-time Grammy nominee, Eric Johnson won the 1991 Grammy Award for Best Rock Instrumental Performance for "Cliffs of Dover.")

FRED FOSTER

 ## TRUSTEES AWARD, 2016

Fred Foster has been one of the most important Nashville music entrepreneurs and creative geniuses of the past 60 years, but that doesn't mean he was solely a country music producer and executive. He launched Monument Records in Baltimore before moving it to Nashville, Tennessee, and some of his most groundbreaking hits were with pop/rock star Roy Orbison.

In the early '60s, Foster signed Orbison and produced all his major hits of the era, including "Only the Lonely (Know How I Feel)," "Oh, Pretty Woman," "Blue Bayou," "Crying," and "Dream Baby (How Long Must I Dream)," among others. While it may seem anyone could have produced hits given Orbison's soaring voice and his haunting songs, MGM Records learned the hard way when they signed him away from Monument in 1965 that there was magic in the Foster/Orbison team. Foster helped bridge pop, rock, and country with his cinemascopic productions of Orbison's records.

Maybe because he was originally a Nashville outsider, Foster was constantly drawn to left-of-center country acts, an instinct that served him incredibly well. He worked very early on with such strong-willed and idiosyncratic artists as Dolly Parton, Tony Joe White, and Willie Nelson, and even if he didn't oversee their biggest hits, he was certainly vindicated by their lasting and hugely influential careers.

Those same instincts led Foster to sign Kris Kristofferson as both a songwriter to his publishing company and as an artist to Monument. Kristofferson would go on to completely change the flavor of country songwriting in the early '70s by injecting doses of raw reality into the storylines, but he wouldn't do it alone. Foster cowrote one of Kristofferson's most influential songs: "Me and Bobby McGee," a hit for Janis Joplin.

Foster's induction into both the Musicians Hall of Fame and Country Music Hall of Fame are monuments to his enduring accomplishments.

FRED FOSTER
Tribute by Dolly Parton
February 15, 2016

I am happy to have the chance to say a few words about Fred Foster. He was like a foster parent (and a good one) to me when I first moved to Nashville in the early '60s . . . just a teenage country sow's ear that Fred tried to make into a silk purse. He never quite succeeded in that, but it was not from a lack of trying. He spent lots of time and money trying to groom me for the rockabilly genre, recording songs with me like the remake of "Happy, Happy Birthday Baby." He even got me a spot on *American Bandstand*. I was a fish out of water at that time in that field, but Fred saw that after a short time and recorded me country. "Dumb Blonde" is still one of my most popular songs. It was my first chart record with Fred.

Fred recorded my first country album, called *Hello, I'm Dolly*. It was Fred's title and a clever one, I might add. He wrote the liner notes on the back of that album and to this day it's one of the best album liners I've ever read. He began it by saying, "Sometimes you just know." Well, Fred had a way of just knowing . . . just knowing talent when he saw it and just knowing exactly what to do with it. I am proud to be part of the discoveries that Fred made and nourished.

He not only was the head of Monument Records and Combine Music Publishing, but was a great record producer as well. He recorded and produced Roy Orbison and his string of great hits. He also produced folks like Boots Randolph, Willie Nelson, Ray Stevens, Al Hirt, and many more that I don't have time to mention here.

Fred also cowrote "Me and Bobby McGee" with Kris Kristofferson, a fact unknown by many. That song has been recorded by so many artists like Roger Miller, Janis Joplin, and even me. It's only fitting that Fred has been inducted into the Musicians Hall of Fame & Museum, as well as so many other awards and accolades that he has received through the years. I am proud to be one of the people to congratulate Fred on receiving the 2016 Trustees Award from The Recording Academy.

I have heard Fred Foster referred to as a genius all through the years and I couldn't agree more. As far as my own thoughts, I will sum it up by using the title of one of my own songs. Fred, I will always love you.

(A seven-time Grammy winner, Dolly Parton was honored with a Recording Academy Lifetime Achievement Award in 2011. She has two recordings inducted into the Grammy Hall of Fame: "Jolene" and "I Will Always Love You.")

THE FOUR TOPS

LIFETIME ACHIEVEMENT AWARD, 2009

Michael Ochs Archives/Getty Images

The Four Tops are one of the most successful and certainly the most enduring of the Motown vocal groups. That's pretty impressive when your labelmates at Hitsville U.S.A. included Smokey Robinson and the Miracles, the Supremes, and the Temptations.

The Tops were the fortunate recipients of some the best songs from the Motown house team of writers Brian Holland, Lamont Dozier, and Eddie Holland, and that's saying a lot: "Baby I Need Your Loving," "It's the Same Old Song," "Reach Out I'll Be There," Standing in the Shadows of Love," and "Bernadette" among them.

But they also had Levi Stubbs, perhaps the grittiest singer in the Motown stable. His delivery was urgent and demanded your attention, even on ballads such as the underrated "Ask the Lonely."

Starting life as the Four Aims (Stubbs, Renaldo "Obie" Benson, Abdul "Duke" Fakir, and Lawrence Payton), the Tops kicked around Detroit, finding their voices on several labels, working in a jazz and supper club vein, but with little success. They finally signed with friend Berry Gordy, who initially planned a jazz album, which was recorded and then scrapped. They would go on to land seven Top 10 pop hits, including the Grammy Hall of Fame-inducted "Reach Out," and enjoy the same lineup for more than 40 years.

To me this is the highest honor you can get in this business, a Lifetime Achievement Award for that which you loved to do. Obie, Levi and Lawrence, and myself, loved every minute of what we've been doing. And they're here today, as they've always been with me.

—Abdul "Duke" Fakir, acceptance speech, 2009

THE FOUR TOPS
Tribute by Lamont Dozier
February 8, 2009

When I learned that I was going to be able to write songs for and produce the Four Tops at Motown Records, I was nervous. They had a reputation for talent and integrity, and I knew that I had to go all out for them.

The Holland Brothers (Brian and Eddie) and I were intent upon creating a sound for the Four Tops that would be everlasting. The challenge was to write hit songs that would be able to showcase their incredible vocal skills and signature dances.

The Four Tops are the quintessential group that all male vocal groups aspire to emulate. They were all my friends and I have deep love for each and every one of them. The Tops—Abdul "Duke" Fakir, Renaldo "Obie" Benson, Lawrence Payton, and Levi Stubbs—were all like brothers to me. We worked together, had fun together, and sometimes fought together as we were trying to harness the creative energy inside each member and allow them to be individuals within a cohesive group. From "I Can't Help Myself (Sugar Pie, Honey Bunch)" to "Reach Out I'll Be There," the stories behind the songs will shape my life forevermore.

I remember when Levi didn't believe he was the right lead to sing the vocal on "Baby I Need Your Loving" and we had to really sit him down and make him do it. This of course was their first Top 10 record that we shared together and now an all-time classic.

Then I remember several years later, after all the hit records, when the Four Tops went back to Motown for one more try in 1983. The Hollands and I got together again and wrote a few songs for the Tops. The album was strategically named *Back Where I Belong* and the single hit the Hot 100, appropriately named "I Just Can't Walk Away," which was how we all felt about each other.

Later, in 1988, when I was writing with Phil Collins for the soundtrack to Phil's film *Buster*, we came up with a song for the Tops called "Loco in Acapulco." Phil and I had Atlantic Records fly them to Los Angeles and we had the time of our lives in the studio recording what would be one of their last significant hits. It was as if time had stood still, and we were back in the 1960s in the Motown days, only this time I was working with Phil Collins and the Four Tops!

I am so proud to have my name on their repertoire of hits. I am so proud to be able to call the Four Tops my friends.

(Along with songwriting partners Brian and Eddie Holland, Lamont Dozier wrote numerous hits for the Four Tops and many other Motown Records artists. He was inducted into the Songwriters Hall of Fame in 1988 and, along with the Hollands, received a Trustees Award from The Recording Academy in 1998.)

GLENN GOULD

 ## LIFETIME ACHIEVEMENT AWARD, 2013

Ullstein Bild/Getty Images

Glenn Gould was one of the most celebrated, not to mention enigmatic, classical pianists of the 20th century. That might be as expected given his place among The Recording Academy's Lifetime Achievement Award recipients. But Gould's accomplishments came in the face of severe hypochondria and antisocial tendencies, which caused him to abandon public performance at age 31 and likely contributed to his early death at age 50 in 1982.

Those afflictions caused many concert cancellations and often captious or sarcastic comments from critics and conductors alike. Conductor George Szell may have summed up both Gould's talents and torments in a succinct sentence: "That nut's a genius."

Born in Toronto, Gould was a musical prodigy who exhibited perfect pitch by age three and who learned to read music before he could read books. He made his first public performance in 1945, and in 1957 he became the first North American musician to tour the Soviet Union since World War II. But he quickly became disillusioned by live performance, preferring the control he could exert in the recording studio.

Gould's career was bookended by two landmark recordings of Bach's *Goldberg Variations*. Both would earn a Grammy pedigree, and both reimagined the works brilliantly. His 1956 recording was inducted into the Grammy Hall of Fame in 1983, and his 1982 version, completely different in pace and tone but viewed as equally accomplished, won the Best Classical Album Grammy for that year.

Gould would go on to both compose and write about music, and he also made a number of TV and radio documentaries in Canada. But ultimately, his hypochondria and very real hypertension would lead to a cycle of ever-increasing prescription medications and finally a massive stroke that precipitated his untimely death. In the years since, the Glenn Gould Foundation and the Glenn Gould School—both based in his hometown of Toronto—continue to reflect his impact and carry on his legacy.

GLENN GOULD
Tribute by Lang Lang
February 10, 2013

Glenn Gould was an amazing personality. Every note he played was so individual, from his groundbreaking first recording of Bach's *Goldberg Variations* (at the age of 23) to his recorded surveys of huge sections of the piano literature. He was perhaps one of the most unusual musicians ever to have performed (he retired from public performance completely at a young age, spending the rest of his performing life in the recording studio), but such was his wonderful musicianship that he is only more beloved by his audience. He performed very little in comparison with the other great soloists, yet his connection with his audience was so incredible that the music-loving public was (and is) devoted to him through the great strength of his musical communication.

Think of Glenn and one word springs to mind: Bach. Glenn had a connection with Bach's music perhaps above all other composers. It was completely suited to his very intelligent approach to music (he always tried to approach a score as a fellow composer, aiming for a freedom and understanding as if he might have written it himself) and he recorded nearly all of Bach's output for the keyboard across his career. The clarity and beauty of sound he brings to this composer is unparalleled. Bach said he wrote his music for the glory of heaven, and Glenn's performances elevate his works to a spirituality that I have never heard equaled. The *Goldberg Variations* recordings that he did at the beginning and end of his career are two thoroughly different, and equally beautiful, interpretations of one of the most magnificent works in the piano literature and every pianist (including myself) that has ever opened the score lives in the shadow of Glenn's performance.

But Glenn was an artist far above and beyond one composer. He recorded music from the classics through Scriabin and Schoenberg to his own works—and was not afraid to be controversial in his delivery (a stated distaste for the music of Mozart, for example, of whom he held the opinion that he died too late, led to some sometimes shocking and invariably brilliant performances). His famous performance of Brahms' D minor concerto led to his collaborator Leonard Bernstein issuing a disclaimer to the audience at Carnegie Hall beforehand, and is a very personal but amazing interpretation. His favorite composer was the early master Orlando Gibbons, whose work he passionately performed both on record and in the concert hall. His artistic heroes ranged from Leopold Stokowski to Barbra Streisand.

Although Glenn Gould died tragically young at only 50, he committed an enormous amount to disc (and film), and it is through his recorded legacy that we can remember him.

Glenn, you were the most amazing musician. We are so lucky to have had you among us. Thank you for leaving behind these wonderful recordings that move and inspire me and countless others. Glenn, we miss you.

(Lang Lang is arguably the most renowned Chinese pianist in history and enjoys superstar status in the classical music world. He was nominated for a Grammy in 2007 for his recording of Beethoven's *Piano Concertos Nos. 1 & 4*, and serves as the Grammy Cultural Ambassador to China.)

GRATEFUL DEAD

LIFETIME ACHIEVEMENT AWARD, 2007

Michael Ochs Archives/Getty Images

The Grateful Dead created their own universe in a number of ways. They're probably the most famous nonmainstream band in history, building an enduring career following only their own road map, and scoring only one Top 10 single, 1987's "Touch of Grey," which came 20-plus years into their career. They were the spiritual leaders of a counterculture community in San Francisco's Haight-Ashbury that spawned the Summer of Love even as violent civil rights and anti-Vietnam protests were spreading across the nation. But most of all, the Dead, or their followers, revolutionized the artist/fan relationship decades before social media, with a vast number of Deadheads traveling from show to show like modern-day disciples.

What they were following was a psychedelic band with Americana roots that espoused peace and consciousness expansion, and whose meandering live shows gave birth to the jam-band aesthetic and probably the tie-dyed T-shirt industry.

The Dead were launched by a banjo-playing bluegrass fan, Jerry Garcia, initially as the Warlocks. Mixing folk, rock, bluegrass, blues, country, and psychedelic drugs, the Dead became the hippie band of choice. By 1970, the band released two classic albums that captured their essence in the studio, the Grammy Hall of Fame-inducted *Workingman's Dead* and *American Beauty*, which contained tracks that would become staples, including "Truckin'" and "Sugar Magnolia."

The band, which continues to perform without their late founding father Garcia, has left an indelible mark and earned a lengthy list of followers, including Phish, Dave Matthews, John Mayer, and many others.

We don't have an address or a P.O. box for the soul. We don't know where it lives but one thing we do know is that music gets us there. And in the groove that we have, and had, we found that joy and that peace and that freedom. And that's what this music was all about.
—Mickey Hart, acceptance speech, 2007

GRATEFUL DEAD
Tribute by Sen. Patrick Leahy
February 11, 2007

It seems like half a lifetime ago (and I guess it was) that my son Kevin, home from school, asked if I'd like to go with him and his buddies to a Grateful Dead concert at Washington's no-longer-there Capital Centre. I'm all for father-son outings, and I said sure. And I loved it.

After a while, word got around to the band that they had a balding fan on Capitol Hill, and they invited me to join them on the stage (in the wings), which I did, several times. I love telling the story of being onstage when a call came in from the secretary of state. He asked if I could turn the radio down. I explained where I was, and after a long pause he asked if I could tune out my "rock music" long enough to chat with the president. Then he handed the phone to Bill Clinton. The president said he wished he could come on over, but the Secret Service thing could have been a problem.

I told Jerry they should go to Vermont, and they did, and 110,000 showed up at Highgate—to this day, still the largest gathering in Vermont's history.

Jerry, Bob, and Mickey and I saw each other often over the years. The last time I saw Jerry, he asked my favorite tune. It was "Black Muddy River," which they then played at the last concert I saw Jerry perform in, the last song of his last set that day, at RFK Stadium.

The music lives on, but millions like me are sad that those concert experiences are gone. Because it was always more than the music, it was also the experience. And it was all for the fans. Though the savviest marketers on the road, the Dead enforced a pander-free zone for the benefit of the Deadhead community. You saw it in the way tickets were sold and in the way they freely shared their music. The stage sets weren't king at a Dead concert, the music was king. And was there or will there ever be a greater concert value? In the mix at a Dead concert might be Bob Dylan, Tom Petty, or Sting. Maybe all of them together.

Nor did the Dead's music cater to the lowest common denominator. It elevated, it embraced, and it inspired. It is a body of work that is at once sophisticated and simple, blending currents of Americana as diverse as rock, folk, and jazz, and salted with nuggets from sources as diverse as Shakespeare and Chinese poetry.

Their influence will live on and on. Even today, when Mickey or Bob get us together again, we aren't Democrats or Republicans first; we are, forever, Deadheads.

(Patrick Leahy is serving his eighth term as Democratic Senator from Vermont, and is the ranking member of the Senate Judiciary Committee. In 2002 he received the Grammys on the Hill Award from The Recording Academy.)

FLORENCE GREENBERG

TRUSTEES AWARD, 2010

Today, a major national political party may have nominated its first woman candidate for president, but in the late '50s, and especially in the music business, a female business leader was all but unheard of. But Florence Greenberg's rise as the first woman to run a significant record label may have been even more unlikely, given her roots as a New Jersey housewife.

Greenberg became intrigued with the music business through a friend of her husband who worked at music publisher Hill & Range. Greenberg's daughter introduced her to her high school friends, who had a signing group called the Poquellos. Greenberg liked what she heard, signed them to her fledgling Tiara Records label, and renamed them the Shirelles. She sold the master of their first song, "I Met Him on a Sunday," as well as the label, to Decca for $4,000 and used the proceeds to start Scepter Records, on which the Shirelles would go on to have their biggest hits, including the Grammy Hall of Fame–inducted "Will You Love Me Tomorrow."

In 1962 songwriter Burt Bacharach brought Greenberg a demo of a new song. Greenberg wasn't impressed by the song, but loved the demo singer. That singer, Dionne Warwick, signed with Greenberg and with a stream of Bacharach and Hal David–written hits, she'd become one of the biggest vocal acts of the decade. Her Scepter recordings "Alfie," "Don't Make Me Over," and "Walk on By" are all in the Grammy Hall.

Greenberg would go on to sign B.J. Thomas, the Kingsmen, the Isley Brothers, and others to her company, building one of the decade's most successful indie labels. She would ultimately sell the company in 1976 and retire from the business, but not before lowering the glass ceiling a few feet.

FLORENCE GREENBERG
Tribute by Dionne Warwick
January 31, 2010

Florence Greenberg was a woman with a great deal of ambition who made and broke many rules in the recording industry. Being a woman who owned and operated her own label, Scepter Records, put her in a class of her own. She could, and did on many occasions, go up against some very tough and aggressive folks in the business during the '60s, and in most cases won the battle and the war.

Her artists—including myself, the Isley Brothers, the Shirelles, B.J. Thomas, and others—earned numerous gold and platinum records with the help of the tireless promotion given to each of us on the Scepter/Wand roster. And for what was considered a "small" record label, she was able to get a few of us into films doing title songs for some very important movies of the time.

We would call her "Mother Hen" because she treated us like our mothers would, and I truly thought at times she really believed she was our mother. She laughed with us, cried with us, went through the births of our children with great joy, and threw great parties, which she loved to do.

I will always remember hearing her voice through the elevator shaft whenever I came to the office, calling for Marvin, or Stevie, or any other person on staff at Scepter, and I am certain the entire building at 254 West 54th Street heard her too.

Remembering the day she called me into her office to let me know she was closing the doors of Scepter still brings a hurt to my heart almost as great as hers must have been. She explained that the "big boys" were buying all of the small independent labels such as Scepter and before she sold to them she would close the doors herself, and that is what she did. I remember her saying to me to look for a label that would be as good for me as Scepter was.

I will always think of her fondly and with gratitude for recognizing my talent and giving me the opportunity to become one of the artists on Scepter Records. She was truly one of a kind, and it is befitting that she is being remembered in this fashion. I know she would be pleased!

(Five-time Grammy winner Dionne Warwick recorded for Scepter Records throughout the 1960s, where she enjoyed some of her most legendary hits, including "Walk on By" and Grammy winner "Do You Know the Way to San Jose?")

BUDDY GUY

LIFETIME ACHIEVEMENT AWARD, 2015

Wireimage.com

Blues guitar great Buddy Guy may be the most direct bridge between the blues and rock and roll, at least judging by his acolytes—rock guitar stars such as Jeff Beck, Eric Clapton, Jimi Hendrix, and Mark Knopfler, among many others.

George Guy was born in Lettsworth, Louisiana, in 1936 and as a youth absorbed the sounds of B.B. King and Lightnin' Hopkins. After migrating to the northern blues capital of Chicago, Guy struggled to find his place. But his impressive playing and the sense of showmanship he learned from watching Guitar Slim in Louisiana would ultimately help him regularly win local talent contests. He befriended all the right people (Muddy Waters, Otis Rush, Freddie King), and in the late '50s signed to Chicago's "it" blues and R&B label, Chess Records, where he cut his own sides as well as played on sessions for Waters, Howlin' Wolf, and others.

Guy didn't record his first album until 1967's *I Left My Blues in San Francisco*, but it was in time to influence the young guard of rock guitarists. Hendrix regularly praised Guy in interviews. In the '80s, players such as Clapton and Stevie Ray Vaughan cited Guy as the biggest influence on rock's electric spin on the blues.

In more recent years, excellent latter-day Guy albums such as early '90s releases *Damn Right, I've Got the Blues* and *Feels Like Rain* would result in two of his seven Grammy Awards. He received the National Medal of the Arts in 2003, and he was recognized with the Kennedy Center Honors in 2012. He was inducted into the Rock and Roll Hall of Fame in 2005, welcomed into the club by both Clapton and B.B. King. And now into his 80s, Guy continues to rock the blues.

I didn't learn nothing from the book. It was watching Muddy Waters, T-Bone Walker, and all the great guys that I got my education from—by looking and paying attention and listening.

—Buddy Guy, acceptance speech, 2015

BUDDY GUY
Tribute by Jeff Beck
February 8, 2015

Buddy Guy, actually born George Guy on July 30, 1936, is a true product of the bayou. Music is in his blood. Now, at the age of 78, his playing still blows me away as much as it did the first time I heard him. He transcended blues and started becoming theater. It was high art, kind of like drama-theater, when he played. He was playing his guitar behind his head long before Hendrix. I once saw him throw the guitar up in the air and catch it, didn't miss a beat.

Buddy's impact on the blues and rock and roll cannot be denied. As a musician, his influence has been evident in the careers of not only myself, but Hendrix and Stevie Ray Vaughan, among many, many others.

I remember seeing him play in the early '60s and saying to myself, "I didn't know a Strat could sound like that," until I heard Buddy's tracks on the *Blues from Big Bill's Copacabana* album—it was the total manic abandon in Buddy's solos. They broke all boundaries. I just thought, "This is more like it!" His solos weren't restricted to a three-minute pop format; they were long and really developed.

I truly cannot think of another instrumental artist who has done so much after coming from such humble beginnings. Buddy's early experiences in the Chicago blues circles to his time at Chess Records sitting in with Muddy Waters all led him to the pinnacle of the blues 'n' rock genre.

For over a half century now, Buddy has blended the genres of blues and rock and roll like no other performer, before or since. His live concerts are legendary and the music world would be a very boring place without his influence. I know that my guitar wouldn't sound half as good if I hadn't heard his first.

(An eight-time Grammy winner, Jeff Beck performed in tribute to Buddy Guy at the 35th Annual Kennedy Center Honors in 2012. Beck and Guy joined forces for a successful co-headlining tour in the United States in 2016.)

CHARLIE HADEN

LIFETIME ACHIEVEMENT AWARD, 2013

Most legendary artists exert their influence because contemporaries and following generations study their style and incorporate the innovations into their own playing. More often than not, this is how next-gen players get "schooled" by their heroes.

That's true of the great jazz bassist and three-time Grammy winner Charlie Haden as well. Many have appreciated not just his skill as a player, but also his instincts, taste, and willingness to explore fresh and sometimes controversial paths in music.

But he's also literally "schooled" other musicians. In 1982 he established a jazz studies program at the California Institute of the Arts where he encouraged students to explore what he saw as the inseparable connection between music and spirituality. For Haden, when making music, one should live only in the moment of creation, with no sense of time before or after. His formal students include tenor saxist Ravi Coltrane, bassist Scott Colley, and trumpeter Ralph Alessi. His informal students include bass players from virtually every walk of music.

Haden was born in Iowa in 1937 into an exceptionally musical family, which gravitated to country and folk music in Haden's youth. He contracted polio at age 15, which affected his ability to sing, leading to his concentration on the bass. He moved to Los Angeles in the late '50s, eventually hooking up with Ornette Coleman, Don Cherry, and Billy Higgins for the quartet that shook the music world with the free-jazz breakthrough *The Shape of Jazz to Come* (Grammy Hall of Fame, 2015).

After that auspicious start, Haden's career became widely varied, playing with wide-ranging artists in styles that would include straight jazz, Latin jazz, folk, and others. And in 1969, he created the Liberation Music Orchestra, whose left-leaning sympathies explored the intersection of jazz and politics.

Before he was done (Haden died in 2014), he left several other legacies: his musician children Petra and Rachel (That Dog), cellist Tanya, and Josh (Spain), as well as son-in-law Jack Black.

> *I tell my students that if you strive to become a good human being with the qualities of generosity, humility, and having reverence for life, just maybe you'll become a great musician.*
> —Charlie Haden, acceptance speech, 2013

CHARLIE HADEN
Tribute by Flea
February 10, 2013

Charlie Haden has made it his life's mission to uplift the lives of others. In my case, he has succeeded dramatically. Time after time, I have listened to his recordings, seen him

WireImage.com

perform, and been touched by the divine truth. When I put on that first *Liberation Music Orchestra* record, or *The Shape of Jazz to Come*, or the recent *Come Sunday*, I vibrate with a feeling that gives me hope for humanity, makes my suffering and complaints feel petty, lets me forgive anyone who has ever done me wrong, and most importantly, makes me aspire to create a light of my own, to put something beautiful out into the universe. This is a humble aspiration, to get a little footlight going, to merge in the large planet of glowing by a great like Charlie Haden. But that's what his music does, that's who he is—a person who brings us all together, who reminds us that we are all connected by our highest selves.

Despite the sophistication and technical brilliance of his playing, which comes from a soul enthralled with the folk and country music he grew up on as a toddler, the bebop he fell in love with as a teenager, a highly intelligent mind and body, a work ethic disciplined enough to learn it, the countless hours of practicing and studying the music he loved . . . despite the highly cerebral music he has played, his music is still for everyone. No matter how far out or evolved he has gotten, his music has always been for all humans, not for academics. His sound is one that touches everyone—it will make you weep, dance like a lunatic, and sit back and listen to the story unfold. The most highly spiritual thing that anyone can do is have faith and be completely in the moment. When Charlie Haden makes music, that's exactly where he is, and that is what enlightenment is.

A few years ago, I had the fortune to play with the great Ornette Coleman. I practiced for months to prepare. I was nervous about it and when the big day came, I was up there with these great jazz musicians with all the chops in the world playing maniacally, and I'm just an uneducated punk rocker, but I did my best. I did OK. I was in awe of Ornette, and did my best to support him with all my heart. A lot of different musicians played that night, all of whom were very well-respected, but at one point, all the many musicians left the stage, Charlie walked on it, and it was just Charlie and Ornette. After all the intense virtuosity that had gone on through the night, Charlie began to play a simple, bluesy, twangy, country riff, a little folk melody, and I felt Ornette really come alive, saw the audience fall into a reverent silence, and Charlie just schooled everybody, shredded everything that came before. He had the ability to play anything, but just came from the gutbucket with the humble truth, and he and Ornette began to dance around each other, and it was the greatest thing I ever saw. These two giants, who turned jazz upside down 50 years earlier, just connecting on the highest level, and the sheer beauty and violence of it reduced me to joyous tears.

When one is playing the kind of improvisational music that Charlie Haden does, he is constantly, through the vehicle of technique and knowledge, channeling magic, the cosmos, letting God speak, whatever you want to call it. To do that at the level of a man like Charlie Haden, one has to have the highest character, the biggest heart, the purest intentions, and utter disregard for commerce. Charlie Haden's motivation has always been to reach for the highest light, brave the depths where one is most vulnerable, to reach that state of ecstasy where time does not exist, where all our world is an illusion, and to bring it on home to us, so we can love. He has done it all his life. I love Charlie Haden and I am so grateful for him. What an awesome fucking dude.

(Six-time Grammy winner Flea is a cofounder of Red Hot Chili Peppers.)

MERLE HAGGARD

LIFETIME ACHIEVEMENT AWARD, 2006

Along with fellow Californian Buck Owens, Merle Haggard altered the course of country music in the '60s working far from its traditional Nashville home base. He was raised in a boxcar by poor dustbowl Oklahomans, and his wild youth included run-ins with the law. As a result, Haggard would create the mold for the outlaw country stars who would follow him, and give his songs an authentic outsider appeal.

Haggard was born just outside Bakersfield, California, and ultimately helped put the California city on the country music map by creating the "Bakersfield Sound" alongside such contemporaries as Owens. Hits such as "The Bottle Let Me Down," "Okie from Muskogee," and "Mama Tried," which was inducted into the Grammy Hall of Fame in 1999, often told the story of recalcitrant antiheroes in music that brought elements of rock, blues, and folk to straight honky-tonk. Unlike the legend that sprang up around Johnny Cash, Haggard really did do time at San Quentin prison, and he put his experiences into songs that would touch millions.

Haggard won the Best Country Vocal Performance, Male Grammy for 1984 for "That's the Way Love Goes" and won Best Country Collaboration with Vocals for 1998 for "Same Old Train," on which he was joined by numerous artists, including some he influenced, such as Dwight Yoakam. Haggard died in 2016, but cast his long shadow over every guitar-slinging country and rock rebel.

MERLE HAGGARD
Tribute by Dwight Yoakam
February 8, 2006

From the mid-1960s, in the midst of cultural upheaval, political turmoil, generational strife, and a collective chaos violently accented and darkly punctuated by the accompanying assassination of three of the most prominent leaders in our nation's history, a solitary and uniquely American voice echoed across the continent from what seemed a memory out of a Steinbeck-described "Okie" and "Arkie" workers camp in central California in the form of a boxcar-born singer named Merle Haggard, who dealt with the love, loss, joy, and longing that co-inhabited the interior of a person whose expression and articulation of human isolation, displacement, and societal exclusion had resonance that belied any time and place.

His voice and words were at once so succinctly pure yet racked with an emotion that was so devastatingly honest it defied comparison or categorization. In a cultural and political time that was as unique as any in America's history, Merle Haggard had the most profound poetic impact and far-reaching artistic influence of any singer/songwriter in country music since Hank Williams Sr.

He had no contemporary equal. Without calculation or contrivance he spoke simultaneously from the hearts and minds of individuals who had been left behind as well as those who had done the leaving. He was as hardcore country a singer as any in history yet was continuously courted and begged by network television producers and pop music moguls to accept the idea of letting himself "cross over." He could at once rant and rail for the working man with a strength that equaled Woody Guthrie's, and then spin and backhand you with a fist that seemed thrown from the right. But what Merle Haggard did for me, and no doubt millions of others, was ease the feeling of being a stranger to love and a fugitive from life.

(Dwight Yoakam has won two Grammy Awards and has been nominated 18 times.)

RICK HALL

TRUSTEES AWARD, 2014

WireImage.com

Like Motown and Stax, Muscle Shoals became an iconic musical outpost that defined a region and a sound in the '60s and '70s. Unlike Motown and Stax, which represented the urban centers of Detroit and Memphis, Muscle Shoals truly was an outpost, a relatively small backwater on the Tennessee River. A seeming nowhere made a somewhere by Fame Studios owner and producer Rick Hall.

Hall was raised in poverty in rural Alabama and was an apprentice toolmaker and music hobbyist when the deaths of his father and new wife within a two-week span sparked an epiphany. He became an itinerant musician and during his travels befriended Billy Sherrill, who would later become one of the giant Nashville songwriters and producers. The pair began writing songs, and along with Tom Stafford, became partners in Florence Alabama Music Enterprises. Acrimoniously, Sherrill and Stafford split from Hall, leaving him with the studio and a little of their publishing rights. The strong-willed Hall then proceeded to build one the world's foremost recording destinations by assembling a crack house band that included Jimmy Johnson, Spooner Oldham, and Berry Beckett (the "Swampers" referenced in Lynyrd Skynyrd's "Sweet Home Alabama") and embracing the soul and southern-fried rock coming out of the South. Recordings cut at Fame represent some of the best of the '60s and '70s, including essential sides by Aretha Franklin, Wilson Pickett, Percy Sledge, and others. Taking note of what was becoming known as the Muscle Shoals Sound, rock acts migrated there to tap into the magic. The Rolling Stones cut "Brown Sugar" and "Wild Horses" there, and the studio gave rise to Lynyrd Skynyrd's "Free Bird."

In 2013 filmmaker Greg "Freddy" Camalier released *Muscle Shoals*, a tribute to the studio's history and a revealing look into the trials surmounted by Hall to preside over a truly American success story.

I want to thank all the musicians, songwriters, producers, and artists who helped me spread this sound of Muscle Shoals music throughout the world.

—Rick Hall, acceptance speech, 2014

RICK HALL
Tribute by Alicia Keys
January 26, 2014

The moment I stepped into Rick Hall's Fame Recording Studios, I felt a buzz. I was giddy like a little girl with excitement. The history, fellowship, and talent of the artists who'd come before enveloped and surrounded me and it was powerful. I tasted it on my lips; it sank down to my heart. I wanted to absorb and revel in the ambiance where this beautiful music was created and has gone on to move generations.

It's hard not to feel overwhelmed by the legacy and the names who walked through Fame Recording Studios' doors and put Muscle Shoals, Alabama, on the music map. As someone who has a real love and appreciation for music, I wish I could have spent just a few moments in the presence of the artists who made magic at Fame. I wish I could have sat in on those sessions with Etta James, Andy Williams, Aretha Franklin, Otis Redding, Wilson Pickett, just to name a few, as they found there was something incredibly special bubbling alongside the rolling Tennessee River. It had southern charm, deep soul, R&B, rock, pop, and just the right dose of funk. It was original and Rick Hall and the musicians he brought together were the very heartbeat of the sounds that came from the now-legendary town.

Hall built Muscle Shoals from the ground up with his determined spirit. Originally an artist and songwriter, Hall understood what it was like to want to share your music with the world. When doors were closed on him, he opened his own with his first small studio and soon after laid down roots as a music producer in Muscle Shoals. Thanks to Hall, the town of about 1000 has since become home to countless musicians, with many getting their first start and a chance to be a part of something completely original.

While the civil rights movement shook the country, the musicians entering Fame Studios were colorblind. Side by side with Hall, they created some of the most unique sounds and lasting music of their generation. Maybe Hall didn't know it then, but he was truly bringing people together through the universal language of music. The name Hall was making for himself with Fame Studios had artists from all over the world heading down south for a chance to be a part of what could come out of that magical studio.

Anyone who creates music knows that any good song comes with little magic, and I am proud to have been able to record at Fame Studios as part of the documentary *Muscle Shoals*. I was filled from being able to learn more about and experience a little bit of what Hall had created. He is a leader and visionary for our industry. His sheer diligence and determination are a lesson in themselves. And his desire to find the magic is the Soul of the Shoals. He is truly the father of Muscle Shoals music.

(A 15-time Grammy winner, Alicia Keys was featured in the 2013 documentary *Muscle Shoals*, and contributed a cover of Bob Dylan's "Pressing On" to the film's soundtrack.)

HERBIE HANCOCK

 ## LIFETIME ACHIEVEMENT AWARD, 2016

Wirelmage.com

A breathtakingly skilled pianist and keyboard player, Herbie Hancock has channeled his virtuosic abilities into a career in which left turns without green arrows were welcomed.

The 14-time Grammy winner was a child prodigy and soloed with the Chicago Symphony at age 11 in 1951. In the early '60s, he joined bop trumpeter Donald Byrd's group in New York and also signed his first recording contract with Blue Note Records. His debut, appropriately titled *Takin' Off*, featured his song "Watermelon Man," which Cuban percussionist Mongo Santamaria took to No. 10 on the *Billboard* Hot 100 in 1963.

That same year, Miles Davis asked Hancock to join his group, and Hancock stayed for five years, recording such Davis albums as *Miles Smiles* and *Sorcerer*, for which Hancock wrote the title track. During this time, Hancock also recorded his own *Maiden Voyage* (Grammy Hall of Fame, 1999).

In 1973 Hancock released *Head Hunters* (Grammy Hall of Fame, 2009), putting him at the leading edge of jazz fusion. *Head Hunters* had as much in common with blaxploitation funk as it did with jazz.

Future Shock, and its Top 10 R&B hit "Rockit," would come in 1983. Hancock was pushing well into the realms of electronic music as well as R&B, and somehow made the mix incredibly accessible, making him likely the only artist who could be claimed by the jazz community who was in regular rotation on MTV.

His sense of adventure has never waned, evidenced by albums such as the genreless *Gershwin's World* in 1998 as well as projects such as the Grammy Album of the Year–winning *River: The Joni Letters*, a jazz interpretation of Mitchell's songs with guests such as Norah Jones and Mitchell herself, both of whom have flirted with jazz traditions in their work.

Now a seemingly ageless elder statesman at age 76, Hancock has won numerous awards and musician polls that confirm his status as one of the great adventurers of jazz.

I know that when I was a young musician coming up, there were those that had the experience that I didn't have who I guess were thinking about me. They encouraged me. They pushed me forward when I was too shy to get up on the stage. They shared their experiences with me and they helped me along the way. Now it's my time to do the same thing. This is a tradition in jazz. In jazz we share. We respect each other. We don't try to hide anything. We uncover in order to discover. And those are the kinds of values that I would like to share with the younger generation because I've learned that from my elders.

—Herbie Hancock, acceptance speech, 2016

HERBIE HANCOCK
Tribute by Chick Corea
February 15, 2016

Herbie Hancock was on the New York City jazz scene making some young musical noise a few years before I arrived in 1959, fresh out of high school in Chelsea, Massachusetts.

I remember seeing him live for the first time when I went to the old Birdland at 52nd Street and Broadway. It was a Monday night. Mondays were the jam session nights at this venerable old club, and there was Herbie onstage with Joe Chambers and some horn players sitting in. I distinctly remember being amazed by the free and creative approach he and the band were taking with the standards they were playing. They were changing the rules and not asking for a license to do it. Right away, I connected with Herbie's sense of adventure and musical exploration, which I myself had just begun realizing.

The amazing thing about this adventure of his is that for a whole lifetime the adventure hasn't stopped. Miles set a powerful example for all of us—and Herbie was an integral part of that groundbreaking quintet that changed the face of jazz and music in general. But he has taken it several steps further by making full use of every new keyboard and sonic possibility, bridging new musical forms to combine the richness of our music's past with the unknown of the new creative ideas from his seemingly infinite imagination. With his ongoing creativeness and successes in movie scores and both pop and classical music, he's certainly never been afraid to explore and to change—and does so frequently and unabashedly.

From his first solo albums *Takin' Off*, *Empyrean Isles*, and *Maiden Voyage*, to his reach-out-to-the-world collaborations such as *Possibilities*, *River: The Joni Letters,* and *The Imagine Project*, his ever-evolving musical creativeness continues to inspire and soothe souls the world over.

Ever since I've known Herbie, he has always inspired me and the music world to be free and reach for greater heights of accomplishment. His validation of the artist's imagination and his demonstration of its ultimate purpose through the amazing music he has created—and continues to create—are a touchstone for every future culture to aspire to.

The world without Herbie Hancock is unimaginable. His contributions to music and to humanity on this planet are immeasurable. Congratulations, Herbie. You are simply the best!

(Chick Corea is a 22-time Grammy winner. His extensive discography includes 1978's *An Evening with Herbie Hancock & Chick Corea: In Concert*, a live album featuring both artists playing acoustic piano.)

GEORGE HARRISON

LIFETIME ACHIEVEMENT AWARD, 2015

Fox Photos/Hulton Archive/Getty Images

In the Beatles, George Harrison was known as "the quiet one." In retrospect, it may have been a forced silence. When you're in a band with a songwriting team like John Lennon and Paul McCartney, it's tough to shine through. But shine he ultimately did.

When the Beatles cut Harrison's songs, they were true gems. On *Help!* there was the irresistible lament "I Need You." On *Rubber Soul*, the jangly "If I Needed Someone," a major influence on the sound of the burgeoning folk-rock scene. From *Revolver*, the angry "Taxman" and trippy "I Want to Tell You." Later albums would give us the stunning "While My Guitar Gently Weeps," and the standards-to-be "Here Comes the Sun" and "Something" (which Frank Sinatra called the greatest love song of the last 50 years).

Harrison's first mainstream solo album, *All Things Must Pass*, was ambitious to say the least, reportedly the first triple album of all-original material by a single artist. Its impact in 1971 arguably exceeded that of records by his former bandmates, McCartney's *Ram* and Lennon's *Imagine*. Its main hits, "My Sweet Lord" and "What Is Life," remain today as the standard by which songs about personal quests for meaning are measured.

It must have been satisfying for Harrison, who in the Beatles was always struggling for his place, to be fully appreciated by his bandmates, and for a chance to expose his songs. But, fittingly for the quiet one, he was never seeking stardom. "I wanted to be successful," Harrison once said, "not famous."

> *I think the best lesson he ever taught me was that anything can be accomplished, as long as you set out to do it with love.*
>
> —Dhani Harrison, son, acceptance speech, 2015

GEORGE HARRISON
Tribute by Tom Petty
February 8, 2015

He never wanted to be the star of anything. But that's the place fate left him. He thought he was best as a team player. But we all know there was just too much great music in him to be contained by modesty.

When the Beatles ended all he had held inside came flowing out, manifesting itself in the 1970 album *All Things Must Pass*—a landmark LP that is still stunning by the quality of the songs and its complete originality. Like it or not, he was now the frontman of the band and more and more great music would flow from him the rest of his life.

It would take volumes to even list his musical achievements and I'm not going to try. His love of Indian music also produced volumes of lovely music, as well as creating a lasting influence on popular music. George truly was the peace and love guy. It wasn't a fad for him. He walked the walk. He dropped some beautiful wisdom on us without preaching, and always keeping a sense of humor, he was forever mindful that we are all so, so, human.

It's my guess that he's the only artist on tonight's program who actually changed the world.

Hare Krishna.

(Three-time Grammy winner Tom Petty, along with George Harrison, won the 1989 Grammy for Best Rock Performance by a Duo or Group with Vocal for *Traveling Wilburys Volume One* by the Traveling Wilburys—a supergroup that also featured Bob Dylan, Jeff Lynne, and Roy Orbison.)

ROY HAYNES

WireImage.com

Author Malcolm Gladwell asserts it takes 10,000 hours of practice to become an expert. As a working musician for some 70 years, drummer Roy Haynes has far exceeded 10,000 hours (if he practiced or played only an hour a day, five days per week, during his career, he'd be at nearly 20,000 hours). But the two-time Grammy winner may have also had a secret weapon: an obsession with drumming.

"I am constantly practicing in my head," he told *DrummerWorld*. "In fact, a teacher in school once sent me to the principal because I was drumming with my hands on the desk in class."

It's that kind of dedication to the craft that has led some to call Haynes the most recorded drummer in jazz. He has, to quote AllMusic, "played with about everyone." Who's everyone? Charlie Parker, Lester Young, Stan Getz, Sarah Vaughan, Thelonious Monk, George Shearing, Gary Burton, Chick Corea, Pat Metheny, Miles Davis, Art Pepper, and Dizzy Gillespie are just some of the higher profiles names.

Born in Boston, Haynes debuted professionally at age 17 in 1942. Through the years, he developed unique styles of playing that have had a wide-ranging impact, including on rock bands such as the Allman Brothers Band and Phish. Haynes used cymbals more prominently than just as accents, and he attacked the snare drum with sharp, rapid strokes, leading to his nicknames "Snap Crackle" and "the Father of Modern Drumming." He also led his own group, the aptly named Hip Ensemble. Haynes was so hip, in fact, that *Esquire* magazine named him one of their best-dressed men of 1960.

Haynes may have received such honors as The Recording Academy's Lifetime Achievement Award in 2011 and induction into *Down Beat*'s Hall of Fame in 2004, but that doesn't mean the 91-year-old has stopped, or maybe even slowed. In his 80s, he began playing with his appropriately named Fountain of Youth band.

ROY HAYNES
Tribute by Page McConnell
February 13, 2011

As a musician with both feet firmly planted in the rock vernacular, the opportunity to perform a set with Roy Haynes and a cast of jazz greats was more than a little daunting. In 2008 at the WaMu Theater at Madison Square Garden, daunting though it may have been, I joined bassist Christian McBride, trumpeter Nicolas Payton, saxophonist James Carter, and the inimitable Haynes for some really amazing takes on my Phish songs "Magilla" and "Cars Trucks Buses."

I was more than a little nervous backstage getting set to jam with some of today's most impressive players, anchored by a drummer who's played with some of music's true giants, guys like Charlie Parker, Bud Powell, and Lester Young.

But a quick rehearsal backstage and any fears were lifted. Graciously, Roy interpreted my tunes with the baddest grooves and a sensitivity that only he could provide.

I probably shouldn't have been surprised by that, or concerned about how the performance would go. Roy has played with so many of the biggest names in jazz that his chops are matched by generous professionalism.

Roy has been in the center of the jazz universe for more than 50 years. His résumé is filled with ridiculously amazing accomplishments. He was a member of the Charlie Parker Quintet, spent time with the great John Coltrane Quartet in the '60s, toured behind everyone from Sarah Vaughan and Stan Getz to Chick Corea and Pat Metheny, and has gigged with Miles Davis, Art Pepper, and Dizzy Gillespie. Quite a résumé.

All the while, Roy was cutting some great recordings of his own, including excellent records like *When It Haynes It Roars!* and the more recent *Fountain of Youth*, recorded appropriately when Roy was a young 79.

Roy was 83 when I played with him that night in New York—still vibrant, still a terrific player, and as always, a tremendous ambassador for jazz and all musicians. That night was one of the great thrills of my professional life.

(Phish keyboardist Page McConnell played with Roy Haynes at the Jammy Awards in New York on May 7, 2008. Phish was nominated for a Best Rock Instrumental Performance Grammy in 2000 for "First Tube," off their *Farmhouse* album.)

BUDDY HOLLY

LIFETIME ACHIEVEMENT AWARD, 1997

Michael Ochs Archives/Getty Images

Like a photograph that fades with the years, even towering legacies can dim over time. It's not that Buddy Holly's achievements have been forgotten. It's more like, after so many years, they're taken for granted, sort of like you know the foundation is under your house, but the four walls it supports seem more immediately consequential.

Charles Hardin "Buddy" Holley probably accomplished more in a shorter career than any other artist in the history of rock. In the span of about 18 months, he charted nine Top 40 singles, altered the way artists chose and recorded their songs, almost single-handedly popularized a brand of guitar, and left a lasting impression on several generations of artists.

Beginning with his first single, 1957's "That'll Be the Day" (Grammy Hall of Fame, 1998), Holly recorded most of his hits in Clovis, New Mexico, with producer Norman Petty rather than in the big record label studios. It provided an opportunity to experiment with the audio and arrangements, resulting in a sound that would presage the next stage of rock and roll, especially the music that would come out of England. Holly was among the very first to write his own hit material, again foreshadowing a trend that would take root in the '60s. His everyman persona (a kind of bespectacled kid next door) was an inspiration to every unlikely rock star, and his trusty Fender Stratocaster become their tool of choice.

After touring England in the late '50s, Holly left a remarkable trail of influence, from the Beatles, the Rolling Stones, and the deferentially named Hollies through Elvis Costello. In the United States in 1971, Don McLean's "American Pie"—which referenced the February 3, 1959, plane crash that killed Holly, Richie Valens, and J.P. "the Big Bopper" Richardson as the "day the music died"—rekindled interest in Holly.

Over the years, Holly has been the subject of major features and documentaries, and often-covered songs such as "It's So Easy" and "Well . . . All Right" will ensure that, in Holly's own words, his legacy will "Not Fade Away."

BUDDY HOLLY
Tribute by Marshall Crenshaw
February 26, 1997

In recent decades, much has been written about early rock and roll's impact on American society and culture. But back in the '50s, when Buddy Holly records were brand new, there was hardly any such thing as a "serious" rock and roll fan. Almost nobody thought about rock and roll in an analytical way. I was only five years old, so I never did. But what I did know was that those maroon-and-orange-labeled 45s with Buddy Holly's name inscribed on them were the ones that got me the most excited, the ones I'd ask my teenage cousins and neighbors to play over and over again.

Especially the B-sides, which in Holly's case could be even more intriguing than the A-sides. Playing "Peggy Sue," I'd hear that jungle drumbeat rumbling in and out of an echo chamber, along with an electric guitar sound (a Fender Stratocaster) that at that time was unprecedented (and to me, unbelievable). Turn it over and there was "Everyday" with its delicate, intimate sounds (a celeste, bare hands on knees keeping time) and half-whispered vocal (something about "going faster than a roller coaster"). Buddy Holly records just seemed to come from their own universe somewhere.

And they did: Holly recorded from Clovis, New Mexico, an environment said to be full of intrigue and subterfuge. (David Lynch should have made *The Buddy Holly Story*.) When I visited Norman Petty's studio there in 1991, I saw the apartment in the back where Buddy and his band, the Crickets, would crash out after sessions, the 10-cent Coke machine, the entranceway where they set up the drums for "Peggy Sue," and all kinds of beautiful Ampex, RCA, Altec, and Neumann recording gear. Buddy Holly was the first rock and roll artist to really set up camp in a studio, approaching the recording process with a sense of adventure and fun while producing a focused body of work all in one place at one time.

One of my favorite things that I've learned about '50s rock and roll is that it was, to a very significant extent, a consciously anti-racist phenomena. People like Buddy Holly, Alan Freed, and Little Richard were all out for a good time, but were aware that they were challenging taboos and breaking rules that needed to be broken. When Buddy Holly took Little Richard and King Curtis to his parents' house in Lubbock, Texas, for dinner (so the stories go), and when he married Maria Elena Santiago, he was doing what his heart told him to do. And that takes a lot of balls sometimes.

Buddy Holly's talents bloomed in an environment that was less than nurturing: Rock and roll artists were being condemned by an establishment that saw them as agents of subversion, and manipulated by businessmen who treated them as disposable commodities ripe for exploitation. And so it was that, hit records notwithstanding, Buddy Holly was broke in January of 1959, and left with no choice but to go out on the Winter Dance Party tour, which, to read about it now, sounds like it was deliberately designed as an instrument of death. The performers traveled through the frozen Midwest in old converted school buses with bad heaters and faulty engines. While trying to (briefly) escape these conditions (and get his stage clothes laundered), Buddy Holly, as everyone knows, died, at the age of 22, in a plane crash along with Ritchie Valens, the Big Bopper, and pilot Roger Peterson. It was a hideous fate for a guy who'd made some of the most joyful, celebratory music in recording history.

Now Buddy Holly's music has endured for almost a half-century and he's recognized as one of the finest American artists of his time. In the words of Keith Richards, "This is not bad for a guy from Lubbock."

(Marshall Crenshaw played Buddy Holly in the 1987 film, *La Bamba*. He has written songs for Bette Midler, the Gin Blossoms, Was [Not Was], and others.)

JAC HOLZMAN

TRUSTEES AWARD, 2008

Like many of his contemporaries, such as Ahmet Ertegun at Atlantic in the R&B world, or Sam Phillips' early rock and roll at Sun Records, Jac Holzman and his Elektra Records label dug deep into the artist community and discovered riches to which the major labels were blind.

He founded Elektra in his college dorm room in 1950, releasing an album of German poems set to music. But as the label progressed, he focused on the burgeoning local New York folk scene. His first major act was singer Judy Collins, who in her early years at the label would expose songs by Bob Dylan, Joni Mitchell, and Leonard Cohen. Soon other important folk artists were drawn to the label, including Phil Ochs and Tom Paxton.

But where the label could have been pigeonholed into folk and fizzled when even that music took an electric turn in the mid-'60s, Holzman proved to have a wide-ranging ear. His label—which would come to be staffed by industry titans in their own right such as Paul Rothchild, David Anderle, and Bruce Botnick—would sign Love, the Doors, and the Paul Butterfield Blues Band, as well as Detroit's MC5 and the Stooges in the '60s, and later Carly Simon, Bread, and Queen.

Holzman sold the label in 1970, and it ultimately became part of the Warner/Elektra/Asylum (WEA) family. Holzman himself, always feeding a curious mind enthused by technology, would go on to work at Warner Communications, where he was instrumental in the adoption of the CD. In 2005 he launched Cordless Recordings, an Internet-only label designed to reduce overhead and the financial pressures on emerging acts. Each step has revealed a remarkably forward-thinking executive who has had a profound impact on music.

I want to thank the Trustees for giving me such a wonderful award—for recognizing that there are crazy people in this world whom you cannot stop from doing what they are meant to do. Even wild horses wouldn't hold them back.

—Jac Holzman, acceptance speech, 2008

JAC HOLZMAN
Tribute by Judy Collins
February 10, 2008

Jac Holzman is one of the most amazing men I have known, in the music business or anywhere. He is enormously gifted and insightful about the artists he looks for, for Elektra and for Cordless Recordings. He has not faltered, not really slowed down, in all his years of creativity and effective executive leadership in the music business. His taste is impeccable and his vision, determination, and sense of fun and adventure are unparalleled. They have said that Jac's taste at Elektra became the world's taste. I don't know what fortune led to our meeting, but I count it the best of all fortunes.

One night in New York in 1960—I was just 21 and had been singing in clubs for a couple of years—I had just come off the stage when a tall, good-looking man approached me, smiling that engaging smile of his. "You don't know me, but I'm Jac Holzman," he said. I certainly knew who Jac was, since I had been listening to, and learning from, the records Elektra had made.

"Dear," he said, "I think you are ready to make a record. And I want you to make it for Elektra."

I thought of myself as a storyteller, not a singer. I had no thought of making a record. But, as I would learn with Jac, in a few minutes we had agreed that he was right. That sort of thing has continued over the 47 years of our friendship and working relationship.

In a short time, I was in the studio in New York. With Jac officiating, we made my first recording—*A Maid of Constant Sorrow*. It arrived in the mail where I was living in Storrs, Connecticut. With it came a check for $1,000, my first advance. I was on my way, and would record for Elektra for the next 24 years.

Jac and I worked on material, took risks, made albums in which we fought and argued and eventually agreed, always working to get it right, to find the center of the thing, to lift the whole enterprise of my music to another level. That is what Jac did for me, and what he did for the artists on Elektra. Those who lived and thrived thank him. Those who died did so with legacies that Jac Holzman, in great part, made possible.

My friendship with Jac has lasted longer than many marriages, and we are close to this day, another gift, I know, of his constancy and ability.

(Judy Collins won a 1968 Grammy for her recording of "Both Sides Now," which was also inducted into the Grammy Hall of Fame in 2003.)

JOHN LEE HOOKER

LIFETIME ACHIEVEMENT AWARD, 2000

Paul Natkin/Getty Images

John Lee Hooker is to the blues what T.J. Hooker was to TV cops, which is to say, very loosely of course, that John Lee became a wise old bluesman who was widely respected by the following generations of musicians and ultimately teamed with them to do some fine and enduring work in the latter half of his career.

The simple, repetitive boogie style that Hooker exhibited in his most noteworthy songs "Boogie Chillun" and "Boom Boom" (both inducted into the Grammy Hall of Fame) would prove influential to such artists as the Animals, Yardbirds, trippy blues collective Canned Heat, Bonnie Raitt, and Robert Cray, among others—nearly all of whom would eventually play or record with him.

A Mississippi native who, like so many other blues greats, migrated north and ultimately found his home and built his popularity in Detroit, Hooker traveled a monumentally winding road in the first part of his career. He recorded for a stunning variety of labels (King, Federal, Chess, Regent, Modern, Specialty, and many others). Even more impressive was the number of names under which he recorded, often perhaps for contractual reasons: Johnny Lee, Delta John, Texas Slim, Little Pork Chops, and the barely disguised John Lee Booker and John Lee Cooker. Playing guitar based on boogie piano, Hooker uniquely retained a delta blues style in the north. It all combined to give him remarkable staying power.

In 1989 he recorded *The Healer*, joined by guests including Raitt, Cray, Los Lobos, Charlie Musselwhite, and other acolytes. "I'm in the Mood" from the album would win the Best Traditional Blues Recording Grammy. His 1997 collaboration with Van Morrison, *Don't Look Back*, would result in two Grammys. He continued as a respected elder statesman until his death in 2001.

If this was an album he'd be thanking individuals and the organizations involved but since this is about John Lee's life, we should be thankful to him, that he shared it with us.
—Mike Kappus, manager for John Lee Hooker, acceptance speech, 2000

JOHN LEE HOOKER
Tribute by Bonnie Raitt with Mary Katherine Aldin
February 23, 2000

John Lee Hooker has been giving me the blues ever since I first heard his records when I was a teenager. His blues is the real deal; it was born in the heart of the Mississippi Delta and bred in the urban centers of Memphis and Detroit. He made his very first record in the Motor City in November of 1948, and in the ensuing five decades he has recorded so many 78s, 45s, LPs, and CDs that even he lost count of them all.

Born the son of sharecroppers in Vance, near Clarksdale, Mississippi, on August 22, 1917, John Lee jumped right into the blues. He ran away from home, landing first in Memphis and then in Cincinnati, where he became a gospel singer. He settled down in Detroit in 1941, working in an auto factory by day and playing in blues clubs at night.

He had developed quite a following by 1948, when legendary bluesman T-Bone Walker gave him his first electric guitar. His unique sound—a mix of Delta blues hotwired into an electric setting—gave John Lee his first hit that same year, the Modern Records smash "Boogie Chillun." It sold several hundred thousand copies, amazing for that time and place. That boogie sound would go on to become the essential inspiration that fueled a series of hit records by the Animals, the Rolling Stones, ZZ Top, and lots of others, including myself. With hits like "Crawlin Kingsnake" in 1949, and my personal favorite, "I'm in the Mood," which sold a million copies in 1951, he remained a successful recording star throughout the 1950s. It's estimated that between 1949 and 1953 alone he had 74 singles issued on 24 different labels using 12 names. He's had over 100 albums under his belt, and when R&B took a back seat to rock and roll in the '60s, he recreated himself as a folk artist and still maintained a successful career. Then, in the '70s he emerged as King of the Boogie, a title he still holds today. One of my proudest moments was sharing the Grammy stage with him in 1989, when our duet recording of "I'm in the Mood" brought him a long-deserved Grammy Award for Best Traditional Blues Recording.

His music has always had a powerful effect on me. It's so darkly erotic, and at the same time sad and lonely, that it forged a permanent bond between me and the blues. All it took was his voice, his guitar, and his foot-tapping and the spell was cast.

Tonight, we see John Lee Hooker in his rightful place among his peers. At 87 years young, he's still healthy, active, and making new music. He's not just coasting on his past accomplishments, although they're significant. He's a member of the Rock and Roll Hall of Fame, has a star on the Hollywood Walk of Fame, has been given a Lifetime Achievement Award by the Rhythm & Blues Foundation, is the recipient of four Grammy Awards, and is the holder of five gold records; these are remarkable accomplishments, and with them he's set standards for future generations to live up to. Already heaped with recognition and richly deserved honors, tonight's Lifetime Achievement Award couldn't be given to a more extraordinary artist. I'm grateful that he's being given this recognition while he's still around to enjoy it.

(Bonnie Raitt has won 10 Grammys, including four for her 1989 album, *Nick of Time*. Mary Katherine Aldin is a blues historian.)

LIGHTNIN' HOPKINS

LIFETIME ACHIEVEMENT AWARD, 2013

Michael Ochs Archives/Getty Images

The great Texas bluesman Lightnin' Hopkins' six-plus decade career, rubbery dexterity, and drawly storytelling made him one of the most important country blues legends and a particular influence on fellow Texas guitar slingers who followed him.

Sam Hopkins was born in 1912 in Centerville, Texas. At age eight he met Blind Lemon Jefferson and would ultimately serve as his guide and get the chance to play with him. Still, it wasn't until he was discovered by a talent scout that he was renamed "Lightnin'" and began recording in 1946. A run of national hits would follow—including "Short Haired Woman," "Shotgun Blues," and "Big Mama Jump"—for Aladdin Records.

He would go on to record for various labels, scoring with "Tim Moore's Farm," "Give Me Central 209 (Hello Central)," and perhaps most notably "Hopkin's Sky Hop," a blazing guitar stomp that was a clear influence on Texas guitarist Stevie Ray Vaughan's "Rude Mood." Nevertheless, by 1959 Hopkins was out of favor and had returned to Texas to play juke joints. But as the folk revival boomed in the '60s, he was "rediscovered" by folklorist Mack McCormick and Hopkins would go on to play the college circuit, make TV appearances, and tour Europe, captivating audiences not just with his guitar work, but with a comic storytelling style. Along the way, Hopkins proved his universal appeal, recording a 1968 album with backing from the psychedelic rock band the 13th Floor Elevators and becoming the subject of alt-rock band R.E.M.'s song "Lightnin' Hopkins."

We knew him as Granddaddy, Uncle Sam, and Lightnin'. He called himself Po-Lightnin'. He was a great artist that did not look for recognition or fame and he didn't receive a fortune. So today, he's getting the recognition that he deserves.
—Bertha Kelly, granddaughter, acceptance speech, 2013

LIGHTNIN' HOPKINS
Tribute by Gary Clark Jr. and Doyle Bramhall II
February 10, 2013

When one becomes deeply familiar with the blues genre it is glaringly evident how the different regional styles connect, evolve, and intersect yet remain very clearly individual in their own personalities. Rural and urban blues, country and city blues, electric and acoustic blues, solo troubadours, small combos, big band blues. And there's Mississippi Delta,

Memphis, Chicago, and Texas blues. All rich with flavorings of their own, all rich with a legendary lineage of mythical names, all rich with a clear musical evolution dating back to the 1920s and further, to chain gangs, field hollers, and experiences deeply rooted in Africa and specifically Mali.

To understand the importance of Sam "Lightnin'" Hopkins requires a look at Texas blues itself. Texas, often referred to as a "country within a country," stays true to its reputation as a century-long hotbed for the blues alongside Mississippi and Chicago. Its style: wide-open, flashy, dangerous, rule-bending, and always swinging. Its lineage, staggeringly rich: Blind Lemon Jefferson, Blind Willie Johnson, Lead Belly, Mance Lipscomb, Lightnin' Hopkins, T-Bone Walker, Lil' Son Jackson, Freddie King, Larry Davis, Johnny "Guitar" Watson, Pee Wee Crayton, Albert Collins, Johnny Copeland, Johnny Winter, Billy Gibbons, Jimmie and Stevie Ray Vaughan, and many others.

Lightnin' Hopkins was born in Centerville, Texas, in 1912. His roots lie in the rural blues sounds of Texas and the Deep Ellum area. His foundational influence was the seminal blues legend Blind Lemon Jefferson. Legend has it that as a young boy he met and followed Jefferson around street corners and church gatherings in Texas, absorbing, learning, and eventually accompanying him. It is believed that Hopkins was the only guitarist to ever play alongside the great Blind Lemon.

Lightnin' was the bridge between ancient and modern, similar to the great legends Muddy Waters and Howlin' Wolf, who bridged the Mississippi Delta style to Chicago blues. What is particularly important to Lightnin's place in this legacy was his bridging of the rural country style characterized by a singular man, wielding his voice, his poetry, and an acoustic guitar into the plugged-in, electric guitar–led, drum-and-bass combos headed by Freddie King, Stevie Ray Vaughan, and others. He carried the primitive rawness and intimacy of his rural Texas blues forefathers into the futuristic and powerful modern and electrified sound of the second half of the 20th century, which is still a part of mainstream Texas blues and Southern rock.

His landmark three-piece combo Herald recordings bear witness to an earthy power that would inform later power trios such as the Jimi Hendrix Experience, Cream, and ZZ Top.

Lightnin's sound was deep, raw, and primitive yet had the flash and swagger of a switchblade knife. His vocals were raspy and rich and his quicksilver guitar playing incorporated hypnotic open-string bass lines and percussive tapping mixed with dynamic fingerpicking and fluid single-note lines across the entire fretboard. His lyrics spoke of heartbreak and love, sexual innuendo, and the racial issues of the Deep South. He had humor and charm in both his lyrics and instrumental prowess. It is speculated that Lightnin' recorded nearly 1000 songs and more albums than any other bluesman.

(Native Texan and Grammy winner Gary Clark Jr. has drawn favorable comparisons to such guitar icons as Jimi Hendrix and Stevie Ray Vaughan. Fellow Texan Doyle Bramhall II is an in-demand guitarist and songwriter whose songs have been recorded by Eric Clapton, among others.)

THE ISLEY BROTHERS

LIFETIME ACHIEVEMENT AWARD, 2014

Several generations of Isleys have enjoyed what may be the most varied career of any R&B group. From gutbucket '50s R&B and Motown soul to throbbing funk and quiet-storm urban ballads, the Isley Brothers haven't just done it all over some 50-plus years, they've done it insanely well.

Their best-known hit from the late '50s, "Shout," was a call-and-response workout that gained even greater fame via National Lampoon's *Animal House* in 1978. Their second hit, 1962's "Twist and Shout," virtually a rock and roll song, spawned a famous cover by the Beatles. In 1966 they U-turned to Motown's Tamla label for the classic Detroit soul song "This Old Heart of Mine (Is Weak for You)." By the late '60s and early '70s, their hits came in more genres than the Top 40 itself: funky empowerment numbers "It's Your Thing" (which won a Grammy for 1969) and "Fight the Power," the fuzz-guitar soul of "That Lady," and spirited folk covers of Stephen Stills' "Love the One You're With" and Seals & Crofts' "Summer Breeze." Factor in the smooth bedroom soul of "For the Love of You" highlighting Ronald Isley's distinctive croon, and listeners had to be wondering if there was anything this group couldn't do.

Add to all this their 1964 invitation to a young guitar player named Jimmy James to join their backing band for a tour that year. James would later change his name to Jimi Hendrix, but after years as one of the most trendsetting groups in urban music, the Isleys' instincts have been well documented.

THE ISLEY BROTHERS
Tribute by Kem
January 26, 2014

The Isley Brothers have been making music for almost six decades. Nearly 60 years in music is tribute enough, but there are artists with long careers whose music never resonates with fans the way theirs has.

When I think about the Isleys' legacy, and what it has meant to me as an artist, I'm reminded of a hot, Kool-Aid-deprived day on Detroit's northwest side, just off of 8 Mile Road. I was holed up in a back bedroom at a friend's house, my face pressed against the speaker of a cassette player, my finger wearing out the rewind button. I played "Don't Say Goodnight (It's Time for Love)," one of their chart-topping singles from 1980, over and over. I was nine years old, and regardless of it being Saturday, Ronald Isley was taking me to school. That was one of my first lessons on the importance of melody, and I was being taught by a master.

Fast-forward to 2013. I'm sitting at the board in a Detroit studio with none other than Ron Isley. Recording a song with him is the fulfillment of a dream. And here he is, in the vocal booth, hitting all the licks. The memory nearly brings tears to my eyes. That session was a moment for me, the closing of a circle through which a student was rewarded with an opportunity to honor a master.

You forget how many hits the Isley Brothers have had until you find yourself in the audience at a sold-out show: "Shout." "Voyage to Atlantis." "Harvest for the World." "Summer Breeze." "For the Love of You." The Isley sound is rooted in gospel, and can be traced to the early 1950s in Cincinnati. But their good news has spread through doo-wop, disco, soul, R&B, and various fusions of sound. An Isley record is to music what *The Godfather* is to film. You've seen it a million times, you know every word by heart and, even if you don't catch it from the beginning, you're captivated until the end.

The last two active members of the Isley Brothers are Ron and Ernie, but their career has truly been a family affair, with many an Isley helping to build the group's legacy, including Rudolph, and late brothers Vernon, O'Kelly, and Marvin. They were also aided by the early encouragement of their father, a professional singer himself, and their mother, a church pianist who accompanied her sons' early performances. Oh yes, and a young Jimmy James played in their band in the '60s (you know him better today as Jimi Hendrix).

When in their presence, I get the sense that for them it has been, and will always be, about the music. In fact, Ron once told me, "We didn't really know it was going to turn into all this. We were just making music the best way we knew how."

How fitting, that at the core of the legacy, and the larger-than-life character Mr. Biggs, there's just a guy who likes to sing, and another who loves to play guitar. Should we be amazed that this perspective made the Isley Brothers' music the unofficial soundtrack to conception? That they've done it masterfully longer than most popular artists have been alive? That they really are your favorite artist's favorite artist? Their resilience, craftsmanship, and ability to survive generations are not the result of commercial machination, but of the love of the music.

(A three-time Grammy-nominated singer/songwriter, Kem was featured on Ronald Isley's 2013 single "My Favorite Thing," which is featured on Isley's album *This Song Is for You*.)

MICHAEL JACKSON

LIFETIME ACHIEVEMENT AWARD, 2010

UPI/Bettmann/Getty Images

As good as the Jackson 5 were (their first four singles went to No. 1), there may still not have been a reason to think that a pre-teen Michael Jackson would go on to change the music world. Or maybe there was.

Jackson was preternaturally talented. He was a precociously gifted performer. And he seemed preordained to become a giant star.

Jackson seemed to come out of the womb with James Brown dance moves and a soulful voice, with empathy for the lyrics he sang that was well beyond his years. Of course, in those early years, the only question was whether he was a simple puppet of his label and producers.

His first album as an adult, 1979's *Off the Wall*, cleared that all up. A towering achievement for any artist at any age, the 21-year-old Jackson wrote some of the album's best songs and seemed clearly in charge of its vision. That was amplified in 1982 with the release of *Thriller*. Its record-breaking sales aside, the album upended R&B music with the same impact that rap would later in the decade, but it did so with its inclusiveness. There was R&B, pop, rock, and unlikely guests such as Eddie Van Halen. With these two albums, Jackson single-handedly broke down the MTV color barrier, and even changed the art of videos. The album cover, with Jackson in a white suit leaning on his left elbow, became a signpost of the era. He would win eight Grammys based on the record, including Album, Record, and Producer of the Year as well as Grammys in the pop, rock, and R&B fields.

It was such an incredible feat that excellent albums that followed, including *Bad* and *Dangerous*, almost seemed like letdowns.

In 1985 Jackson teamed with Lionel Richie to write and lead one of the most impactful philanthropic recordings ever with the Grammy-winning "We Are the World," but as his career progressed, tabloid rumors seemed to gain more traction than his music. Sadly, Jackson died from an accidental overdose in 2009, but his culture-changing career has continued posthumously through such blockbuster efforts as the long-running Cirque du Soleil Las Vegas show "Michael Jackon One" and the 2009 documentary *This Is It*.

[Michael Jackson] was a good friend. He was a funny guy. He had a sense of humor like none of you really know. He loved music; he loved dance. I remember the times he would call me up and say, "Are you watching the Grammys? Do you believe what that person just said?" Then he'd laugh like hell and hang up.

—Frank DiLeo, former manager, acceptance speech, 2010

MICHAEL JACKSON
Tribute by Quincy Jones
January 31, 2010

Every decade in the music business you have a phenomenon. In the '40s you had Sinatra, in the '50s Elvis, in the '60s the Beatles, and in the '70s the innovation of Dolby coupled with the brilliant work of Stevie, Elton, and Marvin.

In the '80s, you had Michael Jackson. For everyone from eight to 80, Michael Jackson was the biggest entertainer on the planet. Together, along with my dream team of Rod Temperton, Bruce Swedien, Jerry Hey, Greg Phillinganes, Siedah Garrett, "JR" Robinson, Louis Johnson, Ndugu, and all the other brilliant members of our gifted family, we shared the decade and achieved heights that I can humbly say may never be reached again, reshaping the music business forever.

I simply loved working with Michael Jackson. This blessed artist, who commanded the stage with the grace of an antelope, shattered recording industry records and broke down cultural boundaries around the world, yet remained the gentlest and most complex of souls. Michael Jackson was a different kind of entertainer. A man-child in many ways, he was beyond professional and dedicated. Evoking Fred Astaire, Gene Kelly, Jackie Wilson, Sammy Davis Jr., and James Brown all at once, he'd work for hours perfecting every kick, gesture, and movement so that they came together precisely the way he intended them.

Divinity brought our souls together on *The Wiz* when I was searching for his missing solo song "You Can't Win," and allowed us to do all that we were able to throughout the '80s. To this day, the music we created on *Off the Wall*, *Thriller*, and *Bad*—as well as the *E.T. Storybook* and the collective that was "We Are the World"—is played in every corner of the world, and the reason for that is because he had it all: talent, grace, professionalism, and dedication. He was the consummate entertainer and his contributions and legacy will be felt upon the world forever.

It is hard for me to acknowledge that Michael is gone. I lost part of my soul when he passed away, and there's not a day that goes by that I don't think of him. We all made incredible music together and in doing so made history. The fact that in the wake of his passing Michael Jackson once again dominated album and download sales around the world for an entire summer is a testament to the deep impact that he had on millions of souls throughout his entire career.

I have a sense that Michael still had much more to contribute as an artist. Sadly, we'll never know. But I promise you in 50, 75, 100 years, what will be remembered is the music. It's no accident that almost three decades later—no matter where I go in the world, in every club and karaoke bar—like clockwork at the witching hour I hear "Billie Jean," "Beat It," "Wanna Be Starting Somethin'," "Don't Stop 'Til You Get Enough," "Rock with You," "Smooth Criminal," "Thriller," "Man in the Mirror," "P.Y.T. (Pretty Young Thing)," "Human Nature," and "The Way You Make Me Feel." In every language, from prison yards in the Philippines to the tribute site Thrilltheworld.com, that is the incredible legacy that he leaves behind, and that's the only thing that matters. Anything other than that is simply noise.

(AllMusic.com calls Quincy Jones the renaissance man of American music. His career stretches from stints in the bands of Lionel Hampton and Dizzy Gillespie in the '50s to the present day, and has included roles as a music, film, and TV producer; publisher; and as an unspoken ambassador for music worldwide. He has a record 79 Grammy nominations and has won 27 Grammys, including awards with Michael Jackson for Album and Record of the Year.)

JEFFERSON AIRPLANE
LIFETIME ACHIEVEMENT AWARD, 2016

Michael Ochs Archives/Getty Images

The Rock and Roll Hall of Fame uniquely summed up the importance of Jefferson Airplane in the bio of their 1996 inductees: "In a sense, San Francisco became the American Liverpool in the latter half of the '60s, and Jefferson Airplane were its Beatles." Call San Francisco the trippy, revolutionary Liverpool, and it's a pretty accurate description.

Jefferson Airplane (original founder Marty Balin, singer Grace Slick, bassist Jack Casady, guitarists Paul Kantner and Jorma Kaukonen, and drummer Spencer Dryden) were born from the same San Francisco folk-rock scene that gave rise to the Grateful Dead, Janis Joplin's Big Brother and the Holding Company, Quicksilver Messenger Service, the Beau Brummels, and others.

But theirs was the first flare fired when the Grammy Hall of Fame–inducted *Surrealistic Pillow* hit in 1967 in the midst of the Summer of Love. Perhaps even more than other area bands, the Airplane epitomized the communal hippie vibe of the Haight-Ashbury district, sharing a house, swapping romantic partners, and espousing revolution, at least musically.

Surrealistic Pillow's two Top 10 hits, "Somebody to Love" and the drug-laced "White Rabbit," have become milestones of a counterculture beginning to pierce the protective white picket fences of Middle America. The Airplane would fittingly have the distinction of being one of the few acts to play the three major '60s music festivals: Woodstock, Monterey, and Altamont.

The flare the Airplane shot up with *Pillow* burned out fairly quickly. The band's last studio album was 1972's *Long John Silver* (not counting a 1989 reunion disc). Spinoffs would abound (Hot Tuna, Jefferson Starship, Starship), but for several tie-dyed, bell-bottomed years in the late '60s, Jefferson Airplane took flight and helped speak for a generation.

> *Fifty-one years ago, my friend Paul Kantner invited me to join a rock and roll band, which at the time was nameless. Against my better judgement, I drove from San Jose to San Francisco to a little club on Fillmore Street, which would soon be called The Matrix. There I had an audition—I guess I passed that audition because I wound up in a band called the Jefferson Airplane.*
>
> —Jorma Kaukonen, acceptance speech, 2016

JEFFERSON AIRPLANE
Tribute by Patti Smith
February 15, 2016

It is said we become whom we love. We who loved Jefferson Airplane shook off our post-war skins, said farewell to the '50s, and marched through the '60s toward the new Jerusalem. It was a Blakean city that was as much a state of mind as architecture, one of unbridled freedom built on the ashes of nationalism, conformity, and materialism. San Francisco was the emblematic meeting ground. Jefferson Airplane, the premiere standard-bearers of the Summer of Love, ushered us through its psychedelic gates.

They were masters of their own ship, and their words and music reflected all the possibilities, kaleidoscopic chaos, and tribal energy of the sea they were navigating. Their modular personnel issued the clarion call of *Surrealistic Pillow,* and it remains a testament to their depth.

The core band of Jefferson Airplane entered the scene as a group of equals, exemplifying the electrifying rise in cultural consciousness. Paul Kantner's science-fictional reaches for the cosmos. Jorma Kaukonen's plugged-in virtuoso fingerstyle folk blues. Jack Casady's fluid and stalwart bass lines entwining the propulsive creativity of Spencer Dryden's drums. And there was vocal anarchy in the midst of mystical beauty, projected through the soaring combination of Grace Slick's acerbic wit and fearless charisma and the romantic purity of Marty Balin.

How *Surrealistic Pillow* served in the transformation of an entire generation is well documented. For myself, a 20-year-old girl in rural New Jersey, hearing the voice of Grace Slick on the radio was a revelation. "Somebody to Love" and "White Rabbit" both contained the emotional trajectory of an aria. Make no mistake; we all owe her a debt. She was like no other and opened a door that will never close again.

On my worktable is a small orange button with the words "Jefferson Airplane loves you" in green. It is nearly half a century old. How fortunate we were to be loved by them. Their banner was also our own. They gave us anthems of love. They gave us instructions for action—feed your head! Got to revolution! And within *Crown of Creation*, a requiem for a time all too brief. Yet their message enduringly calls, for all who listen, to unite once more through the collective consciousness of love.

(A three-time Grammy nominee, Patti Smith recorded Jefferson Airplane's "White Rabbit" on her 2007 covers album, *Twelve.*)

FLACO JIMÉNEZ

LIFETIME ACHIEVEMENT AWARD, 2015

WireImage.com

And you thought the accordion wasn't cool.

Texas native Flaco Jiménez turned his ebullient accordion style and love of such local music styles as conjunto into a career of international reach. He's played with countless mainstream rock and country music acts and has been a part of more supergroups than Eric Clapton.

Jiménez formed his first band at age 15, inspired in his own playing by Zydeco star Clifton Chenier. By the early '60s, Jiménez was well known in Texas and had won a fan in Doug Sahm, founder of the Sir Douglas Quintet. For his 1973 solo debut, Sahm recruited Jiménez on accordion, providing the latter's first exposure to a more mainstream audience. It would lead to all kinds and flavors of guest appearances with acts ranging from Ry Cooder and Dwight Yoakam to the Mavericks and even the Rolling Stones.

Jiménez' work on Yoakam and Buck Owens' No. 1 country hit "Streets of Bakersfield" in 1988 provided a huge springboard that helped lead to his first supergroup, the Texas Tornados, with old friend Sahm along with Freddy Fender and Augie Meyers. The group won a Grammy Award for 1990.

In the early '90s, Jiménez would join Fender, Joe Ely, and members of Los Lobos in Los Super Seven, and win another Grammy for 1998. In all, Jiménez has won five Grammys.

At age 77, Jiménez continues to tour and record and prove that the joys of Tex-Mex music will tear down walls both real and figurative.

FLACO JIMÉNEZ
Tribute by Raul Malo
February 8, 2015

His influence is undeniable. Even if you don't know the name, you know the sound.

Whether accompanying seasoned veterans, young upstarts, or on his own iconic recordings, Flaco Jiménez has the talent and musical wisdom to turn great songs into masterpieces. Whether it's a country song or a traditional "ranchera," his accordion is always the perfect accompaniment. His music has combined worlds I never thought could be combined. Perhaps they would have never collided had it not been for Flaco orchestrating and manipulating this beautiful cosmic orchestra. He would never admit to such things of course, for he is a humble man. He lives to serve the music.

Through the years his music has made us dance, cry, love, drink, party, mourn, and fight. He's created a song and a sound for just about every piece of the human condition. As part of any of the acclaimed bands he has played with (Texas Tornados, Los Super Seven) or as a solo artist, Flaco's music has stood the test of time. His collaborations with Doug Sahm, Ry Cooder, Linda Ronstadt, and Dwight Yoakam (just to name a few) are some of the most important and undeniably influential recordings of all time. His path has been his and his alone.

As a young Latin musician I was always looking for that place where cultures would and could blend naturally. I was looking for a link between two separate and distinct musical worlds. Whether out of necessity or just because, it does not matter. Flaco is that place. He is that connection. He is that link. He is the one who blurred the lines. And all the while staying true to the one thing that matters most of all: his music.

Thank you Flaco for being an inspiration and a mentor to many.

(A Grammy winner as a member of the Mavericks, Raul Malo appeared on Flaco Jiménez's 1994 self-titled album as a guest vocalist on "Seguro Que Hell Yes.")

ANTONIO CARLOS JOBIM

LIFETIME ACHIEVEMENT AWARD, 2012

In the late '50s, the laid-back Brazilian beach life conspired with songwriter and musician Antonio Carlos Jobim to lay the groundwork for a pop/jazz hybrid that would become a worldwide rage by the early '60s. When Brazilian singer/guitarist João Gilberto recorded Jobim's songs on his debut album *Chega de Saudade*, bossa nova—a music that would come to represent Brazil in much the same way reggae has helped define Jamaica—found a wide audience.

When Gilberto and Stan Getz won the Grammy for Album of the Year for their bossa album *Getz/Gilberto*, bossa nova was truly a phenomenon, and Jobim's songs were the centerpiece. "The Girl from Ipanema" (sung by Gilberto's wife Astrud in a lilting style that would come to define the relaxed delivery of bossa songs) won Record of the Year, and other Jobim songs would become signposts of the style: "Desafinado," "Chega de Saudade," "Wave," and "Corcovado (Quiet Nights of Quiet Stars)," among others.

By 1967, bossa and its unofficial international ambassador Jobim had reached an almost unprecedented pop/jazz crossover audience, which led to the sublime duet album *Francis Albert Sinatra & Antonio Carlos Jobim*, on which Sinatra shows impeccable form primarily singing Jobim's songs.

Jobim's own records were just as inviting as those who covered him, featuring tastefully complex instrumentals combined with his softly swinging vocals inspired by Chet Baker.

By the time of his death in 1994, Jobim—who has been called the George Gershwin of Brazil—had firmly established himself as one of the great composers of his generation.

ANTONIO CARLOS JOBIM
Tribute by Sergio Mendes
February 12, 2012

Antonio Carlos Jobim (in Brazil we called him Tom Jobim) is one of the most important composers of the 20th century. His beautiful songs, such as "The Girl from Ipanema," "Desafinado," "Corcovado (Quiet Nights of Quiet Stars)," "Wave," and "Waters of March," to mention a few, became standards all over the world and were recorded by the greatest singers and musicians of our time.

Tom Jobim's music is unique—his melodies are haunting and the harmonies extremely sophisticated. He is responsible for introducing Brazilian music to the world.

Jobim is the primary founder of a Brazilian musical style that became known as bossa nova in the late '50s. He gained worldwide attention in 1959 with his contributions to the soundtrack for the film *Black Orpheus*. Shortly after, artists such as João Gilberto began enjoying hits with Jobim's songs. Stan Getz and Astrud Gilberto's version of "The Girl from Ipanema" won the Grammy for Record of the Year for 1964. Soon, jazz artists and music lovers the world over would embrace bossa nova.

I was privileged to work with him on many occasions and fortunate to become his personal friend. He was my mentor and helped me a lot during the first years of my career. I have the fondest memories of the times we spent together at his home in Ipanema, Rio de Janeiro. As he was doing all the arrangements for my first album, we would spend many hours, not only working, but also talking and laughing at his wonderful stories into the night.

Jazz musicians such as Getz, Charlie Byrd, Dizzy Gillespie, and many more were seduced by Tom's harmonies and original style. Frank Sinatra, Ella Fitzgerald, Sarah Vaughan, and Tony Bennett were some of the iconic singers who became enchanted by his melodies. His songs continue to entrance young artists of today, including will.i.am, John Legend, Diana Krall, and many others.

I know he would be thrilled by the distinction of receiving a Recording Academy Lifetime Achievement Award. I'm sure his music will continue to touch the hearts of many generations to come.

(Sergio Mendes first gained fame with Sergio Mendes & Brasil '66, a group that played their own pivotal role in bringing international recognition to Brazilian music. His album *Brasileiro* won the Best World Music Album Grammy for 1992 and his *Herb Alpert Presents Sergio Mendes & Brasil '66* was inducted into the Grammy Hall of Fame in 2012.)

STEVE JOBS

TRUSTEES AWARD, 2012

What's a nice (or not-so-nice, depending on your viewpoint) tech industry titan like Apple's Steve Jobs doing in a place like this? In the 21st century, Jobs didn't just reimagine the distribution and consumption of music; for a struggling music industry, he helped to ensure it would continue to create revenue for artists.

With the iPod and iTunes, Jobs aimed his user-friendly focus on creating a commercially viable digital music service at a time when digital pirate outlets such as Napster were potentially bankrupting the music economy. Sure, Jobs knew if he could solve the problem there would be a nice payday for Apple, but he also viewed the online music dilemma as a fan, having come of age with the music of his most revered artist, Bob Dylan.

"I was very lucky to grow up in a time when music really mattered," Jobs had said. "It wasn't just something in the background; it really mattered to a generation of kids growing up. It really changed the world." To suggest his own drive to change the world sprang from this relationship to music wouldn't be a stretch.

Launched in 2001 about eight months apart, iTunes and the iPod were instant hits. By 2012 Apple reported it had sold more than 350 million iPods and as of February 2013, the iTunes store had sold more than 25 billion tracks worldwide. Jobs' famous compulsive, hands-on style was responsible for the iconic look and feel of the iPod. And while music consumers seem to be moving toward a streaming music model, for nearly a decade and a half, Jobs' inventions did indeed change the music world.

Steve was focused on bringing music to everyone in innovative ways. We talked about it every single day. When he introduced the iPod in 2001, people asked, "Why is Apple making a music player?" His answer was simple: "We love music and it's always good to do something you love."

—Eddy Cue, Apple senior vice president of Internet software and services, acceptance speech, 2012

STEVE JOBS
Tribute by Yo-Yo Ma
February 12, 2012

Before I met Steve, I first had to say no to him. In the early '90s, I was touring like a madman, trying to juggle professional commitments and a home life with a young family, when a call came in. Steve Jobs was getting married at Yosemite and he wanted me to play. I declined with great regret. When we met, years later, I was also introduced to his wife and children. The simplicity, directness, and openness of his family really struck me. Steve showed me the things he cared about, and I shared the music I would have played at their wedding. From there, the friendship grew.

There were many more meetings, sometimes for a picnic dinner before concerts, other times grabbing lunch after one of his legendary presentations. Steve was ever eager to share the latest "one more thing." I will never forget how he pulled out a prototype of the iPhone for me and the astonished members of the Silk Road Ensemble at UC Berkeley, or the conversation about intuition versus intelligence and the importance of stimulating disciplined imagination in our students to ensure an innovative workforce. His life's work was a reflection of his father Paul's lesson: "When you make something, make sure the back is as beautiful as the front, even if nobody sees it."

This last year we had three visits, and in the spring Steve asked me to play at his funeral. I said I would, if he would speak at mine. Needless to say, Steve got his way. I, like so many others, will always be grateful for the impact he had, for the beautiful tools that have helped change my thinking, but even more so for his extraordinary friendship.

(Cellist Yo-Yo Ma is a 17-time Grammy winner. This appreciation was originally published in *Entertainment Weekly*.)

HANK JONES

LIFETIME ACHIEVEMENT AWARD, 2009

Pianist Henry "Hank" Jones was the eldest of three accomplished jazz instrumentalist brothers—drummer Elvin and trumpeter Thad rounded out the trio—but given his incredibly full biography, it was as if he was all three brothers. The nine-time Grammy nominee, who died in 2010 one year after receiving his Lifetime Achievement Award, seemingly played everywhere with everyone in the world of jazz.

By age 13, Jones was playing regionally around his Pontiac, Michigan, home. As a result, he was invited to New York to work at the Onyx Club with trumpeter Hot Lips Page. Soon, his live and recording dates were as constant as Model Ts rolling off an assembly line. In 1947 he toured with jazz entrepreneur Norman Granz' Jazz at the Philharmonic. From 1948–1953 he accompanied Ella Fitzgerald. All the while he played with the likes of Billy Eckstine and Coleman Hawkins. He made recordings with Charlie Parker, Lester Young, Cannonball Adderley, and Wes Montgomery, among others. And that was just phase one of his career.

From 1959–1975 he was the staff pianist at CBS Studios, which included work on *The Ed Sullivan Show*. Throughout the next two decades he made many of his own recordings as well as records with Benny Golson, Nancy Wilson, and Charlie Haden.

So omnipresent was Jones, he was the accompanist when Marilyn Monroe sang her famous birthday salutation to President John F. Kennedy on May 19, 1962, at Madison Square Garden. His breadth of career work truly epitomizes a lifetime of achievement.

HANK JONES
Tribute by Christian McBride
February 8, 2009

American culture in the last 40 years has increasingly tended to celebrate the manu-factured iconoclast, rather than the artist who has done the true study, preparation, and grind at his or her craft behind closed doors. Musicians who have transcended generational gaps and genres have consistently strived for—first and foremost—*respect*, I believe, from their fellow artists rather than the expectation of excessive temporary mainstream glory. Longevity and timelessness are what creative artists strive for. It's very difficult by any stretch of the imagination to think of an artist from any genre whose artistry and creativity and performance excellence have remained vibrant and relevant for more than three-quarters of a century. Did you hear me? *Three-quarters of a century!*

It is my honor on behalf of all of his many fans and worshipers to congratulate the great Hank Jones on his Lifetime Achievement Award. Mr. Jones' zest for beauty in creativity has transcended the many styles of jazz that he has witnessed and been a part of. From swing to bebop to modal to avant-garde and back again, his piano stylings have seeped into the blood of any and every important pianist after him.

It was one of my greatest thrills as a young bassist, having been in New York for just about three years, to receive a call from Mr. Jones to play with his trio. Not only was it a great honor for me, but my stock rose significantly with my peers. All of my fellow 20-something friends were highly impressed that the great Hank Jones would bother calling a 19-year-old kid. I'll never forget walking into Tavern on the Green dressed in my tuxedo waiting to start the gig. I knew that this was an experience that I would not get from anyone else. I can remember so many different pianists coming to hear Mr. Jones during the week. George Shearing even sat in one night. Boy, what a great week that was.

About six months later, we would record together with Benny Carter, Doc Cheatham, and Lewis Nash. Even as I write this, I can't help but think, "What was I doing there?" Then there was the trio recording with Jimmy Cobb a few years back, and, of course, the thrill of having Mr. Jones participate on my duets project.

I cannot begin to thank Mr. Jones enough for not only teaching and inspiring me so often in my career, but for also teaching generations of musicians that simple beauty, elegance, and kindness are the key to longevity. May God bless you, and it is my wish that we all can be like you when we grow up!

(Bassist Christian McBride has won five Grammy Awards. He collaborated with Hank Jones and drummer Jimmy Cobb for the 2006 album *West of 5th*.)

JANIS JOPLIN
LIFETIME ACHIEVEMENT AWARD, 2005

Michael Ochs Archives/Getty Images

In a remarkably short career, Janis Joplin changed the game for women in rock and became a counterculture touchstone. Even as her life was beset by school-age trauma and ongoing drug and alcohol addiction, onstage and on record she was rearranging the musical universe, especially as its laws pertained to female vocalists.

Born in the small town of Port Arthur, Texas, Joplin felt like an outcast in her conservative community. She ultimately found her way to San Francisco's Haight-Ashbury, where free expression was the rule and she could explore her wilder tendencies. As a singer, her style was full of abandon and unabashed sexuality, her voice a cross between the raunch of a male rock singer and the blues power of Bessie Smith.

Between her work with Big Brother and the Holding Company and her solo recordings, she released only four proper albums, three in her lifetime (Joplin died of an overdose in 1970). Yet three of her titles reside in the Grammy Hall of Fame: the posthumously released *Pearl*, "Me and Bobby McGee," and the Big Brother track "Piece of My Heart."

It was these works, as well as her historic turn at the Monterey Pop Festival and renowned live performances, that would inform everyone from Melissa Etheridge and Joss Stone to Stevie Nicks and Florence Welch. Indeed, virtually every female rock singer (or maybe every singer, period) who has followed Joplin owes her a debt of gratitude for the barriers she bulled over.

JANIS JOPLIN
Tribute by Melissa Etheridge
February 13, 2005

I remember the first time I heard Janis Joplin. I was 10 years old and my parents had just purchased the album *Pearl*. I remember listening to the songs as I studied the album cover, wondering about this crazy woman in feathers and beads smiling and laying on that couch. I had never heard the blues. I had never heard Bessie or Odetta or Lead Belly, but I was hearing them then. When I was 19, I discovered her other work and it grabbed me. I wanted to explode like that. I wanted to feel like that, and I wanted to sing like that.

Janis was like a light for me. I finally had hope that I didn't have to fit any cookie-cutter mold as a female singer. A woman could sing of her heart and sex. She could rock, and she could rock hard.

She was part of the rock and roll revolution. She blended the blues into rock and roll. She inspired the other singers of her time. She was strong and unique before women's lib. She had her own style and lived at her own speed.

She left such a mark on rock and roll and culture that to this day whenever a strong-voiced female artist is described, you will more often than not find a comparison to Janis Joplin. I, for one, always take it as a very high compliment.

(Singer/songwriter Melissa Etheridge has won two Grammy Awards.)

CAROLE KING

LIFETIME ACHIEVEMENT AWARD, 2013

When it comes to the Brill Building—the '60s music factory that turned out precision-crafted songs that have stood the test of time—Carole King was certainly among the elite few who produced hit after memorable hit. Not one of the elite *women*, because the Brill Building was seemingly gender-blind. One of the elite, period. Writing mostly with her then-husband Gerry Goffin, her songs consistently charted: the Shirelles' "Will You Love Me Tomorrow," the Drifters' "Up on the Roof," Maxine Brown's "Oh No, Not My Baby," Aretha Franklin's "(You Make Me Feel Like) A Natural Woman," the Everly Brothers' "Crying in the Rain," the Chiffons' "One Fine Day," and many more.

If that was all she did in her career, she'd be a rock and roll hall of famer (which she is, alongside Goffin). But in the early '70s she embarked on a second career as a performer and recording artist that arguably topped that phenomenal songwriting track record.

With her solo album *Tapestry*, she not only released one of the biggest albums ever (it holds the record for the most consecutive weeks on the *Billboard* 200 for a female artist), she became one of the centerpieces of the decade's singer/songwriter movement. In addition to her own major hits (*Tapestry* and its huge single "It's Too Late," which won the Album of the Year and Record of the Year Grammys, respectively), James Taylor scored with her "You've Got a Friend."

Ultimately, she has become a source of inspiration and aspiration for female songwriters *and* artists who follow her, and the subject of tribute albums (*Tapestry Revisited: A Tribute to Carole King*) and a dedicated Broadway musical (*Beautiful: The Carole King Musical*).

One thing that I've gotten to observe about Carole over the years is that she never was concerned with popularity. She always went to the beat of her own drum. She was, at the age of 14, very rebellious and has retained that nature to this moment as if nothing's really changed.

—Louise Goffin, daughter, acceptance speech, 2013

CAROLE KING
Tribute by Diane Warren
February 10, 2013

I have such a clear memory of this: I was probably no more than seven years old. There was a 45 of a song one of my older sisters had. It was my favorite song. I looked at the name in the parentheses; oddly, not at the name of the artist who sang the song, but to see who wrote it. The song was "Up on the Roof" and the names in parentheses were Goffin/King. I would look at a lot of my favorite songs and see those same names.

Carole King, along with Gerry Goffin, or on her own, has written some of the greatest and most enduring songs of the last 100 years, and that will last hundreds more. Songs such as "Will You Love Me Tomorrow," "(You Make Me Feel Like) A Natural Woman," "It's Too Late," and "You've Got a Friend," and so many more. Later she went on to make history with her own album *Tapestry*, showing the world it all comes down to the simplicity of a great song sung as only the writer of those songs could sing them. Perhaps not with the virtuosity and vocal gymnastics of some of the singers who sang them or could have sung them, but with more *heart* and *soul* than anyone else could ever bring to them.

I met Carole King at Duke's Coffee Shop when I was a starstruck 20-year-old and I stuttered something to her about being a fan and I'm a songwriter too. And she was very nice to me, even though I'm sure the last thing she wanted to do was talk to me. At that time I was frustrated by not yet having a hit and she told me to keep on writing and it will happen.

People use terms like "she is one of the greatest 'female' songwriters." Fuck that. Carole King is one of the *best* songwriters. Ever.

On a personal note, I want to thank her for the kind words she took her time to say to an annoying person interrupting her breakfast. And also thank her for so many songs that have touched me and so many others. Congratulations on this award, Carole. No one deserves it more.

(Songwriter Diane Warren has been nominated for 14 Grammy Awards and eight Academy Awards, winning a Grammy for 1996 for "Because You Loved Me." She was inducted into the Songwriters Hall of Fame in 2001.)

THE KINGSTON TRIO

LIFETIME ACHIEVEMENT AWARD, 2011

Michael Ochs Archives/Getty Images

Bob Dylan may be the rock era's most defining, and no doubt most important, folk artist, at least until he went electric anyway. But it was arguably the success of the Kingston Trio that provided Dylan's launching pad. Without the group's massive success, major labels may have been far less interested in guys with acoustic guitars in the post-Elvis era.

The Trio—original members Dave Guard, Nick Reynolds, and Bob Shane—formed in the San Francisco Bay Area in the late '50s, establishing a following at the city's Purple Onion nightclub. Capitol Records A&R rep Voyle Gilmore signed the group, and their 1958 debut album hit No. 1 as did the massive first single, "Tom Dooley." Coincidentally, 1958 was the first year Grammy Awards were presented and "Tom Dooley" won Best Country & Western Performance, further building the Trio's acclaim.

Before long, as is often the case in pop culture where imitation is easier than originality, folk-flavored groups began springing up like weeds. The Highwaymen, the Journeymen, the New Christy Minstrels, the Serendipity Singers, and the Halifax Three, among others, were suddenly in the sights of label A&R reps, and a vast amount of talent would emerge from them, including Denny Doherty, Cass Elliot, and Gram Parsons.

Despite folk's left-wing roots, the Trio were not an especially political act, but in 1962 they scored a hit with Pete Seeger's "Where Have All the Flowers Gone," adding an anti-war song to their repertoire. Other hits included "M.T.A." and "Greenback Dollar."

The Kingston Trio, or at least their name and songs, have been incredibly enduring. The group, minus any original members, continues to perform today.

THE KINGSTON TRIO
Tribute by Peter Yarrow
February 13, 2011

When I was at Cornell as a freshman I was a nerd, an outsider, and a square. I was immersed in (perhaps "obsessed with" is the right phrase) traditional folk music. Yet, when I heard the undeniable joy and pleasure of three voices, meeting in midair to create the sound of the Kingston Trio, all of a sudden I was no longer out of step. In an insensitive, biased, selfish era, and a highly stratified society, these three bridged the gap between the wealthy and the rest of us who had to be satisfied with leftover scraps until, and unless, we bootstrapped our way out.

The Kingston Trio transcended this clearly dismal aspect of those times without moralizing, without philosophizing, and without preaching. They brought us together by simply being comfortable in their skin, and being together, united as friends. They offered a more hopeful, brighter path to me and, I suspect, to many others.

Their music was a balm to the growing angst of a generation that was soon to turn our country and our world upside down. They tossed off renditions of song gems that felt effortless yet genuine, cool yet caring, sympathetic yet "no big ting." Sometimes they were wistful as in "Sloop John B;" sometimes they sang a great, happy joke, as in "M.T.A.;" sometimes they were oddly, at least for men in those times, sensitive, as in "Tom Dooley;" and sometimes they were wonderfully cutting-edge "hip," as in Bob Shane's classic rendition of "Scotch and Soda."

In college, I imagined them, only a very few years older than me, to be devoid of malevolence or unkindness. And I was right. I met the Kingstons for the first time with Noel Paul and Mary at our first club gig outside of New York, at Boston's mainly jazz club Storyville, owned by George Wein. We were opening up for the immortal Josh White.

I was self-conscious, and secretly blown away by the fact that they had come to see us perform. They were, all three of them, somewhat shy, gracious, and oh so just plain nice.

Ah, we were all so young then. We were wide-eyed and green. Singing together was intoxicatingly wonderful. And the Kingston Trio had come to see us perform. Wow!

History has a way of allowing the truth of each era to become trivialized and marginalized, as the "gods" of the next thing obscure what has come before. However, we of the folk family know what we know. We know how much we learned from each other, how we inspired one another, and how indebted we are to those who brought us along in our similar paths.

Let us take our hats off to the Kingston Trio and the wonderment of a new chapter of American life to which they brought us closer. They showed us a very special and never-out-of-style path to love, life, music, and joy. Like the sound of a banjo, their music will always remain one of the best ways, ever, to announce that we are, indeed, a family.

(Peter Yarrow is a cofounder of Peter, Paul, and Mary, who won five Grammy Awards.)

KRIS KRISTOFFERSON

LIFETIME ACHIEVEMENT AWARD, 2014

"You can look at Nashville pre-Kris and post-Kris, because he changed everything," Bob Dylan said during a captivating acceptance speech when he was honored in 2015 as the MusiCares Person of the Year during Grammy Week. Dylan was ruminating about all the good and bad he had experienced in the music business. His good list was very specific: Nina Simone, Johnny Cash, Elvis . . . and Kris Kristofferson.

Indeed, Kristofferson landed in Nashville at a time when country songs had become safe and formulaic. With songs such as "Sunday Morning Coming Down" (a hit for Cash), "Help Me Make it Through the Night" (Sammi Smith, Best Country Song Grammy for 1971), and "Me and Bobby McGee" (Janis Joplin), Kristofferson turned the country songwriting factory upside down. In place of happy endings, love songs, and novelty records came alcohol-binge hangovers and devil-be-damned sex to cure a lonely soul. In other words, real-life songs.

As a recording artist, Kristofferson, like Dylan, sang with an unvarnished delivery, focusing on the truth in his songs rather than the technical execution—another spanner in the works of the Nashville assembly line.

Many know that Kristofferson has had a successful career as an actor, starring with Barbra Streisand in the 1976 remake of *A Star Is Born*, among other roles. What's less known are his master's degree in English literature, status as a Rhodes Scholar, career as a boxer, and his helicopter-pilot military training. (He once landed a helicopter on Johnny Cash's front lawn to deliver a demo tape.) All of his experiences have no doubt informed his renegade approach to music.

KRIS KRISTOFFERSON
Tribute by Rodney Crowell

January 26, 2014

When in 1971 the news reached my small corner of the world that there was this helicopter-piloting, William Blake-quoting Rhodes Scholar by the name of Kris Kristofferson, whose songs were transforming the country and popular music airwaves, I was marooned six nights a week in an East Texas Holiday Inn lounge, fielding requests for "Scotch and Soda" and "99 Bottles of Beer" from a handful of traveling salesmen and gin swills whose nightcap needs did not include meaningful music. Fortunately, recent recordings of "Help Me Make It Through the Night," "Me and Bobby McGee," "Sunday Morning Coming Down," "For the Good Times," and "Why Me Lord" had begun seeping into the disinterested listeners' nonmusical psyche, and, practically overnight, introducing even the most obscure Kristofferson tune seemed to trigger in the Old Mill Club clientele something resembling audience refinement.

Despite the cold fact that the typical Mill crowd consisted of, maybe, six inebriated tractor suppliers, a table full of box tape wholesalers, and a couple of recently divorced medical assistants, experiencing this subtle shift in the public's taste bolstered in me the notion that I too could someday carve out for myself a career as an artist.

Forty-three years later, having gotten to know the man and his wife, Lisa, I feel modestly qualified to scribble down these few words framing his extraordinary musical legacy: By creating a narrative style that introduced intelligence, humor, emotional eloquence, spiritual longing, male vulnerability, and a devilish sensuality—indeed, a form of eroticism—to country music, Kris Kristofferson, without compromising the content and quality of his work, did as much to expand the mainstream accessibility of an all-too-often misunderstood art form as Roy Acuff, Hank Williams, Johnny Cash, Roger Miller, Willie Nelson, Ray Charles (I'm thinking of *Modern Sounds in Country and Western Music*), and, more recently, Garth Brooks. And, lest we forget, the man is one hell of an accomplished actor.

(A two-time Grammy-winning singer/songwriter, Rodney Crowell was featured on the 2006 album *The Pilgrim: A Celebration of Kris Kristofferson* with a cover of "Come Sundown," which is featured on Kristofferson's Grammy Hall of Fame–inducted debut album.)

BRENDA LEE

 ## LIFETIME ACHIEVEMENT AWARD, 2009

WireImage.com

Even before Taylor Swift crossed over to pop, it's no wonder she was looking to Brenda Lee as a spiritual mentor. Early in her career, Lee could, and was allowed to, do it all: ballads, country, rockabilly, and pop. And she was already making a name for herself right around driving age. Today, she's often viewed as a teenaged teen idol, but that does a disservice to the remarkable presence she had on both the pop and country charts in the '60s, and to her precociously mature singing and phrasing.

Though she was recording in Nashville, in her heyday from the early to mid-'60s, Lee charted primarily on the pop charts, including two No. 1s, the Grammy Hall of Fame–inducted "I'm Sorry" and "I Want to be Wanted." Working with producer Owen Bradley, who was already going about changing the sound of Nashville, Lee even put records on the R&B chart. She was so free of boundaries in those years, she had one of the era's biggest holiday songs, the rockabilly-meets-pop "Rockin' Around the Christmas Tree," and a rock and roll hit with "Is It True," cut in the U.K. with Jimmy Page on guitar.

Later she would concentrate on country music, landing numerous hits on the country chart, and cementing her status as child prodigy turned graceful music legend.

As a member of the Rock and Roll, Country Music, and Rockabilly halls of fame, it's no wonder the 4' 9" Little Miss Dynamite has served as a role model for other young women looking to build powerful careers without being bound by the expectations of others.

BRENDA LEE
Tribute by Taylor Swift
February 8, 2009

November 19, 2008. I'm curled up in my mother's bed, staring intently at my laptop. I'm watching a video of a familiar-looking man wearing a black tuxedo. The video seems to be of a televised award show. The tape is grainy, but the man steps up to the mic and his words are clear:

"Now I'm gonna deal you a queen from the winning hand. Her voice is full like solid gold, with some platinum blended in. Sometimes you'll hear silver when she twists and twirls her notes but gold is Brenda's metal in this song I wish I'd wrote. Ladies and gentlemen . . . Brenda Lee."

The camera then focuses on a woman in her late 30s. The music starts and she's looking down at a framed picture. She's at ease. She is theatrical. And she is beautiful, in a sparkling gown that matches the twinkle in her eye. Lights, camera, action. She starts to sing. That's when you hear the gold, and you watch her as she holds the crowd in the palm of her hand. The performance ends and the crowd goes wild. The lovely lady graciously takes a bow. She smiles out into the vast darkness, taking it all in with grace and composure. The video ends, and I reflect back on what I just saw. It was a timeless performance, but here are the facts: The year is 1983. The song is "Someone Loves You Honey." The man in the tuxedo is Johnny Cash. And the woman in the beautiful dress with the honey-like voice is none other than Brenda Lee.

Brenda Lee, who was born in 1944 near Atlanta, used her prodigious singing talent to support her family after the tragic death of her father. Brenda Lee, the little girl who took over the music world with chart-topping hits when she was still a child. Brenda Lee, the woman who ushered in a new style of rock and roll and was one of the early musical artists to find her fame through television. Brenda Lee, the artist who later went back to her country roots, proving that she could create classics and break down barriers no matter what genre or category her music fell under. Brenda Lee, the singer who mastered the sound of heartbreak so flawlessly, she made audiences not only identify with her, she made them believe her.

I watch the look on her face as she ends her song and first hears that applause. There's a reason she's been able to move people to their feet for more than 60 years. Brenda Lee is grace. Brenda Lee is class and composure. And when she hears the roar of a crowd, Brenda Lee smiles like she's five years old and receiving her first standing ovation. Brenda Lee is someone I will always look up to because of the way she shines. As Johnny Cash said in 1983, it's almost like she's *golden*.

(Tribute written by Taylor Swift, when she was 18 years old, for the Grammy Awards program book in 2009 celebrating The Recording Academy Special Merit Award presented to Brenda Lee. A 10-time Grammy winner, Swift is the first woman in Grammy history to win Album of the Year twice. She performed Lee's "I'm Sorry" on *The Grammy Nominations Concert Live!!* TV special in 2008.)

ROGER LINN

TECHNICAL GRAMMY AWARD, 2011

Songs using electronic instrument and effects developer Roger Linn's most famous innovation, the LinnDrum, form a veritable "Best of the '80s" playlist: Madonna's "Lucky Star," Pat Benatar's "Love Is a Battlefield," Tears for Fears' "Everybody Wants to Rule the World," Queen's "Radio Ga Ga," the Cars' "Drive," A-Ha's "Take On Me," Don Henley's "Boys of Summer." The list is nearly endless. In fact, the LinnDrum is perhaps a bigger signpost of the '80s than mammoth shoulder pads, parachute pants, and "I Want My MTV" video clips.

Linn came to his role as an electronic instrument designer from a music background. He is an accomplished guitar player who toured with Leon Russell at age 21 and a songwriter whose biggest hit was his cowrite (with Richard Feldman) of Eric Clapton's Top 10 smash "Promises."

The LinnDrum was actually the successor to Linn's first creation, the LM-1 Drum Computer—the first programmable drum machine to sample actual drums, which he introduced in 1979. Despite the fact that the LinnDrum helped revolutionize the way records were being produced, the company shuttered in 1986, but Linn himself was far from done innovating.

Working with Akai, he introduced the MPC60, an integrated digital sampling drum machine and MIDI sequencer, in 1988. The Akai MPC products would become especially popular with hip-hop producers.

In 2001 Linn launched Linn Design and his AdrenaLinn products, digital multieffect guitar pedals, which have been used on such recordings as John Mayer's "Heartbreak Warfare" and Green Day's "Boulevard of Broken Dreams."

To this day, Linn continues to bring new products to market, including the Tempest Analog Drum Machine and LinnStrument Expressive MIDI Performance Controller, revealing an unquenchable thirst for design perfection.

Most importantly I'd like to thank my wife Ingrid, who is here with us tonight. Ingrid is not only a constant source of love and inspiration but also, unlike me, she is a real engineer and she helps me with the higher math algorithms that I don't understand very well.

—Roger Linn, acceptance speech, 2011

ROGER LINN
Tribute by Todd Rundgren
February 13, 2011

My first LinnDrum fascinated and frightened me. I had been pretty unimpressed with the state of programmed drums, the tinny analogue sounds that propelled the disco music that was glutting the airwaves in the late '70s. Yet, here was a device that, in the proper hands, could be a suitable replacement for a real drummer—that most troublesome of all instruments and instrumentalists!

What frightened me was the ease with which I and my contemporaries could perform such a substitution. Soon a recording would not be considered radio-worthy without the fat, precise sound that the LinnDrum provided. We were moving into a world where few could tell the difference between live and programmed performances.

Innovation was nothing new to Roger Linn. In 1979 he introduced the LM-1 Drum Computer, the world's first programmable sampled-sound drum machine. The drum sounds created by his machines were heard on countless recordings, including my own, and those by Prince, Madonna, Michael Jackson, and Peter Gabriel, to name a few.

He has since continued to develop cutting-edge products, including the Linn 9000 and more recently a tool for guitarists, AdrenaLinn. Appropriately, he is a fine guitarist and songwriter himself, having cowritten songs for Eric Clapton and Mary Chapin Carpenter, and toured with Leon Russell. Based in Berkeley, California, he and his wife Ingrid operate Roger Linn Design out of their home and will no doubt continue to churn out high-tech products designed for musicians.

Of course, not telling the difference between a machine and a real person is moot today. The revolution started by Roger Linn and his rhythmical box is complete. Drummers have not disappeared, but you can't listen to the radio for five minutes without hearing a drummer who may not actually be a drummer.

(A singer/songwriter, musician, and producer, Todd Rundgren's hits include "Hello It's Me," "I Saw the Light," and "Can We Still Be Friends?" With a career spanning more than four decades, Rundgren was also a member of Nazz, formed the progressive rock band Utopia, and produced for artists such as Badfinger, Grand Funk Railroad, and the New York Dolls.)

THE LOUVIN BROTHERS

 ## LIFETIME ACHIEVEMENT AWARD, 2015

Michael Ochs Archives/Getty Images

Like the Delmore Brothers before them and the Everly Brothers who followed, the Louvin Brothers' heavenly familial harmonies made them huge stars. Ira Louvin had a remarkable high tenor, and when he combined it with younger brother Charlie Louvin's warmer tone, they made one of the most pleasing sounds in gospel and country music in the '50s and '60s.

The brothers, originally named Loudermilk (Nashville Songwriters Hall of Fame member John D. Loudermilk is their cousin), began in gospel music, establishing and perfecting their harmony singing. With the minor hit "The 'Get Acquainted' Waltz," they made their foray into secular music. After a number of tryouts, they finally joined the Grand Old Opry in 1955. They would go on to enjoy signature hits such as "Cash on the Barrelhead" and "When I Stop Dreaming."

Despite a lengthy and influential career, the brothers would become almost as noteworthy for a single album, *Satan Is Real*, and its quirky album cover. Designed by Ira and featuring the brothers navigating through fire and brimstone in front of a cartoonish Satan—who looks anything but real—the cover has made many lists of the strangest album covers of all time and added a colorful chapter in the Louvin story.

But the sentiment of the album was real. The brothers were active Baptists who often railed in song against sin. Still, Ira's troubled life would split the brothers. He was a heavy drinker, and in 1963 Charlie tired of Ira's abusiveness and left for a solo career. Ira would die in a car crash in 1965 at age 41. Charlie died in 2011 at age 83. But their approach to music would later resonate with the Everlys, Gram Parsons, and the Byrds, among others.

Ira Louvin's achievements came from a tormented yet loveable man, against all odds and under intense scrutiny. Many stories tell of his troubled childhood, his shortcomings, mistakes, and tragedies, as do a lot of his songs. But a great deal of his music tells a different story. These were often songs of hopes and reverence and victory—the story he wanted told, the legacy he wanted spoken of. Louvin Brothers' music speaks volumes.

—Kathy Louvin, Ira Louvin's daughter, acceptance speech, 2015

THE LOUVIN BROTHERS
Tribute by Jerry Douglas
February 8, 2015

The sound of the Louvin Brothers' harmony is so captivating that it has reached and influenced a cache of performers—from the Everly Brothers, the Beatles, and the Byrds to Dolly Parton, Gram Parsons, the Rolling Stones, and Emmylou Harris. I first heard the Louvins at age six and, even then, I *knew* they were good. That physical and psychological expression going into the mix when siblings sing together is something that cannot be surpassed. Listening to others attempt to emulate the Louvins' style, it is the brother and/or sister acts who come closest to capturing that magic. Just consider: the Jackson 5, the Staple Singers, and the Everly Brothers.

Ira and Charlie Louvin (originally Loudermilk) were born and raised in Depression-era Alabama near the southernmost slope of the Appalachian Mountains. The boys grew up poor, chopping cotton and working their family's plot of dusty land. Discovering a love of singing together in church, it was soon evident the brothers had something special in their vocal harmonies, and they began making appearances on local radio programs. Following Charlie's active military service in World War II and the Korean War, the gospel-singing brothers, yearning to be famous, shifted from the sacred sector to the world of country music. The duo shared stages and record bins with Chet Atkins, Bill Monroe, and Patsy Cline.

While they could astound audiences with harmonic chemistry, the Louvin Brothers were also known for their rowdy ways, with alcohol and personal demons fueling Ira's deep rage. Still, the pair created some of country music's best religious anthems: "I Steal Away and Pray," "There's a Higher Power," and "The Christian Life." The brothers joined the Grand Ole Opry in 1955, opened for Elvis Presley in 1956, and made records with producer Ken Nelson throughout the golden age of country music. That recording partnership yielded "When I Stop Dreaming," "I Don't Believe You've Met My Baby," "Cash on the Barrelhead," "You're Learning," and "Knoxville Girl," songs that continue to inform country and alt-country rock repertoires. By 1963, Charlie found himself no longer able to abide Ira's frequent fury, and the duo ceased to be.

The Louvin Brothers were inducted into the Country Music Hall of Fame in 2001. No one ever deserved it more, in my estimation. If only there was an Album Cover Hall of Fame that would recognize their incomparable cover art on the LP *Satan is Real*.

(Dobro master Jerry Douglas is a 14-time Grammy winner. Douglas was a featured artist on the 1997 tribute album, *Songs of the Louvin Brothers*. In 2010 he performed at an all-star benefit concert for Charlie Louvin, who succumbed to pancreatic cancer in 2011.)

BRUCE LUNDVALL

TRUSTEES AWARD, 2011

Wirelmage.com

Widely regarded as not just a consummate industry figure but also a protector of the jazz tradition, Bruce Lundvall's 50-plus-year career was marked by an impressive business track record as well as a legacy of goodwill.

Lundvall took an entry-level marketing job at Columbia Records in the early '60s, rising some 15 years later to president of the label's domestic division. While there, he signed artists as varied as Dexter Gordon, Herbie Hancock, Stan Getz, Wynton Marsalis, and Willie Nelson.

After leaving Columbia, Lundvall, who always recognized the ambassadorial role music plays, mounted an ambitious concert in Havana, Cuba, with artists such as Billy Joel, Stephen Stills, Weather Report, and Kris Kristofferson on the U.S. side, together with such Cuban acts as Irakere and Orquestra Aragón, resulting in two albums and the filmed documentary *Havana Jam '79*.

Shortly thereafter, he was invited to run the new pop-oriented Manhattan Records, as well as revive the venerable jazz label Blue Note. Manhattan's acts included Richard Marx, the Pet Shop Boys, Natalie Cole, Queensrÿche, and Lila Downs. For Blue Note, Lundvall personally took a chance on a young singer who came from out of the blue with a multimillion-selling debut album. Since then, Norah Jones has continued to prove herself a remarkably adventurous and accomplished artist.

Over his career Lundvall hasn't just won awards, he's inspired them. The Montreal Jazz Festival's Bruce Lundvall Award and *JazzTimes* magazine's Bruce Lundvall Visionary Award both honor nonmusicians who have left a mark on the world of jazz, as Lundvall did himself.

Lundvall died in 2015, but is remembered by artists and colleagues today not just as an accomplished and supportive music executive, but as a friend and mentor.

When I worked at Columbia Records, there was a man named Goddard Lieberson. He was the visionary former president of Columbia Records and taught me, among other things, that we have a very serious business responsibility to our parent company, as well as a greater responsibility, actually, to an art form that happens to be called music. If we get the art form right, he said, the business will come right along with it. That mantra is as relevant today as it always was.

—Bruce Lundvall, acceptance speech, 2011

BRUCE LUNDVALL
Tribute by Herbie Hancock
February 13, 2011

Bruce Lundvall, a music powerhouse, is the heart and soul of jazz. His lifetime dedication and devotion to jazz, coupled with his expert ability in orchestrating all facets of Blue Note Records, have bestowed upon the world a priceless gift—some of the greatest music ever created.

His stalwart support for the master musicians who have been fortunate to work with him has been instrumental in the continuation and development of modern jazz because, to Bruce, the music and the artists are paramount.

My gratitude to Bruce is immense because he was responsible for events that became cornerstones in my life's work and passions. He has championed my music, whether he was involved in the production or was just cheering me on from the sidelines. Bruce played a crucial role in advancing my career when he brought me to Clive Davis at Columbia Records. They released *Head Hunters* in 1973, a pivotal recording for me, and a defining moment in jazz fusion. And, it was Bruce who suggested me to the iconic film director, Bertrand Tavernier, to create the score for the film *'Round Midnight*, for which I subsequently won an Oscar.

For almost five decades Bruce has steered the music world by shepherding a plethora of jazz, pop, Latin, and country icons into successful recording careers. He can identify emerging artists destined for success, like Norah Jones, or champion a gifted musician who is worthy of respect and wider attention, exemplified by his recent signing of the gifted guitarist Lionel Loueke.

His stable of past and present artists reads like a musical history book: Willie Nelson, Natalie Cole, Dexter Gordon, James Taylor, McCoy Tyner, Paquito D'Rivera, Stan Getz, Wynton Marsalis, Bobby McFerrin, Rubén Blades, Stanley Jordan, Dianne Reeves, Joe Lovano, Gonzalo Rubalcaba, Max Roach, Cassandra Wilson, Phoebe Snow, Bob James, Rosanne Cash, Toto, and Stephen Stills, to name a few. Whew!

And, I am proud and greatly honored to be a member of his extraordinary musical family.

Bruce has received numerous awards from his peers, and has been praised for his charity work and his lifetime service to world culture. Receiving the Trustees Award from The Recording Academy adds a prestigious accolade to his long list of achievements.

(A 14-time Grammy winner, Herbie Hancock received a Recording Academy Lifetime Achievement Award in 2016.)

BARRY MANN AND CYNTHIA WEIL

 ## Trustees Award, 2015

A team as both wife and husband and songwriters, Cynthia Weil and Barry Mann were two of the most successful writers in New York's Brill Building, the '60s songwriting and music publishing house that was home to other writers such as Carole King, Gerry Goffin, Burt Bacharach, Hal David, and Neil Diamond, among others.

The pair met on a writing session and quickly embarked on a professional and personal relationship, both of which continue to this day. And while a number of Brill writers penned a catalog of hits, Weil and Mann's is as lengthy, and impactful, as any.

Writing with producer Phil Spector, the pair authored "You've Lost That Lovin' Feeling" (inducted into the Grammy Hall of Fame in 1998) for the Righteous Brothers, arguably setting the tone for blue-eyed soul acts to follow. Songs such as the Drifters' "On Broadway" (written with Jerry Lieber and Mike Stoller, Grammy Hall of Fame 2013), the Crystals' "Uptown," and Jay and the Americans' "Only in America" shook off the Brill Building's focus on teen love to address economic and racial inequality.

In fact, the range of their songs and the artists who recorded them is pretty remarkable: the fun-loving "Blame It on the Bossa Nova" for Eydie Gorme; "We Gotta Get Out of This Place" (Grammy Hall of Fame, 2011), embraced as an anti-Vietnam war anthem, for the Animals; the drug commentary of "Kicks" for Paul Revere & the Raiders; and "Rock and Roll Lullaby," the vastly underrated tale of teen motherhood, for B.J. Thomas.

And well into the '80s they were scoring hits by helping to introduce singer James Ingram with "Just Once" and "Somewhere Out There" (written with James Horner) for Ingram and Linda Ronstadt.

The pair has won two Grammys and were inducted into the Rock and Roll Hall of Fame in 2010 and the Songwriters Hall of Fame in 1987. Now that's a successful marriage.

It all begins with the song. Without the song, there are no singers, no musicians, no recording artists, no record labels, no business managers, no publishing companies, no music business.

—Cynthia Weil, acceptance speech, 2015

BARRY MANN AND CYNTHIA WEIL
Tribute by Lionel Richie
February 8, 2015

Oh my God—I am a fan. No, no, let me rephrase that: I am a *huge* fan. The Brill Building: birthplace of the sound and songs that shaped a generation of music and influenced countless more. This wonderful place, where composer Barry Mann and lyricist Cynthia Weil first met and tried their hand at crafting songs together—a decision, I might add, sparked by destiny—is where they fell in love, married, and wrote more than 50 hit songs together over the next four decades.

Now, one hit song—from my point of view—one hit song is great! But 50 hit songs? Now that is *amazing!* My favorite song of theirs, "You've Lost that Lovin' Feeling" (written with Phil Spector and performed by the Righteous Brothers), was the most played song of the 20th century, with more than eight million plays.

I can remember the first time I met Barry and Cynthia. I showed up at their house knowing I had a good melody and a good idea for a title, but I needed help. My title was "Strangers in the Night." Cynthia said to me, "Would you be upset if I change the title to 'Running with the Night'?" And after a few blows to my ego, I said, "Sure." The rest . . . is history.

Barry and Cynthia are the masters of their craft and to be recognized with this prestigious honor, well, no one can be more deserving of this award than the two of them. I have admired them for years and I am happy to call them my friends.

(Grammy-, Oscar-, and Golden Globe Award–winning singer/songwriter Lionel Richie cowrote his 1983 Top 10 hit "Running with the Night" with Cynthia Weil. Richie has won four Grammy Awards, and was honored as the 2016 MusiCares Person of the Year.)

ARMANDO MANZANERO

 ## LIFETIME ACHIEVEMENT AWARD, 2014

Wirelmage.com

When you're considered the finest composer of romantic songs in a culture where romance and passion are calling cards, you know you're going to be, well, popular. Mexican composer and singer Armando Manzanero has written hundreds of songs that have established him as *el rey* of romantic ballads not just in his native Mexico, but internationally as well. Many of his songs have become worldwide hits, including arguably his best-known composition, which when translated into English became the standard "It's Impossible." Perry Como's version helped the title earn two Grammy nominations for 1971, including Song of the Year.

Manzanero studied music in Mexico City. His first song, "Nunca en el Mundo," written at age 15, has been recorded more than a dozen times in multiple languages, signaling an auspicious start. In 1957 he became a creative executive at the Mexican branch of CBS International, and began accompanying singers such as Raphael and Lucho Gatica. In 1959 he was convinced to record his own album, beginning a string of dozens of albums and hit records.

Over the years, his songs have been recorded by artists including Christina Aguilera, Tony Bennett, Andrea Bocelli, José José, Lucero, Luis Miguel, Elvis Presley, Frank Sinatra, and many others.

In 2011 he became president of the Asociación Nacional de Autores y Compositores (the Mexican National Association of Authors and Composers), and has worked to strengthen copyright laws to help songwriters continue to thrive.

To paraphrase his own song, can you overestimate the impact of Armando Manzanero? It's impossible.

ARMANDO MANZANERO
Tribute by Lucero
January 26, 2014

How easy it seems to talk about music and songs. They have been part of our lives since we can remember. But rarely do we stop to think about where these songs come from. Those songs that make us fall in love, that give us goose bumps, that make us want to cry or laugh, and that have been with us in so many memorable moments of our lives.

It's then that I think of the master, Armando Manzanero. And automatically, in my mind, the melody and lyrics to "Adoro," "Somos Novios," "Contigo Aprendí," "Esta Tarde Vi Llover," "Voy a Apagar La Luz," and "No," among many others, begin to play. They are a part of my life and my surroundings—the pure romanticism reflected in their lyrics. Writing and singing of love, Armando Manzanero has become part of millions of us, although some are not as lucky as I am to know him.

Talking about him and his songs is like talking with family at our kitchen tables. He has taken over our hearts with such ease. He has entered our lives to fill it with wonderful sounds, accompanied by his piano, his voice, and the vast amount of talented singers who have interpreted his songs with pride for decades. We've heard his songs in many languages and many countries, delivering the flavor of his native Yucatán to unexpected places. He makes me proud to be Mexican like him. It was a delight to have performed a duet with him on his song "No Existen Limites," and it is a joy to hear him tell his stories.

He is a remarkable man, whose every word gives us the opportunity to feel and vibrate with his inspiration. How many times have we dedicated his songs? How many times have we used his songs as the soundtrack to our love affairs and heartbreaks? How often have we hummed at least one of his songs? I seem to lose track.

That's how music is. It has to do with math, but math doesn't explain what we feel or what occurs within us when we hear his melodies. Thus, the number of hits that Don Armando Manzanero's musical legacy continues to leave many generations is truly staggering.

With these few humble words I try to express my admiration, respect, and love for a man who is measured from the land to the sky, for a man who has given us his talent and inspiration, more than he can perhaps imagine himself. Long live our Armando Manzanero.

(A native of Mexico City, Emmy-winning actress, singer, and former Latin Grammy Awards show host Lucero performed "No Existen Límites" with Armando Manzanero on his 2001 duets album, *Duetos*.)

ARIF MARDIN

TRUSTEES AWARD, 2001

Wire Image.com

On the surface, it might be tempting to attribute producer/engineer Arif Mardin's success to a kind of nepotism. He was, after all, a fellow Turkish countryman of Atlantic Records founder Ahmet and Nesuhi Ertegun. Mardin ended up going to work as Nesuhi's assistant, and while his geographic familiarity may have factored into his hiring, he also brought with him a Berklee College of Music degree and a love of jazz and R&B.

Of course, nepotism doesn't create the kind of dynamic career Mardin enjoyed. Only talent and instincts can do that.

Mardin began working with Atlantic jazz acts such as Mose Allison and Freddie Hubbard. But he really emerged as an essential figure in R&B in 1967 when he arranged the music for Aretha Franklin's *I Never Loved a Man the Way I Love You* and its single "Respect." Until then, Franklin had spent more than half a decade on Columbia Records trying on styles that didn't seem to fit her. Mardin and producer Jerry Wexler began a string of recordings with Franklin that would earn her the title of the Queen of Soul.

But that was truly the beginning. With the Rascals, Mardin produced some of the finest blue-eyed soul of the '60s. In 1969 he teamed with the great Tom Dowd to produce Dusty Springfield's classic *Dusty in Memphis*. He'd go on to work with artists such as Hall & Oates, Roberta Flack, Donny Hathaway, and John Prine.

In 1974 he was given the assignment of creating an American R&B sound for an Anglo-pop group that was exploring new directions. The result was the Bee Gees' *Main Course* and the seminal white disco hit "Jive Talkin'."

Mardin never truly had a down period. He earned 11 Grammys—his last coming nearly 30 years after his first. As late as 2003, he helmed Norah Jones' breakthrough *Come Away with Me*, just three years before his death.

ARIF MARDIN
Tribute by Ahmet Ertegun
February 21, 2001

As a young boy, many years before I had ever met or even heard of Arif Mardin, I was very much aware of the importance of the Mardin family in Turkey. In some ways, they could be described as the Rockefellers or the Vanderbilts of the Ottoman Empire. They were statesmen, diplomats, and industrialists.

Years later, my brother Nesuhi told me that there was this young jazz arranger who had befriended Quincy Jones while he was on a State Department tour of Europe with the Dizzy Gillespie orchestra and who had also written charts for various bands—including that of Count Basie. And when he told me that his name was Arif Mardin, I was amazed that this aristocratic family had produced a "black sheep" whose life, love, and passion were devoted to American jazz music. Nesuhi wanted to invite Arif to join us at Atlantic Records and, of course, I instantly agreed.

Born in Istanbul, Arif had graduated from Istanbul University and then studied at the London School of Economics. In 1958, five years before he joined Atlantic, he had come to America as the first recipient of the Quincy Jones Scholarship at the Berklee College of Music in Boston. After graduation, he had taught at Berklee for a year. (Years later, he became a trustee of the school and was awarded an honorary doctorate.)

So, in 1963, we hired Arif at Atlantic, and it wasn't long before he became a guiding musical light of our growing company. He not only became a very important member of our Atlantic family, but of the Ertegun family as well. His great musical skill, combined with his immense personal charm and self-effacing manner, made him a favorite with every artist with whom he worked. Arif started out as Nesuhi's assistant, was soon made studio manager, and then became our house producer and arranger. He was subsequently named vice president and then senior vice president of the label.

In 1966 Arif's first full-fledged production assignment was a new group called the Young Rascals. Right off the bat, Arif landed his first No. 1 hit, "Good Lovin'." Since then, he has worked with many of the most illustrious artists in the history of modern music, including the Average White Band, the Bee Gees, Eric Clapton, Judy Collins, Phil Collins, Michael Crawford, Roberta Flack, Aretha Franklin, Hall & Oates, Donny Hathaway, Jewel, Chaka Khan, Manhattan Transfer, Bette Midler, John Prine, Diana Ross, Carly Simon, Barbra Streisand, and many, many more. He has also been involved with a number of original cast albums and soundtracks. Alongside these extensive accomplishments, Arif is a gifted composer and artist in his own right.

In a business often driven by trend and fashion, Arif has remained a beacon of quality, taste, and consistency. In contrast to many other producers, he does not have one sound which dominates his records or overshadows the artists he is recording. On the contrary, Arif creates an environment unique to each performer, bringing out the best qualities of those artists. As a result, over the decades he has helped singers and musicians of very different musical styles do the best work of their careers. At the same time, he has the rare ability to create records which are at once timeless and utterly contemporary. Arif has won six Grammy Awards, including Producer of the Year for 1975. In 1997 he received the Heroes Award from the New York Chapter of The Recording Academy.

Above all, Arif remains a true gentleman, and his great ears are matched only by his great heart. I am privileged to have had him as a valuable colleague and close friend for the past four decades. But, much more importantly, the music world has been truly blessed by his immense talent and his wonderful presence.

(Ahmet Ertegun was the cofounder of Atlantic Records and co-chairman/co-CEO of the Atlantic Group. He was honored with a Trustees Award in 1993. He died in 2006.)

JIM MARSHALL

TRUSTEES AWARD, 2014

He was there at Woodstock. He was there when Jimi Hendrix burned his guitar at the Monterey Pop Festival. When Johnny Cash flipped the bird at San Quentin State Prison. And backstage at the Beatles' final concert at Candlestick Park in San Francisco. Though he does seem omnipresent, he's not God. But he may be the god of rock and roll photography.

Jim Marshall shot those iconic scenes and many more, including hundreds of album covers, concerts, and music stars in their natural habitats. He was raised in San Francisco and came of age with its rock and jazz communities. His first notable assignment was shooting John Coltrane at the home of noted jazz critic Ralph J. Gleason.

He moved to New York in 1962 and shot album covers for Atlantic, Columbia, and ABC-Paramount Records and covered the Newport Folk Festival before returning to the Bay Area in 1964 in time for Monterey, the Summer of Love, and the dynamic cultural shift being driven by music. His goal was to shoot his subjects as they lived and worked, and his own embrace of the rock and roll lifestyle and willingness to pursue any avenue for a great shot gained him unique access to the personalities and turning points that formed a generation—artists such as the Grateful Dead, Janis Joplin, the Allman Brothers, and Miles Davis and the major music events of the '60s.

His work would continue through the decades, culminating in numerous exhibitions and books of his photos prior to and following his death in 2010, allowing us to view music history through his famed Leica lens.

Jim always said, "It's never just been a job. It's been my life."
—Amelia Davis, beneficiary of Jim Marshall's estate, acceptance speech, 2014

JIM MARSHALL
Tribute by Henry Diltz
January 26, 2014

Jim Marshall was my guru. He told me so himself. He was the guru of most of today's music photographers because he was one of the first and one of the best. His mantra was "Get the picture!"

I met him in the mid-'60s. He worked mostly in San Francisco and I worked mostly in L.A., but our paths crossed at the Monterey Pop Festival and at Woodstock, and then more often as the years went by.

There are many colorful adjectives that come to mind when remembering Jim: irascible, impatient, explosive, but always very, very kindhearted. He liked to drink and tell stories and he loved pretty women. "Cars, guns, and cameras always get me into trouble," he used to say. He brooked no denial as he waded right in with his little Leica clicking quietly and constantly. His eye was amazing as he caught the essence of each scene before him. His subjects loved his energy and commitment to the moment. He was always very much in the moment.

I had always known Jim for his photos of San Francisco's rich music scene: the Grateful Dead, Jefferson Airplane, Janis Joplin, and Santana. I knew his famous photo of Johnny Cash giving the finger (a message to the warden of the San Quentin State Prison), but I was totally unprepared for the breadth of his subject matter the day I walked into a gallery in L.A.'s Bergamot Station that was exhibiting his work. There were several big rooms with walls completely covered with his photos from floor to ceiling with no space in between. I saw old blues singers, civil rights marches, baseball players, famous comedians, beatniks, hippies, and jazz musicians. I never saw so many pictures on a wall in my life. That huge collection of images is his living gift to us all.

Jim had no family as long as I knew him; his family was his friends, all of whom have hilarious and harried "Jim" stories they love to share. Some involve guns, some involve drugs, all involve the F word (his favorite), and all include an awe and a warm feeling for the man we all loved.

We still love you, Jim!

(With a career spanning more than 40 years, photographer Henry Diltz is responsible for capturing iconic images of historic events such as Woodstock and artists including Blondie; Eric Clapton; Crosby, Stills, Nash & Young; the Doors; and Led Zeppelin, among countless others. In 2001 Diltz cofounded the Morrison Hotel Gallery, which represents some of the most renowned photographers in music.)

Tribute by Graham Nash

The world is a better place because of the talent and vision of my friend Jim Marshall. He, of course, took countless iconic photographs over the years and always brought a deeper insight into the world of photography and music. His images can be likened to haiku poetry: everything in its proper place . . . no "extra" information . . . only the very essences necessary to convey what he wants us to see. Never one to be dissuaded from a good shot, he opened our eyes to the wonders of his portraits. Jim's images always have a sense of completeness and his ability to compose instantly is renowned. It's possible that I took the last portrait of Jim shortly before his untimely passing. Jim may be gone but his images will absolutely stand the test of time and be around for us to see and enjoy for years to come.

(A Grammy-winning founding member of Crosby, Stills, and Nash and the Hollies, and two-time Rock and Roll Hall of Famer, Graham Nash is also a photographer and published author. His photographic work is collected in the book *Eye to Eye: Photographs by Graham Nash*. In 2008 he curated others' photographic work in *Taking Aim: Unforgettable Rock 'n' Roll Photographs Selected by Graham Nash* (2009). Since 2005 the first IRIS 3047 printer owned by Nash's digital printing company, Nash Editions, and one of its first published works—his 1969 portrait of David Crosby—have been in the permanent collection of the Smithsonian Institution's National Museum of American History.)

DEAN MARTIN

 ## LIFETIME ACHIEVEMENT AWARD, 2009

Few entertainers have been so successful in as many different areas of the business as Dean Martin. He was among the rarified few who became such a pop culture fixture that it was hard to distinguish the entertainer (hard-drinking, fun-loving ladies' man with the velvety croon) from the caricature (hard-drinking, fun-loving ladies' man with the velvety croon).

His career began in the mid-'40s on the Atlantic City boardwalk when almost accidentally he and comedian Jerry Lewis hit upon a team act that propelled them to the height of fame, making them among the most popular and highly paid stage and film acts in the business. But by the mid-'50s, the pair's relationship had deteriorated and the partnership ended. The future was uncertain for Martin, whose music career had only been mildly successful to that point.

But in 1956, he scored a No. 1 hit with "Memories Are Made of This," and followed it with the 1958 smash "Volare (Nel Blu Dipinto di Blu)." The 1958 film *The Young Lions* proved he had acting chops. Soon, his solo talent would turn him into an iconic personality who would ultimately knock the Beatles out of the No. 1 spot on the *Billboard* Hot 100 in 1964 with the Grammy Hall of Fame–inducted "Everybody Loves Somebody," become part of Frank Sinatra's Rat Pack in Vegas, star in his own long-running variety show and a series of very '60s James Bond-lite spy-spoof Matt Helm films, and emcee *The Dean Martin Celebrity Roast* franchise, which is still hawked through Time Life Entertainment.

It all added up to a larger-than-life career and persona that touched anyone who didn't live under a rock.

> *My 10-year-old grandson, the fortuitously named Deano, wanted a brand new skateboard for Christmas . . . and he called the day after Christmas, he was so excited. He said, "I got my new skateboard and you'll never guess whose picture's on it. It's grandpa Dean with two of his friends!" Really priceless. How great a career is it when you make your first recording in 1948 and you're still so popular that your picture is on a skateboard in 2009? That's a lifetime achievement.*
>
> —Gail Martin, daughter, acceptance speech, 2009

DEAN MARTIN
Tribute by Steven Van Zandt
February 8, 2009

As a kid I didn't really get Dean. His partner Jerry Lewis was the one I was supposed to get. Jerry was the greatest and so when he credited Dean as the reason the thing worked, we believed him. But we didn't really get it.

It wasn't until later, in the '60s Rat Pack years, that a certain unique quality began to show through the many protective layers of the never-to-be solved mystery of Dean's true personality. I would identify it as I began to see his complexities and start to relate to him. It was a thing called dignity. That was it. That's what made him different than the other straight men.

Yes, Jerry would talk about the man's expertise at his craft. But Bud Abbott, in truth, was equally adept. Oliver Hardy. Dan Rowan. Tommy Chong—pick your straight man, they all made the act work.

But the reason why Martin and Lewis were one of the four showbiz phenomena of the 20th century—along with Sinatra, Elvis, and the Beatles—was not just craft. While Jerry was reinventing silly slapstick and arrested adolescence at its most hilariously obnoxious, Dean was counterbalancing it all with dignity.

Classic cool suave sophistication. Picture-perfect juxtaposition. And always with a little, "Hey folks, let's not take this showbiz thing too seriously, after all I should have been just another hood from Steubenville." For that matter he didn't even take the mob seriously, which almost got him whacked on more than one occasion.

Alright, so maybe I was the only one of my generation to not get upset when he famously made fun of the Rolling Stones on *The Hollywood Palace* TV show as my past and my future met. But that's what he was supposed to do! He was just fulfilling his obligation as a representative of the showbiz generation about to be replaced. Just getting his last licks in. Even his best friend Frank had to give in and host a show for Elvis when Presley got out of the service, which must have made him gag.

But a funny thing happened on the way to the generation gap. Dean (and by the way, Frank) didn't get replaced. Underneath all the jokes, the drunk act, the no rehearsals, the do it on the first take, the "I do not care," was a solid foundation of quality and dignity.

The Young Lions, *Some Came Running*, *Rio Bravo*, *Ocean's Eleven*, *Robin and the 7 Hoods*. And, oh yeah, he sang real good too. "Everybody Loves Somebody," "That's Amore," "Sway," "Return to Me (Ritorna-Me)," "Ain't That a Kick in the Head."

His TV shows, his records, his Vegas act—all consistently great, funny, always entertaining, and for real rebels, inspiring. That doesn't happen by not caring, not paying attention, or by accident. The fact was, his consummate professionalism wouldn't let him break character. You like him drunk? He'll stay pretend-drunk for you. A very smart businessman and caring artist just isn't as interesting.

And now as generation after generation discover him, his sales continue to break records. His irreverence continues to inspire and will do so forever.

Cool, it turns out, is timeless.

(Steven Van Zandt is a longtime member of the E Street Band, who were inducted into the Rock and Roll Hall of Fame in 2014. He hosts the syndicated radio show *Little Steven's Underground Garage* and played Silvio Dante on the HBO series *The Sopranos*.)

COSIMO MATASSA

 ## TRUSTEES AWARD, 2007

Besides having one of the rock era's truly great given names, New Orleans recording engineer and studio owner Cosimo Matassa was a vital part of the Crescent City's rock and R&B scene, working with the area's legendary producers (Dave Bartholomew and Allen Toussaint) and helping develop what came to be known as the New Orleans Sound.

In the mid-'40s, Matassa noted there were dozens of talented musicians in New Orleans, but no place to record them. When he opened his J&M Studios (originally in the back of his appliance store), Bartholomew and Toussaint in particular began recording national hits there: Fats Domino's "The Fat Man," Little Richard's "Tutti Futti," Smiley Lewis' "I Hear You Knockin'," Shirley and Lee's "Let the Good Times Roll," Lloyd Price's "Lawdy Miss Clawdy," Ernie K-Doe's "Mother-in-Law," Roy Brown's "Good Rockin' Tonight," and Big Joe Turner's "Shake, Rattle and Roll," among dozens of others.

Matassa's studio and miking techniques were credited with developing the New Orleans Sound—heavy on drums, guitar, bass, and vocals, with a lighter touch on the piano and horns. In a 1999 *Goldmine* interview, Matassa said his role "was to get the performance and the performer on the tape with the least interference and the least resistance." And while those who recorded with him credit him with far more than a passive role, if creating the means to capture this essential music on tape was all he did, he'd qualify as a rock and R&B giant.

You know when I started recording 70 years ago the only people doing digital were proctologists.

—Cosimo Matassa, acceptance speech, 2007

COSIMO MATASSA
Tribute by Allen Toussaint
February 11, 2007

Right has never been righter as far as the right man for an award: Cosimo Matassa!

As they say, behind every great this, there's a great that. Well, behind every recording, there's an engineer. And, in the world of recording engineers, like in any other field, there are pioneers; the backbone, the trailblazers. Unlike others who have been honored and truly have the right to be listed on the scrolls of the elite but who have been long since gone, we are fortunate to still have with us Cosimo Matassa.

I don't know if he does or not, but if he has two dollars for every recording he's engineered, and throw in a couple of bucks for careers he's started and/or helped, he and Bill Gates just might be socialite buddies.

Speaking of starting out in our recording industry, some success stories, truthfully so, tell of how people got started on a simple eight-track or even four-track machine. Well, let's consider recording sessions Cosimo did where if someone makes a bad enough mistake to have to stop, the engineer takes the partially recorded disc off, breaks it and throws it in the trash can and puts on a fresh one; Cos' knows about that.

What you heard at the end of the take was the record, nothing more, nothing less. Speaking of how many tracks, how about one?

But more importantly, Cosimo Matassa grew at the luxury of a New Orleans pace, but he grew. Already having superior intelligence, he was not intimidated by the growth of technology and he led us through decades of progress, changes, and successes, and sent us onward into the future with an undeniable history.

Cosimo owned J&M Studios and Cosimo Recording Studio, and Little Richard and Fats Domino were just two of the many artists who made hits there. And folks like myself and Dr. John started to make our reputations in those studios.

Thank you, Cosimo Matassa. The fruits of your labor have touched every continent. You played an essential part in creating the New Orleans Sound.

(Musician, songwriter, producer, and one of New Orleans' towering talents, the late Allen Toussaint worked extensively with engineer and studio owner Cosimo Matassa. Among Toussaint's varied compositions were Herb Alpert's "Whipped Cream," Lee Dorsey's "Working in a Coal Mine," and the Pointer Sisters' "Yes We Can," among others. He received his own Recording Academy Trustees Award in 2009.)

THE MEMPHIS HORNS

LIFETIME ACHIEVEMENT AWARD, 2012

GAB Archive/Redferns/Getty Images

Though the name sounds like a large brass section, the Memphis Horns were primarily associated with trumpeter Wayne Jackson and saxophonist Andrew Love, though over the years the group also included saxophonists Lewis Collins, Ed Logan, and James Mitchell and trombonist Jack Hale, among others.

The Horns were an essential part of the sound coming out of the Stax Records soul-music factory in the '60s, augmenting Stax house band Booker T. & the MG's' rhythmic groove with punctuated accents. They played on virtually every Stax recording (at least those that called for horns, which were many), as well as on classic recordings by soul stars such as Aretha Franklin. They would ultimately make appearances on pop recordings by artists ranging from the Doobie Brothers to U2 and also worked closely with blues artist Robert Cray.

The Grammy Hall of Fame is rife with recordings that bear their signature playing, from Sam & Dave's "Soul Man" to Otis Redding's "I've Been Loving You Too Long."

The prominence of their role at Stax was such that they were given the opportunity to record their own albums, including their well-regarded self-titled 1970 debut.

Love was diagnosed with Alzheimer's in 2002, discontinuing his role in the group. He died in 2012. Jackson continued on with former member Jack Hale, playing with Jack White and Alicia Keys, among others, through the 2000s, before dying in 2016.

I'm not afraid to say thank you. That's about what you got left. I thank all of you. I'd like to thank my mother and father for somehow knowing that that trumpet would carry me through life, and it did. I've had a wonderful time with that thing. And I ain't through with it yet.

—Wayne Jackson, acceptance speech, 2012

THE MEMPHIS HORNS
Tribute by Booker T. Jones
February 12, 2012

If you've ever heard the brilliant unison horns that play the starting phrases on records such as "Knock On Wood," "Hold On, I'm Comin'," or "In the Midnight Hour," then you've experienced the excitement that the Memphis Horns can stir when opening a song.

The enthusiasm exhibited by these extraordinary session players appears on every recording take, every rehearsal, and every live show that they have been involved with. If you call the Memphis Horns, you know what you're going to get: solid horn lines and warm, flowing harmonies to accentuate the vocals or highlight the melody.

I had the pleasure of working with founding members Wayne Jackson and Andrew Love during my days at Stax Records as a fellow session player. Nicer guys, or more hardworking and reliable people, you just couldn't find. They were true team players.

I remember working with them on the introduction to Otis Redding's version of "Try a Little Tenderness." Otis said he wanted to begin with a horn part that was reminiscent of a traditional southern ballad for this slow romantic song. What at first seemed a simple request morphed into a maze of musical possibilities. This note or that? Start in unison and develop into harmony. Build here, a decrescendo there.

As the Horns patiently entertained and played through Otis' ruminations, which he hummed to them, as well as the ideas of other musicians, including myself, I witnessed their endurance and professionalism. The process of inclusion and elimination, which in times past might have taken only a few minutes, stretched out for more than an hour, but the simple, beautiful gem that resulted was well worth it, and we started the song with this longing, emotive phrase.

Only the horns are heard during this introduction. Plainly presented and arguably one of history's most moving showpieces, they pave the way for Otis' aching vocal performance.

An essential element of the Stax family, and a unit unto themselves, they put their distinctive mark on the Memphis sound before they expanded to the wider musical community.

Aside from Otis, the Memphis Horns played on Stax records by Eddie Floyd, Wilson Pickett, Sam & Dave, and Rufus and Carla Thomas. You can also hear them on recordings by the Doobie Brothers, Al Green, Neil Diamond, Elvis Presley, the Robert Cray Band, U2, and Neil Young. They are members of the Musicians Hall of Fame.

And now the time has finally come for the recording industry to play a unison note in tribute to the men that defined what a horn section should be.

(Booker T. Jones played on countless hits as a member of Stax Records' house band, Booker T. & the MG's. The band also recorded its own gold records, won a Best Pop Instrumental Performance Grammy in 1994 for "Cruisin'," and received their own Recording Academy Lifetime Achievement Award in 2007.)

CHARLES MINGUS

LIFETIME ACHIEVEMENT AWARD, 1997

Tom Copi/Michael Ochs Archives/Getty Images

While many 20th-century jazz greats are best known for their instrumental facility—and Mingus was no doubt a highly skilled double bassist and pianist—his rank as a legend may lie more in his abilities as a composer and bandleader. Award-winning composer/historian Gunther Schuller has identified Mingus as one of the essential American composers, genre aside, and he has been called jazz's most important bassist bandleader. But none of those fair-weather accomplishments came without Mingus' own periodic storm front.

By all accounts, Charles Mingus wasn't just a formidable musical presence, but also an imposing physical one with a forceful and sometimes hot-tempered personality. During his lifetime, his intensity often resulted in confrontations with other musicians as well as audiences. At least part of his behavior may have been driven by his deep-seated dissatisfaction with the business side of music (he started several labels to release his own work as well as that of other musicians pursuing hard-to-market music) and the way he processed his reactions to racism.

With regard to the latter, he exorcised some of those emotions through music with tunes such as "Fables of Faubus" from his 1959 album *Mingus Ah Um* (Grammy Hall of Fame, 2013), a poke at segregationist Arkansas Governor Orval Faubus.

But while his personality may have played a part in Mingus' genius not being fully recognized until after his death, it didn't stand in the way of his towering musical achievements. Starting in the mid-'50s and over the next decade, Mingus released dozens of albums, many of which have taken on the status of classics, including *Mingus Dynasty* (Grammy Hall of Fame, 1999), *Oh Yeah,* and *The Black Saint and the Sinner Lady.*

In the mid-'70s, Mingus was diagnosed with amyotrophic lateral sclerosis. During his illness, Mingus served as the impetus for Joni Mitchell's 1979 album *Mingus* when he requested she write songs with him for an unrelated project. After Mingus' death in 1979, the formation of the Grammy-winning Mingus Big Band aided in a continued appreciation of the unique legacy he created.

CHARLES MINGUS

By Charlie Haden

February 26, 1997

I really loved Charles Mingus as a person and as a musician. Being a bassist, I was imme-diately struck by how he phrased the instrument like a horn instead of a bass. But it was as a bandleader and composer that I knew Mingus best: He had charisma, leadership quality, and a very strong compositional vision. He sounded like no one else—the way he voiced his chords, his arrangements, and his melodies—all of them have that Mingus identity.

I remember what a revelation it was hearing the *Jazz at Massey Hall* with Mingus, Charlie Parker, Dizzy Gillespie, Bud Powell, and Max Roach making beautiful music together. Mingus the bandleader always had a great talent for drawing together amazing players with compatible musical voices. He would integrate them into his compositions: If he wrote a drum part, it might be with Dannie Richmond in mind, while a trombone part would be perfectly suited for Jimmy Knepper. That's another reason great musicians would stay with him for years.

All of Mingus' tunes are very vital to the language of jazz. A lot of them were political too, having to do with the struggle of the African-American (which is why his "Fables of Faubus," for instance, was one of the earliest censored records).

After Mingus passed away, Sue Mingus formed the Mingus Dynasty Band, and I had the honor of playing in its earliest incarnation. We recorded the first album (*Chair in the Sky* on Elektra) with Jimmy Knepper, Joe Farrell, John Handy, and a lot of other great mu-sicians, and performed some of Mingus' most beautiful and inspired compositions, includ-ing "Peggy's Blue Skylight" and "Goodbye Pork Pie Hat."

I remember that first rehearsal most of all: It was held at Mingus' apartment, where Sue still lived. As I took my bass cover off, I could feel this presence. I turned to look be-hind me, and there was a portrait of Mingus staring right down at me. Man, was I nervous!

(Composer, musician, educator, and bandleader Charlie Haden won three Grammy Awards. He received the Lifetime Achievement Award in 2013. He died July 11, 2014.)

WILLIE MITCHELL

 ## TRUSTEES AWARD, 2008

WireImage.com

Anyone who hears Al Green's sensuous '70s soul hits—the peak of what may have been soul music's finest hour—can at least partially thank bandleader/trumpeter/producer Willie Mitchell. Mitchell was the de facto leader of Memphis' Hi Records and Green's producer and arranger. Together they created a lifetime worth of hits from 1971–1974: "Tired of Being Alone," "You Ought to Be with Me," "Look What You Done for Me," "Let's Stay Together," "I'm Still in Love with You," and "Here I Am (Come and Take Me)" among them.

Mitchell was a bandleader and solo artist in Memphis in the '60s. He scored a couple of minor hits, including "Soul Serenade" in 1968. He turned his attention to producing, and opened Royal Studios. He signed on with Hi, which was founded in the late '50s, and took the reins at the label as the '70s were dawning. With Green, as well as other Hi artists such as Syl Johnson and Ann Peebles, Mitchell created the Hi sound: a solid bass drum, steady beats, and tasteful horn and organ fills.

His effective leadership of the label and sessions in the studio earned Mitchell the nickname "Poppa Willie." (The compilation *Poppa Willie: The Hi Years, 1962–1974* collects Mitchell's own best work.) Green's Mitchell-produced tracks "Let's Stay Together" and "Take Me to the River" have been inducted into the Grammy Hall of Fame. Mitchell died in 2010, but left the legacy of an era-defining sound.

WILLIE MITCHELL
Tribute by John Mayer
February 10, 2008

The first time I ever knowingly heard Willie Mitchell was on Buddy Guy's recording of the Otis Redding classic "I've Got Dreams to Remember." I had played on the song but hadn't heard it finished until Steve Jordan (who produced both mine and Buddy's records) came back from a trip to Memphis and excitedly sat me down to hear it. Behind Buddy's pleading vocal was a small brass ensemble, kind of ghostly in a way, hovering over the track, behind the beat in some places and ahead of it in others. It's one thing to hear a classic recording, and it's another thing to witness a classic art form take place.

These days the word "authentic" is used to mean "seemingly real," as if to trick the brain into believing that it's not 2008, or 2040, and it's not in a shopping mall food court. What I heard come through the studio monitors didn't have authentic undertones, and it didn't remind me of something classic. It was, by definition, authentic, created by the real deal, Willie Mitchell.

I can't say for sure whether I happened to write a song some months later that was perfect for Willie's arranging or if I made sure that I did, but there I was, with a hole in the tune sized perfectly for a soulful yet pensive-sounding Memphis horn arrangement. It didn't take much deliberation before we realized a trip to Willie's Royal Studios was in order.

I'll never forget that day, sitting in the dimly lit Royal Studios, amongst the tape boxes and the analog equipment, some in use and others resting in the shadows, surely with a story to tell. Willie handed out the sheet music he'd written to "I'm Gonna Find Another You," which made me wonder if my silly tune was worth him sitting up at night and stacking notes in his mind and on paper for, but the question didn't last for long because when the music started playing, it wasn't my song anymore. It was my tribute to Willie Mitchell.

Most people don't get the experience of immersing themselves in an artists' repertoire the way I did Willie's that afternoon. I sang the vocals through the very microphone that Al Green sang through on cuts like "Let's Stay Together," one of a string of classic Top 10 hits Willie produced and arranged horns for. I stood in Willie's office, a small room that seemed never to have grown or shrunk relative to his success but rather served as the understated workstation for a career and a life that has spanned more than 40 years and has seen his success as a trumpet player, bandleader, arranger, producer, and record label owner, each one of his endeavors having proven to be an authentic success.

Willie Mitchell is a pillar of classic soul music, and one that I am beyond proud to say stands not only in the annals of modern American music, but on my album as well.

(John Mayer is a seven-time Grammy winner, including for Best Pop Vocal Album in 2006 for *Continuum*, which features "I'm Gonna Find Another You.")

(ORIGINAL) CARTER FAMILY

LIFETIME ACHIEVEMENT AWARD, 2005

GAB Archive/Redferns/Getty Images

A.P., Sara, and Maybelle Carter may not have invented country music, but they were arguably its first major stars and first musical soap opera.

Alvin Pleasant Carter met wife-to-be Sara Dougherty when he was a traveling fruit tree salesman. They were joined by A.P.'s brother's guitar-playing wife Maybelle. The trio found their first success after a 1927 road trip from their Maces Springs, Virginia, home to Bristol, Tennessee, to make some recordings for music executive Ralph Peer. They were paid $50 plus a half-cent for each song on which they owned the copyright. The recordings became successful. By 1930 they had sold 300,000 records and A.P., who didn't always perform on the records but who quickly realized the value of copyrights, would soon after write many of the Carter's best-known songs, as well as embark on song-finding expeditions, transcribing what he heard to Sara and Maybelle upon his return.

Many of those songs have become country standards, including "Keep on the Sunny Side" (Grammy Hall of Fame, 2006), "Can the Circle be Unbroken (Bye and Bye)" (Hall of Fame, 1998), "The Wabash Cannonball," "Wildwood Flower" (Hall of Fame, 1999), and "I'm Thinking Tonight of My Blue Eyes." The latter's melody would eventually be appropriated for a number of other groundbreaking country hits, including Roy Acuff's "Great Speckled Bird" (Hall of Fame, 2009) and Kitty Wells' "It Wasn't God Who Made Honky Tonk Angels" (Hall of Fame, 1998).

But A.P.'s travels around the Virginia area in search of songs left Sara feeling neglected, and she would find solace in A.P.'s cousin, Coy Bayes, for whom she would leave A.P. and move to California. But for a while after the breakup, the group would still perform together, until their final dissolution in 1944.

But the Carter dynasty would live on. Maybelle and her daughters, including June Carter, became a successful act, and June's marriage to Johnny Cash resulted in a line of country royalty that stretched from the original Carters through Rosanne Cash and today's Carter Family III with Maybelle's grandson by way of Johnny and June Carter Cash, Grammy winner John Carter Cash.

(ORIGINAL) CARTER FAMILY
Tribute by Gillian Welch

February 13, 2005

The Carter Family is the undisputed first family of country, and yet their impact on modern music is easily taken for granted. But remove them and the foundations of American music quickly start to crumble, for their sound is the sound of our music, and their songs are our musical heritage and identity. Their music is the recorded beginning of that great American confluence of white, black, religious, secular, old, and new—that same alchemy that would later be repeated in the forging of rock and roll.

They were a perfect trinity and all marvels in their own right. A.P. was the visionary song man and arranger, taking tunes that had been heard across the hills for years and elevating them to new forms, creating a timeless canon of American folk songs. Maybelle was the innovative guitar prodigy who created a new style born out of necessity and self-invention, setting a benchmark for the instrument that still stands. And Sara, the voice of the people, a naïve singer of startling honesty and depth, whose voice earned them the RCA Victor recording contract, and made their music a beacon for people in dark times.

When we hear them together as the Carter Family we hear time and distance (and surface noise) fall away, leaving only the essential elements—the sound of the human struggle laid bare, the spirit in adversity, shining, plain spoken, and frankly poetic—and we remember why we make music and why we need it in our lives.

(Singer/songwriter Gillian Welch won a Grammy for 2001 for her work on the *O Brother, Where Art Thou?* soundtrack.)

DOLLY PARTON

 ## LIFETIME ACHIEVEMENT AWARD, 2011

Kevin Winter/Hulton Archive/Getty Images

To say Dolly Parton may have single-handedly busted the myth of the dumb blonde probably has a seed of truth, but even that noble accomplishment doesn't tell the whole story of Dolly Rebecca Parton. Perhaps more notably, she may be the most accomplished country music star ever, having achieved wide success in film, on the stage, and on TV, as well as in her towering music career.

Parton's earliest records revealed a self-assured female singer/songwriter, putting her in the fairly rarefied company of Loretta Lynn as women writing their own material. Songs such as "Dumb Blonde," "Something Fishy," and "Just Because I'm a Woman" established a strong female perspective.

Through the '60s and into the early '70s, Parton would enjoy a string of duet hits with Porter Wagoner, on whose TV show she regularly appeared, while having moderate hits of her own, including "Coat of Many Colors," which would become a signature.

In 1974, she had her first crossover hit when "Jolene" (Grammy Hall of Fame, 2014) hit No. 60 on the *Billboard* Hot 100. The album of the same name contained her version of her song "I Will Always Love You," which would become one of the best-selling singles of all time when Whitney Houston recorded it for *The Bodyguard* soundtrack.

In 1980 she'd star in *Nine to Five* and become an instant film star. The movie was, fittingly, a nod to female empowerment. The title song would result in two of her seven Grammys. After that, Parton would truly become her own cottage industry, even creating her own amusement park, Dollywood. Her impact on female singers has been impressive, her impact on the wider culture nearly incalculable.

DOLLY PARTON
Tribute by Miranda Lambert
February 13, 2011

When it comes to the headline of this tribute, it could have been just one word . . . Dolly.

Dolly Parton is an icon among icons. She defines the word "entertainer." Yet somehow she never let go of her East Tennessee roots and infectious humor, which makes her the lady we all adore.

With a career spanning more than five decades, Dolly has proven that there is nothing she can't do. She's a singer, songwriter, author, actress, philanthropist, and straight-ahead businesswoman.

Dolly has proven herself well beyond the boundaries of country music, but she has carried the banner for country music no matter where her career has taken her. From her days getting started on *The Porter Wagoner Show* to topping the country music charts to her critically acclaimed bluegrass albums and winning every award in between, Dolly has become timeless.

And then there is her gift for songwriting, which is just that: a gift. Being a songwriter myself, one of the qualities I love most about Dolly is her ability to craft a song in such a way that you feel every note she's singing. With hits such as "Jolene," "Coat of Many Colors," and "I Will Always Love You," which has been a hit in three different decades, including a best-selling single for Whitney Houston, you could say that songwriting loves Dolly.

And you know, Dolly couldn't stop at just singing and songwriting; she had to find other ways to entertain us, so she tried her hand at acting. In true Dolly fashion, she won our hearts with her wit and humor in movies such as *Nine to Five* and *Steel Magnolias*, among many others.

Even with her incomparable awards and accolades over the years (she's won seven Grammys and earned an impressive 45 nominations to date, among other awards she's received), Dolly has stayed true to herself and who she is. She has endeared us with stories from her childhood and proven to all of us who look up to her that anything is possible, no matter where you are from, and that dreams really do come true.

There is no one more deserving of The Recording Academy Lifetime Achievement Award than Dolly Parton.

(Miranda Lambert has garnered two Grammy Awards, including Best Country Album for 2014's *Platinum*.)

TOM PAXTON

LIFETIME ACHIEVEMENT AWARD, 2009

Independent News and Media/Hulton Archive/Getty Images

Part of the Greenwich Village folk scene of the late '50s and early '60s, Tom Paxton was among the first to expand from covers of traditional folks songs to his own original material. According to fellow Village folkie Dave Van Ronk in his memoir *The Mayor of MacDougal Street*, "[Bob] Dylan is usually cited as the founder of the new song movement, and he certainly became its most visible standard-bearer, but the person who started the whole thing was Tom Paxton . . . he found that his own stuff was getting more attention than when he was singing traditional songs . . . Dylan had not yet showed up when this was happening."

Paxton's best-known songs—which ranged from romantic ballads to political satire—got early important cover recordings that made them part of the cultural dialogue of the times. The venerable Pete Seeger cut the satiric patriotism of Paxton's "What Did You Learn in School Today":

What did you learn in school today
Dear little boy of mine?
I learned that war is not so bad
I learned about the great ones we have had
We fought in Germany and in France
And someday I might get my chance

His oft-recorded "Whose Garden Is This" was an early environmental song. And his ballad "The Last Thing on My Mind" was among Dolly Parton's first country hits in a duet with Porter Wagoner in 1968.

Other songs that became standards included "Bottle of Wine" and "Ramblin' Boy," and his songs enjoyed hundreds of covers by the Carter Family and the Kingston Trio to Stephen Stills and Norah Jones. His own recording career has been long and consistent, if not overwhelming in sales, but both his serious and farcical observations of the world remain as rich today as when they were first written.

I'm supposed to be able to express myself but I'm tongue-tied. Maybe it's by the stature of my fellow honorees. I feel like the fellow who ran with H. Ross Perot and said in the vice presidential debate, "Who am I? What am I doing here?"
　　　　　—Tom Paxton (read by Kate Paxton, daughter), acceptance speech, 2009

TOM PAXTON
Tribute by Jac Holzman
February 8, 2009

Tom Paxton has accomplished what few singer/songwriters can claim. He has become his own tributary of oral tradition, creating a body of songs that delight, amuse, and breathe joy into his worldwide community of listeners.

I doubt that Tom ever planned it long-term because he has always been a singer/songwriter matched to the moment. He has crafted some of the most exquisite love songs, children's songs, talking blues, road songs, and salutes to those who have inspired him. Tom does this with wit, deceptive ease, and with a consistency of style and a congruence of purpose we recognize in the work and life trajectories of Woody Guthrie and Pete Seeger.

I first heard Tom sing in 1962 at the Gaslight, a basement coffeehouse in Greenwich Village. Next, in my little home office/studio where I agreed to record a full-on session with him, mostly to see if his songs held up in the non-visual, recording realm, without the sway of his persuasive personality. It must have gone well because we made six classic albums together.

Tom sang of love and the human condition and wrote fierce protest songs. Protest (or "topical" songs) were revived during the Vietnam War and became anthems for disaffected young people who saw the political deception but had yet to achieve the right to vote.

Together with Phil Ochs and Pete Seeger, Tom confronted the war using his own best weapons: intellect, irony, the well-wrought phrase . . . and the truth. His lyrics, absent the melodies, were corrosive without being venal. When matched to a lilting tune, these lyrics became even more devastating. "Lyndon Johnson Told the Nation" became so widely known that others added new lyrics and the "enhanced" song then migrated into the classic oral folk tradition, being passed on from one person to another.

Ironically, Vietnam became the potent catalyst to the adoption of the 26th Amendment to our Constitution in 1971, lowering the voting age to 18 and giving the ballot to the next generation.

Several years ago I caught Tom at Santa Monica, California's wonderful folk den McCabe's. We were now a bit grayer and carrying a few extra pounds but as we surrendered to Tom and his music he connected us with our vital, youthful selves, placing his songs in a context of emotion and shared experience that had shaped our young lives.

(Jac Holzman is the founder of Elektra Records and recipient of a 2008 Trustees Award from The Recording Academy.)

RICHARD PERRY

TRUSTEES AWARD, 2015

When the activities in the later stages of your career include dating Jane Fonda, you know you've had a pretty good career. But as a producer and industry executive, Perry's career has been much more than pretty good. In fact, in the '70s, Perry was the producing world's gold standard—or maybe more fittingly, platinum standard.

Perry's early associations included working at Jerry Leiber and Mike Stoller's Red Bird Records. Leiber and Stoller had written and produced some of the biggest hits for artists such as Elvis Presley, the Drifters, the Coasters, and others, and served as mentors to producers including Perry and Phil Spector.

Early in his production career, Perry's credits included making an acclaimed record with early rock great Fats Domino (*Fats is Back*), as well as working with pop weirdo Captain Beefheart (*Safe As Milk*) and cutting his first hit album, *God Bless Tiny Tim*, with the eccentric and falsetto-voiced one-time TV talk show regular.

But in the '70s he got on a roll that put him in the sphere of the most elite pop producers of all time. Harry Nilsson, Leo Sayer, Art Garfunkel, Diana Ross, Barbra Streisand's mainstream pop breakthrough *Stoney End*, virtually all of Carly Simon's hits, and even after all that, former Beatle Ringo Starr's most impressive and lasting album, *Ringo*.

In the '80s, he'd have huge hits with the Pointer Sisters, which came on his own Planet Records, where he also embraced the decade's new wave genre with acts such as the Cretones and the Plimsouls.

Perry would later help guide Rod Stewart's more recent traditional pop albums—oh, and date Jane Fonda. His most essential work remains among the most esteemed of its era.

RICHARD PERRY
Tribute by Carly Simon
February 8, 2015

Just 400 words? Which ones? Richard Perry is worth hundreds of thousands.

I first met him in New York at my apartment on 35th Street.

"You're really a rock and roll singer, you know. I want to show everybody."

I was not convinced but I loved his enthusiasm. "My voice just doesn't do that. When I try, I last only two songs at most."

"Let's just ignore that now, shall we?" he said. "Show me anything new you've been working on."

Reluctantly, I played him "Bless You Ben," a song about a man who had rescued me while I was hiding up in some loft. The song made little sense lyrically. When I went into the chorus, playing on my aunt's upright "tonk" piano, I went into a low register in my voice in the key of C.

"You're so vain, you probably think this song is about you."

I finished the chorus and then stopped: "That's really all I have for now, and the verse and the chorus have nothing to do with each other," I explained.

"It's a hit" said the tall, dashing, luscious, and fascinating, tense, and daring madman who made statements like "it's a hit" just to encourage me into believing that I was a rock and roll singer. Was this a joke? I didn't know him yet.

Weeks passed and I wrote an entirely different verse, but kept the chorus. We went to London and set up at Trident Studios. Richard kept me at work on this song for weeks. There were, of course, songs in between, but he kept going back to "Ballad of a Vain Man."

Richard toyed with the tempo, the percussion, my vocal performance, background parts, and the drum fills. We made a bet. I relented and vouched: "OK, if this is a 'hit,' I'll fly you (and I hate, and hated then, to fly) first class with me to Hawaii!"

I don't know how many artists Richard Perry has sat with during writing or recording sessions and made those positive predictions, but it's probably an inordinate number. Richard has brought it out of so many singers. First in 1968 with Tiny Tim's debut album *God Bless Tiny Tim* and Fats Domino's *Fats is Back*. About the latter, *Rolling Stone*'s Jann Wenner said something that I think is true of Richard Perry all through his years of making records: "The past and present have been precisely, masterfully, and tastefully combined . . . ."

He brought a new light to Barbra Streisand on *Stoney End* as well as *Barbra Joan Streisand*. In 1976 Leo Sayer's "When I Need You" and "You Make Me Feel Like Dancing" played endlessly on the radio without ever getting cloying, and Artie Garfunkel, whose 1975 hit "I Only Have Eyes for You," from his brilliantly novel *Breakaway*, arrived at No. 1 on the Adult Contemporary chart. (I wonder if Artie promised Richard a trip to Hawaii?) And Harry Nilsson's breathtaking "Without You," "Coconut," and "Jump into the Fire" were all Top 40 hits. (Surely they went vacationing.) We also heard a whole new side of Rod Stewart on his *American Songbook* albums.

And that is only the beginning. I recommend adding to your collection, if they are not already there, all the albums Richard made for his own label, Planet Records. Primarily the ones that come to mind first are *Break Out* or any of the Pointer Sisters' other amazingly hot albums that were riddled with hits. (I think I like "Slow Hand" best, but maybe it's "Fire," or "I'm So Excited.")

All that and a Beatle too. Richard's work on 1973's *Ringo* led to the No. 1 singles "Photograph" and "You're Sixteen."

I never fulfilled my promise to take you to Hawaii, but thank you, Richard, for so many of my own albums, singles, specials, and movie songs (including my James Bond theme); long conversations into the night sharing stories, laughter, advice; and the enormous appreciation we have for each other. You know you are adored.

(Carly Simon is a two-time Grammy winner, including Best New Artist for 1971. Many of her biggest hits, including "You're So Vain," were produced by Richard Perry.)

ANDRÉ PREVIN

LIFETIME ACHIEVEMENT AWARD, 2010

Composer/conductor André Previn is among the very few artists to make important contributions to the pop, jazz, and serious classical music canons. That's impressive on its own, but maybe even more so for someone who really saw himself as a conductor first.

He learned film music and jazz very early, playing piano in jazz clubs and accompanying films in movie theaters before he was of the age to drive. Though his family fled Nazi Germany, he did have one leg up when they landed in Los Angeles. Previn's uncle was the head of music at Universal Studios, and André was hired to arrange and orchestrate film music at age 14.

All of this wasn't just great preparation for his career to come, it was proof that Previn's precocious talent made him a prodigy of sorts. When he composed his first film score at age 18 (*The Sun Comes Up*), he found himself on a podium conducting the score and realized he had found his true love, though serious conducting positions would have to wait. Meanwhile, he recorded accomplished jazz albums and film scores that by 1964 would earn him four Oscars for scoring films such as *Gigi* and *My Fair Lady*.

Despite the success, Previn wanted to pursue serious conducting roles. His first came with the St. Louis Symphony, and ultimately he'd spend more than a decade as the principal conductor of the London Symphony Orchestra in addition to other appointments.

Still, he was a noted member of the West Coast jazz scene, and in 1968 when Dionne Warwick recorded his "(Theme from) *Valley of the Dolls*" (written with his then-wife Dory Previn), he had a No. 2 *Billboard* Hot 100 hit on his hands.

He's remained active into the 2010s, a musical elder statesman and living testimony to the wisdom of pursuing one's dreams.

ANDRÉ PREVIN
Tribute by Anne-Sophie Mutter
January 31, 2010

The Lifetime Achievement Award for André Previn is overdue. In fact, one would have to give him several because of the immense diversity of his talents.

This formidable creator lived the life of a pianist and jazz musician from the early age of 16 when he started to perform with such legends as Ella Fitzgerald and Ray Brown. His four Oscars from his intermezzo in Hollywood are a recognition of the fact that first-rate music has often saved movies. Soon after in the '70s he became the longest-standing principal conductor of the London Symphony Orchestra. Positions with such illustrious orchestras as the Royal Philharmonic, Pittsburgh, Houston, and Oslo followed.

We met in the mid-'80s and since then there has been nobody in my life I have admired more for his many genius facets in music.

I will always remember the morning when, after my longtime collaborator Lambert Orkis and I had frustratedly given up on it, André walked onstage, put on his reading glasses and played for us, with amazing ease, his "Tango Song and Dance." There it was. That innate ease with even the most complex and difficult rhythms, and what a wonderful touch!

Above all, André's music incorporates the best of the old and the new worlds. Although the music was written with refined knowledge and always relentlessly difficult, he has never shied away from profound beauty and the many sound colors expressing even the most intimate emotions.

"Tango Song and Dance" was the first of many wonderful pieces he has since written for me. Lately a second sonata for violin and piano followed, as well as a second violin concerto and a gorgeous nonet. But let's not forget that he is also the composer of such outstanding works as "Honey and Rue," "Diversions," "Owls," his opera "A Streetcar Named Desire" (probably the most played contemporary opera on this planet), followed this year by the premiere in Houston of his very moving second opera, "Brief Encounter."

I cannot hide the fact that his works for violin hold a very special place in my heart. The greatest present a man ever gave to me is his violin concerto "Anne-Sophie," in which the third movement has variations on my favorite German children's song. That our recording received a Grammy makes this piece even more special.

I am glad to have found a small niche next to André. The only things he is not great at are playing the fiddle and cooking!

Thank you, very dear André. You have given yourself so intensely to music.

(Celebrated violinist Anne-Sophie Mutter won one of her four Grammy Awards for 2004 in the Best Instrumental Soloist(s) Performance (with Orchestra) category for *Previn: Violin Concerto "Anne-Sophie"/Bernstein: Serenade*.)

RICHARD PRYOR

LIFETIME ACHIEVEMENT AWARD, 2006

The stature of comedian Richard Pryor's legacy as an important social critic isn't even funny, though Pryor certainly was. The five-time Grammy winner was a fearless voice for oppressed African-Americans, a controversial funnyman who nevertheless won over both black and white audiences, and fellow comedians as well. Jerry Seinfeld called him "the Picasso of our profession" and Denis Leary said Pryor "was probably the best, most gifted stand-up comedian who will ever live."

Though he started out in New York in the early '60s as a funny but fairly conventional comic, he had an epiphany at a Las Vegas casino performance in 1967, asking rhetorically "What the fuck am I doing here?" and walking off the stage. When he returned to performing, it was as an uncompromising social satirist who used vulgarity and racial epithets as a tool to open eyes and minds. Grammy-winning albums such as 1974's *That Nigger's Crazy* and 1976's *Bicentennial Nigger*, on which he jabs at whites' perceptions of the black experience, as well as the black experience itself, were indicative of the voice Pryor found and used to shock America with laughter. The echoes of those performances can be heard in the comedy of Eddie Murphy, Chris Rock, Bernie Mac, and others who followed in his wake.

Pryor also had success in TV and film, writing for *Sanford and Son*, appearing in films such as *Lady Sings the Blues*, *Silver Streak*, and *Car Wash*, and cowriting Mel Brooks' *Blazing Saddles*.

Pryor dealt with several misfortunes in life, including serious burns, which were reported as drug related, and a 1986 multiple sclerosis diagnosis. He died in 2005, but clearly the taboos he broke gave new freedom to subsequent comedians.

RICHARD PRYOR
Tribute by Whoopi Goldberg
February 8, 2006

The first time I met Richard Pryor, I was tongue-tied for hours. I literally would turn to say something, and it would just come out "grchxvgrrhjr." When I was finally able to speak, I said, "I want to be like you." He said, "You need to be like you." That's all I needed to hear; it was validation.

Richard was an original and that doesn't come along that often. He didn't raise or lower the bar—he expanded it. His performances, from albums like *Craps (After Hours)*, were all so free and they talked about things that were present in life, like Big Bertha; they weren't abstract. You know, like the size of someone's behind and how it moved when they walked down the street. The idea that you could talk about your experiences in life and make it interesting was mesmerizing for me. Richard was a great storyteller and he was funny. Not jokey funny, but *funny* funny. With Richard, it was like " . . . and the ground shook and she turned around really fast and took out eight people with her left cheek . . . ." It was just wonderful. And when his mind expanded into politics, when he started talking about what was going on in the world, he made you laugh and think and then laugh again.

What made him great was the fact that he was fearless. He really just said what he thought, about white people, about black people, about politics. That's wonderful freedom in your art, freedom from caring whether someone else thinks it's good or relevant. Richard shaped what I do, and he continues to shape what I do, how I do it, and why I do it.

(Oscar-winning actress/comedian Whoopi Goldberg, a previous host of the Grammy Awards, won a Best Comedy Recording Grammy for 1985.)

TITO PUENTE

LIFETIME ACHIEVEMENT AWARD, 2003

Santana took Tito Puente's "Oye Como Va" to the Top 20 in 1971, the band's second major hit, following "Evil Ways." With those two songs, Carlos Santana and his band virtually created Latin rock, and proved the universal appeal of Puente, the King of Latin Music.

It's no surprise that Puente factored into Latin music's crossover to rock. A New York–based bandleader since the '50s, Puente was raised in Spanish Harlem and was at the epicenter of the explosion of Latin jazz, mambo, and salsa in America. His approach was both studied (he trained at Juilliard) and hands-on (he was in the band of Machito, whose merging of musical styles would lead to Latin jazz and salsa). Puente was the bridge over which acts such as Santana and later Los Lobos would travel.

Puente may also have succeeded because of his warm and effervescent stage presence and persona. Google images of Puente, and hardly a photo comes up on which he's not wearing his broad smile. That infectious energy carried over to his stage performances, especially at New York's Palladium, where Puente helped grow America's fascination with the mambo and cha-cha dance crazes.

As he had apprenticed with Machito, Puente and his bands helped grow the careers of other important figures in Latin jazz, including Mongo Santamaria, Willie Bobo, and Johnny Pacheco.

Puente won six Grammy Awards, his last—for *Masterpiece/Obra Maestra*, a teaming with pianist Eddie Palmieri—coming nine months after his death in 2000.

> *For those who knew my father, or were his friend, he was a fun guy to be with. But those who worked with him appreciated the genius that he was as a musician. For those who never met my father, I feel bad for you in a way. [laughter from the audience] Because he was truly an icon—he was big, a very friendly man, yet very humble.*
>
> —Ronnie Puente, son, acceptance speech, 2003

TITO PUENTE
Tribute by Sheila E.
February 23, 2003

My first recollection of Ernesto Anthony "Tito" Puente Jr. was in 1963, at the age of six at our home on 13th Avenue in East Oakland, California. My dad, Pete Escovedo, was one of Tito's best friends, and I would soon know him affectionately as Grandpa.

Tito was born April 20, 1923, at Harlem Hospital in New York City to Ernesto Sr. from Guanadillas, and Ercilia Ortiz from Coamo, Puerto Rico. As a toddler he would use forks and spoons to create rhythms on the furniture and window sills of his home, revealing his early love of music. At age seven he began taking piano lessons for 25 cents a session. By the age of 10, inspired by his hero Gene Krupa, he realized his true love and began playing drums (this was his first percussion instrument, not the timbales as most expect). At age 16, Tito played his first paying gig with the Noro Morales Orchestra. Before the draft of WWII, he played with the great Machito and his orchestra. In 1945, after serving in the Navy, Tito attended the Juilliard School of Music, studying conducting, orchestration, and theory. In 1950 he recorded his first album, *Tito Puente and Friends*, on Tropical Records.

Grandpa Tito was a frequent visitor at our family's home. He would come for dinner whenever his orchestra performed on the West Coast. I immediately fell for Grandpa Tito. He was as charming as royalty and his smile would light the darkest day. My parents realized my love for Grandpa Tito and allowed me to tag along to the Sands Ballroom in Oakland where they shared my elation with what I was hearing. It was a day I'll never forget.

One of my first and favorite albums I ever heard was *Puente in Percussion*, recorded in 1956 on Tico Records. Imagine this little six-year-old experiencing the sounds of Grandpa Tito, Willie Bobo, Mongo Santamaria, and Carlos "Patato" Valdez in the heart of her living room. I was amazed by the Latin percussive sounds and rhythms that came from my parents' record player. Little did I know then that these sounds and experiences would influence the musical course of my life and so strongly impact the musical culture.

During the '50s, Tito helped establish a new style of music and dance craze called the mambo. He became known as El Rey, "The King," and held court at the Palladium in New York. During this era, Tito played a major role in the cross-fertilization of jazz and Latin music, which became known as Cubop.

In 1971 at the historic Jack Tarr Hotel in San Francisco, Grandpa Tito invited me, at the tender age of 14, to sit in with him and his orchestra. Every percussion player in the Bay Area attended this concert as the King and I made beautiful music together. Though nothing could top this, in 1989, my dad, brother Juan, and I shot our video "La Familia" featuring Tito Puente, which was an amazing and exhilarating experience.

Tito recorded over 118 albums, won six Grammy and two Latin Grammy Awards, and has always delighted audiences young and old. What his life and gift brought to this world can never be duplicated—his smile moved millions and his rhythms changed the course of music. His family continues to honor Tito, as his wife Margie and daughter Audrey are dedicated to keeping his memory alive, while his son, Tito Jr., keeps the Puente musical flame burning.

The joy we experienced together as a family with Tito will live in our hearts forever, and I am honored to have known this great man, musician, and family friend.

(Sheila E. is a performer, producer, composer, and business executive, president of Heaven Productions Music, and cofounder and chair of the Lil' Angel Bunny Foundation for abused and abandoned children.)

PHIL RAMONE

TECHNICAL GRAMMY AWARD, 2005

WireImage.com

To those who casually follow the professional lives of record producers, Phil Ramone is probably best known as the man behind the glass for many of Paul Simon and Billy Joel's most memorable works. As a producer, he would go on to collaborate with some of pop's most towering talent, including Barbra Streisand and Frank Sinatra.

Nevertheless, his producer credits tell just part of the story. Ramone was a child-prodigy violinist who attended Juilliard while still in high school. Despite his musical talent, he found greater joy in the studio. In the late '50s, Ramone founded A&R Recording studios with business partner Jack Arnold. He would soon become a top-notch engineer, winning the Best Engineered Recording Grammy for 1964 for the Album of the Year–winning bossa nova classic *Getz/Gilberto*. Working out of A&R, Ramone would become the go-to engineer for producers such as Burt Bacharach, and in the early-to-mid-'70s for artists including James Taylor and Bob Dylan.

When he transitioned to producing, there was no looking back. He produced no less than three Album of the Year winners: Simon's *Still Crazy After All These Years* (1975), Joel's *52nd Street* (1979), and Ray Charles' *Genius Loves Company* (2004). In all, he won 14 Grammys.

But that still doesn't tell the whole story. Ramone was always an innovator. *52nd Street* was the first commercially released CD. He introduced optical surround sound for films. And he pioneered recording over fiber optics from different locations for Sinatra's *Duets* album. Ultimately, he would serve as a consultant to Lucent Technologies as they worked to innovate digital downloads, and launched a record label, N2K Encoded Music, in the early Internet days with the goal of marketing artists through an online retail experience. All of which also resulted in a Trustees Award in 2001 and a Technical Grammy Award in 2005.

PHIL RAMONE
Tribute by Paul Simon
February 13, 2005

Phil Ramone has been my friend for 30 years now, yet it's still hard to distill in a few paragraphs what he has meant to me as an artist. As you undoubtedly know, Phil's career has spanned five decades and he's worked with many of the legends, from Sinatra to Pavarotti, Streisand to Ray Charles.

Let me tell you what it was like working with Phil Ramone. As a producer he created an atmosphere that was both relaxed and exciting. He has the natural ear of a musician and the technical skill of a great engineer. He introduced me to unknowns who went on to become legends in their own right: drummer Steve Gadd and keyboardist Richard Tee, among others. He could call established superstars like Quincy Jones to add their gifts to the projects we were working on.

He was always upbeat and encouraging; still he wasn't afraid to speak up when things started to go south. I never heard him make a snide comment, express envy or resentment. His studios always had an aura of warmth and solitude, as if the outside world didn't exist during the hours of those sessions. How can you not want to be friends with a guy like that? Easy to hang with, funny, with an encyclopedic knowledge of musicians and genres. I count it as one of the blessings of my life to have known Phil Ramone. Congratulations on your Technical Grammy! You deserve it and every award they've got as well. Love to you, Phil.

(Paul Simon has won 16 Grammy Awards combined, as a solo artist and part of the duo Simon & Garfunkel, who earned their own Lifetime Achievement Award in 2003. Phil Ramone produced Simon's Album of the Year winner *Still Crazy After All These Years*.)

RAMONES

 ## LIFETIME ACHIEVEMENT AWARD, 2011

Michael Ochs Archives/Getty Images

If the development of rock and roll could be simplistically broken down into three waves—the first coming when Elvis and his friends at Sun Studios melded R&B and country music into early rock and the second when the Beatles refracted their vision of those early roots through an Anglo prism—the Ramones were arguably the flash point of the third wave. The Queens, New York–bred rock misfits took 20-plus years of the growing sophistication—and some might say indulgence—of rock and brought it back to its primitive roots.

In virtually everything they did they thumbed their noses at the prevailing conventions of rock. Glam rock created alien characters in otherworldy costumes; the Ramones dressed in torn jeans and leather jackets. Prog rock brought the intricacies of classical and jazz music to extended, thematic songs; the Ramones played three-chord, two-minute music blitzes. Singer/songwriters wrote sensitive, thoughtful songs of deep meaning; the Ramones were deliberately stoopid.

They were one of the earliest bands playing regularly at New York's CBGB, the New York punk mecca that would serve as the nexus of the growing punk movement.

The Ramones released a string of albums that proudly showed almost no evolution musically or conceptually. *Ramones* (1976; Grammy Hall of Fame, 2007), *Leave Home* (1977), *Rocket to Russia* (1977), and *Road to Ruin* (1978) made mostly small dents on the pop charts, but in both America and the U.K., they were having an explosive impact. U.K. acts such as the Sex Pistols and the Clash were soaking up the Ramones' aesthetic, while in the U.S. the band would serve as the inspiration for an attitude-over-chops approach to music.

In sadly quick succession, Joey Ramone (Jeffrey Hyman) died in 2001, Dee Dee Ramone (Douglas Colvin) in 2002, and Johnny Ramone (John Cummings) in 2004. Tommy Ramone (Tom Erdelyi) died in 2014, but the D.I.Y power of the Ramones lives on.

Joey [Ramone] always used to say to me, after we'd recorded every album he'd come and say, "Hey Richie, this is going to be the one, this is going to be the one." I can't help thinking that he's watching this right now with a little smile on his face behind his rose-colored glasses. You know Joey, "Yeah, this is the one, man, this is the one." So congratulations. We miss you. Peace.

—Richie Ramone, acceptance speech, 2011

RAMONES
Tribute by Seymour Stein
February 13, 2011

Being head of Sire Records, which turns 45 in 2011, I was responsible for all artists, and as hard as it was not to show favoritism, for the most part I succeeded. It was hardest with the Ramones, partly because soon after I signed them their manager Danny Fields asked my wife Linda to be his partner. It was harder still because I admired the band's total dedication to their music, despite the fact that selling millions of records eluded them throughout their career.

With Linda as their comanager, the Ramones knew my every move. One Sunday within 10 minutes of returning after a 10-day trip to London, I received a call from Johnny. "Seymour, we got some great songs, ya know, we want you to hear 'em, ya know."

I said, "Great, just got home. Come in anytime you want on Tuesday."

"No, we want you to hear 'em live, ya know, and we know you're not doing anything Wednesday night, ya know, so we booked ourselves into CBGB."

That evening proved monumental. The opening act was supposed to be the Shirts. I had seen them many times before and was standing outside the club with Lenny Kaye.

The opening act goes on and I hear a screeching voice: "When my love, stands next to your love . . ." and all of a sudden as I'm sucked into CBGB, I say, "That's not the Shirts." Lenny says, "No, they got another gig, that's the Talking Heads."

Armed with the Ramones and Talking Heads, amid the buzz building around the Bowery and CBGB, Sire finally got the distribution deal I always wanted with Warner Bros. Records, where we have been for the past 35 years.

Thank you Johnny. Oh yes, and thank you Joey, thank you Tommy, and thank you Dee Dee.

Over the years I can't tell you how many artists were lured to Sire by the Ramones, and yes, also Talking Heads.

The Ramones made it seem easy and as such were an inspiration to bands as varied as U2, the Red Hot Chili Peppers, Green Day, Pearl Jam, the Offspring, Motörhead, Metallica, the Undertones, the Strokes, Bad Religion, Black Flag, Dead Kennedys, Sonic Youth, Bad Brains, and many others.

I remember when we first brought the Ramones to London back in 1976. Members of the Clash and Sex Pistols, both only semiprofessional at the time, attended the second show and it was said both bands turned pro right after that.

According to Danny Fields, Johnny Ramone asked the Clash's bass player Paul Simonon, "Are you in a band?" Paul said, "Well, we just rehearse. We call ourselves the Clash, but we are not good enough." Johnny said, "Wait 'til you see us. We stink, we're lousy, we can't play. Just get out there and do it."

Joey Ramone had the biggest heart ever and was always trying to help new acts. Last time we spoke, two weeks before he died, Joey called to tell me he had just sent a new band's CD.

Bono once said at a Madison Square Garden gig, "We love New York City. . . New York City has given us a lot of things, but the best thing it ever gave us was a punk rock group called the Ramones, without whom a lot of people would never have gotten started; certainly us!"

Eddie Vedder might have set a Rock and Roll Hall of Fame record by speaking for more than 20 minutes when he inducted the Ramones back in 2002. "The Ramones didn't need Mohawks to be punk. They're visually aggressive. They were four working-class, construction-worker delinquents from Forest Hills, Queens, who were armed with two-minute songs that they rattled off like machine-gun fire. And it was enough to change the Earth's revolution."

I've been to Beijing twice this past year to check out China's emerging punk music scene. There is a club called D-22, reminiscent of CBGB, and aspiring young bands like Carsick Cars, P. K. 14, and Rustic are carrying on the tradition, further proof the Ramones' music is truly global and will endure forever.

(As founder of Sire Records, Seymour Stein signed to the label the Ramones, Talking Heads, the Pretenders, and Madonna, all of whom have been inducted into the Rock and Roll Hall of Fame, as well as Depeche Mode, Echo and the Bunnymen, Ice-T, the Replacements, the Smiths, k.d. lang, Erasure, the Cult, the Cure, Seal, the Undertones, and Barenaked Ladies, among many others. He was inducted into the Rock and Roll Hall of Fame in 2005.)

LINDA RONSTADT

LIFETIME ACHIEVEMENT AWARD, 2016

Ron Galella, Ltd/WireImage/Getty Images

Linda Ronstadt remains closely, and rightfully, associated with the Southern California rock scene of the early '70s. And it isn't just because her own remarkable career sprang from that dust-and-glitter landscape. Her early backing band would eventually become the Eagles, and in the mid-'70s she was even the state's unofficial first lady when she was dating California Gov. Jerry Brown.

But this characterization sells the singer far short. Yes, she was at the nexus of the fertile Laurel Canyon/Troubadour scene, performing or associating with virtually every artist of consequence in L.A., from Neil Young and Frank Zappa to the Eagles and early boyfriends such as songwriter J.D. Souther. And when she connected with producer/manager Peter Asher, she became what many considered the top female singer in rock through the '70s.

But to end the story there would be to dismiss the inquisitive and wide-ranging second half of her career. She cut the classic country harmony album, *Trio*, with country star Dolly Parton and folk queen Emmylou Harris. She was among the very first rock-era artists to record albums of standards, starting with 1983's *What's New*, arranged and conducted by the great Nelson Riddle. And she made a series of Spanish-language albums inspired by the music of her Arizona childhood. And in between these projects, she proved she could still create some of the best pop, especially in duets with Aaron Neville such as "Don't Know Much."

Ronstadt's 10 Grammys include wins in the country, pop, and Latin fields.

Ronstadt was diagnosed with Parkinson's disease in 2013, which has prevented her from singing, but thanks to an adventurous career, one in which she was willing to deviate from pop albums at her commercial height, we have a lasting record of the breadth of her talent.

Thank you for helping me to explore different kinds of music even when you thought it unwise and making it all work somehow.

—Linda Ronstadt, acceptance speech, 2016

LINDA RONSTADT
Tribute by Aaron Neville
February 15, 2016

Linda Ronstadt is one of the premier singers of any time, and also a beautiful person. I'm so glad to have her music to listen to. It soothes me on long flights. From her songs with the Stone Poneys and her songs with Nelson Riddle to her mariachi music and *Cry Like a Rainstorm—Howl Like the Wind*, you can feel every emotion.

I'm thankful that we are on the planet at the same time and it was an honor and a privilege to record with her. She's a strong singer who could belt it out, and then come down to the sweetest most intricate part of her voice. It's like her voice is a painting meant to be here forever, and she made it so easy to sing with her. She told me that our voices were married.

The first song we actually sang together was "Ave Maria" in harmony. The Neville Brothers were playing at Pete Fountain's club during the World's Fair in 1984 in New Orleans. After her show with Riddle, Linda came to see us. Someone told us that she was in the audience and I dedicated a song to her and called her up to sing some doo-wop. She told the press that it was the highlight of her tour. She felt like Cinderella at the ball because we were her favorite band.

When I asked her to come back to New Orleans to join myself and Allen Toussaint for our annual concert to raise money for New Orleans Artists Against Hunger and Homelessness, a nonprofit I founded with Toussaint in 1985, she quickly agreed. We have so much respect for each other's voices.

She and Peter Asher said that we should record together, and now our songs are a part of history. I can remember being at the studio to record with Linda and I couldn't wait. I had fallen in love with the songs that we were going to record; I was ecstatic. It was five years from the night I called her onstage to sing with us in New Orleans. George Massenburg was the engineer and Asher and Steve Tyrell coproduced. Linda and I sang "Don't Know Much" and when we finished I said to her, "Meet you at the Grammys." I was joking, and yet not joking because it was that great of a song, and also a great performance. So, like I said, the rest is history.

I don't know much, but I know that Linda deserves to be honored with The Recording Academy's Lifetime Achievement Award.

(A cofounder of the Grammy-winning band the Neville Brothers, Aaron Neville has garnered four Grammys, including two with Linda Ronstadt for Best Pop Performance by a Duo or Group with Vocal for "Don't Know Much" (1989) and "All My Life" (1990). Neville's 1966 solo hit "Tell It Like It Is" was inducted into the Grammy Hall of Fame in 2015.)

RUN DMC

LIFETIME ACHIEVEMENT AWARD, 2016

As the first truly hard-edged rap group, Run DMC helped change the sound of rap as it headed into its '80s prime, adding some menace through aggressive, spare beats, as well as blasts of electric rock guitar. The sound made the group a beacon for gangsta rappers to come and earned them the distinction of being the first rap act to receive a Recording Academy Lifetime Achievement Award.

The group received a Best R&B Performance by a Duo or Group with Vocal Grammy nomination for 1986 for arguably their best album, *Raising Hell*. Despite not winning (the award was taken by Prince & the Revolution's equally groundbreaking "Kiss"), the nomination was another distinction: the first Grammy nomination for a rap recording.

Run DMC came onto the scene with a pedigree (or at least a pedigree-to-be). Group member Joseph "Run" Simmons was the brother of up and coming hip-hop mogul Russell Simmons, and with *Raising Hell* the group began an association with producer Rick Rubin, who was key in infusing the rap with rock, as he would do with the Beastie Boys. *Raising Hell* is credited with launching an explosion in the mainstream viability of rap, and the reported $1.6 million sponsorship deal the group got from shoemaker Adidas based on the track "My Adidas" showed corporate America sensed the coming revolution.

Run DMC raised hell and left an imprint on the American psyche the devil would kill for.

They were young boys and Jason [Jam Master Jay] lived with me. And I always believed that if my children is home, I know where they are. But if he'd been somewhere else doing his music I wouldn't have known what he was doing or where he was, so my home was open to them and all the noise, and the music was loud. For my ears it was loud.
—Connie Mizell, Jam Master Jay's mother, acceptance speech, 2016

RUN DMC
Tribute by Ice Cube
February 15, 2016

I became a rap music fan in 1979 when the Sugarhill Gang released "Rapper's Delight." I was also a fan of groups like Grandmaster Flash & the Furious Five and Afrika Bambaataa & Soulsonic Force. Although those groups did great records, I could not relate to them as much as I could relate to three guys out of Queens, N.Y., who looked like the older homies from around my block. Black hats, black leather jackets, and that confident attitude.

The first time I heard "It's Like That," I almost had a seizure it was so good, and on the B-side it was "Sucker M.C.'s." My homie Sammy Dennis wore out his speakers playing that song relentlessly on repeat. By 1983 Run DMC released their second single, "Hard Times" and "Jam-Master Jay." Then I knew there was a God and I had found my new favorite group.

Run DMC were the first group that I obsessed over. Their debut album, *Run-D.M.C.*, was the first album I ever saved up to buy with my own money. As a matter of fact, me and my friend Ronnie bought the record together. I would keep it four days; he would keep it three days. Our parents thought we were crazy when we took all the shoestrings out of our shoes. Run was my favorite MC. I thought he had 1000 percent more swagger than any rapper of today. Ronnie loved DMC's voice. He said nobody could ever sound like the Devastating Mic Controller. I remember the day that Dr. Dre played me the *Raising Hell* album. We knew we had to step our game up.

Run DMC took hip-hop to rock star status. They showed us how to do everything, especially how to perform with songs like "Here We Go." They showed us if you had a dope DJ you didn't need no band, and that rappers from the hood could be the Kings of Rock too. I wouldn't be a rapper today if Run DMC didn't show me how to do it with class.

In 1985 I went around to every movie theater I could find looking for a movie called *Krush Groove* because Run DMC were in it. In 1987 I saw them perform in Phoenix. After the show we went by their hotel and DMC needed a ride to the store. After buying 40 ounces with DMC, I thought I died and went to heaven.

A few years back I had a bucket list moment when BET asked me to do a cypher with my two sons and Run with his two sons. There's nothing like being on a rooftop in Brooklyn with a little alone time with one of my heroes. I had a chance to thank him for inspiring me to be great and showing me that it's cool to rap about the world around you.

It's been a blessing getting to know these guys over the years as their peers. I remember when someone said hip-hop was dead. I didn't believe them until I heard that they killed Jam Master Jay. Then I believed them. A part of hip-hop died that night, but the spirit lives on. I will always love and be totally indebted to and grateful to the phenomenal Kings from Queens, Run DMC.

(Jam Master Jay was shot and killed in Queens, N.Y., on October 30, 2002.)

(Ice Cube is a rapper, producer, actor, and filmmaker. He is an original member of 2016 Rock and Roll Hall of Fame inductees N.W.A, who were the subject of the 2015 biopic and box-office smash *Straight Outta Compton*, named after the group's seminal debut album. His solo work includes hit albums such as *AmeriKKKa's Most Wanted* and *Death Certificate*.)

AL SCHMITT

TRUSTEES AWARD, 2006

Whether or not most casual observers realize it, "Al Schmitt" is actually a synonym for "recording engineer." Schmitt has engineered so many recordings—20 of them earning him Grammy Awards—the list rolls on longer than all 9,000 miles of Australia's Highway 1.

Schmitt's initial tutelage came under Atlantic Records great Tom Dowd in New York. In the late '50s he moved to Los Angeles and became a staff engineer at Radio Recorders and then at RCA, both in Hollywood, California. At the latter he worked with Henry Mancini, Sam Cooke, Rosemary Clooney, and many others.

In the mid-'60s he became an independent producer and worked on such noteworthy projects as *Crown of Creation* and *After Bathing at Baxter's* for Jefferson Airplane and *On the Beach* for Neil Young.

But primarily, Schmitt is an engineer at heart and he's served in that role for Grammy wins such as George Benson's *Breezin'*, Steely Dan's *Aja*, Toto's *Toto IV*, Quincy Jones' *Q's Jook Joint*, Diana Krall's *The Look of Love*, Ray Charles' *Genius Loves Company*, and Paul McCartney's *Kisses on the Bottom*.

Schmitt was awarded a star on the Hollywood Walk of Fame in 2015 and is in the TEC Awards Hall of Fame. But for a guy inclined to the technical side of recording, Schmitt's success may lie in his empathy for the artistic side. "Do you know anybody who buys a record because the snare drum sounds a certain way?" Schmitt said during an interview with *Mix with the Masters*, a video seminar series. "People buy a record because it emotionally touches them."

This has been an incredible voyage for me and the boat hasn't docked yet. I'm still working and I know a lot of my engineer friends out there are trying to break an eardrum or something so I can retire early. But I wouldn't know what to do. I lie to my wife every single day when I tell her I'm going to work. It's a labor of love.

—Al Schmitt, acceptance speech, 2006

AL SCHMITT
Tribute by George Benson
February 8, 2006

My first studio recording in Los Angeles was one of the most incredible experiences of my life. The band and I arrived at Capitol Recording Studios in Hollywood on a sunny winter's day to begin recording my first album for Warner Brothers Records. Everything was new for me. I had a first-class producer in Tommy LiPuma; I was recording in the same studio my mentor, Nat King Cole, had recorded in (Studio A); and we were joined by a very quiet man who happened to be the most competent engineer you could ask for: Al Schmitt. I later dubbed him "Job" because of his patience in helping us put together the landmark album of my career—*Breezin'*. I cannot fail to mention that the very first take we recorded (which I thought was a test recording) was so good it turned out to be one of the best recordings I ever made. This was the song "Affirmation." The success of the album brought deserved attention not only to Tommy, but also to his longtime friend, and now *my* longtime friend, Al Schmitt. Al was awarded a well-deserved Best Engineered Recording Grammy for the *Breezin'* album.

We have since recorded many outstanding records and CDs together, which have received even more Grammy nominations. Al has become an icon recognized by many who have experienced his recordings and by those whose careers he has helped catapult to the top of the charts. I'm proud to say that Al and I remain the best of friends and I am very proud of his achievements. I congratulate my friend Al on his Trustees Award.

(George Benson has won 10 Grammy Awards, including Record of the Year for 1976 for "This Masquerade" from the *Breezin'* album.)

GIL SCOTT-HERON

LIFETIME ACHIEVEMENT AWARD, 2012

Tom Copi/Michael Ochs Archives/Getty Images

On the occasion of his death in 2011, the kindling that Gil Scott-Heron gathered to help build the raging political fire of rap was acknowledged by Public Enemy's Chuck D: "RIP GSH," he tweeted. "And we do what we do and how we do because of you."

Starting in the '60s, Scott-Heron's mix of hard soul and jazz with spoken-word poetry was among the earliest antecedents of rap, and his recorded report cards on America's racism weren't lost on the likes of Public Enemy and N.W.A.

His best-known song, the Grammy Hall of Fame–inducted "The Revolution Will Not Be Televised," was an indictment of a country distracted by a media focused on lightweight sitcoms and advertising while the inner cities were brimming with economically and politically oppressed minorities.

Scott-Heron came by his political views through experience. He was one of a handful of African-American students chosen to integrate the elementary school near his grandmother's Tennessee home. After much abuse, he moved to the Bronx to live with his mother, which no doubt inspired his first collection of poetry and other writings. In 1970, the same year "Revolution" was released, Scott-Heron published his first novel, the well-received *The Vulture*.

In the mid-'70s he would score R&B chart hits with uncompromising tracks such as "Johannesburg" and "Angel Dust."

In addition to his influence on rap and hip-hop, Scott-Heron has been credited as the godfather of poetry slams, and his work with collaborator Brian Jackson has been cited as an important stepping stone to acid jazz, which briefly enjoyed a successful run in the U.K.

Even if he was here, I'm kind of glad it's not televised because he would have said something that was probably going to be bleeped and gotten CBS fined.
— Nia Kelly Heron, daughter, acceptance speech, 2012

GIL SCOTT-HERON
Tribute by Common
February 12, 2012

Gil Scott-Heron was a leader, a leader in revolution. He had the courage, strength, heart, will, sense of sacrifice, and selflessness that few embody in this world. Gil was a leader who possessed a powerful but soothing voice, a voice that had the tone and texture of standing up for the people. He represented the people from the ghetto, the people who were oppressed, and the people who were standing up for justice and equality for all. Gil Scott-Heron was the embodiment of millions; their voices and their spirits were alive in him.

I remember the first time I heard Gil as a young boy. My best friend played his record "The Revolution Will Not Be Televised." I was intrigued, excited, and amused by this inspirational piece. At the time, I was unaware of the mighty influence the song's empowering message would have on me not only as an artist, but as a human being. From that point on, every time I listened to Gil's music he truly left footprints on my soul. He left footprints of joy, footprints of resistance, and footprints of power and love. Gil gave us a chorus of power to chant to. And he gave us shoes of positive change and upward mobility to walk in.

What was so beautiful about Gil's gilded gift of artistry was that he blessed the world with messages that impacted the paradigms of the youth in such a dynamic way. What makes this truth so magical is that in the eyes of our youth we find our development and progress as a collective human race. We find our future. I was a member of that youth at one period of time. I represent the generation Gil influenced and crowned with his wisdom, style, and musical genius.

In college, as I was being exposed to more and more types of music, I was reintroduced to Gil Scott-Heron. It was then, after having the same intrigue and excitement as hearing him the first time, that he officially became one of my favorite artists. I loved the depth of his voice, the soul he sang with, the music that he created, and the words that sparked illuminating thoughts. I loved the beautiful experience I had every single time I listened to Gil's music and felt the movement that naturally shined through the lyrics.

I found myself taking pieces of him and placing them into my own music because he represented something bigger than us and of the spiritual realm. I would quote him, sample him, and use his lyrics for inspiration in my songs. On my single "The 6th Sense" I quoted "The Revolution Will Not Be Televised." On my single "Real People" we sampled "We Almost Lost Detroit," and it felt great to connect my work to the work of such an iconic poet and artist as Gil Scott-Heron.

To make it all even more mesmerizing, in August 2010 I was afforded the blessing to connect with Gil personally during a performance we had together in Central Park. I remember the day vividly. First, I went to Gil's home in New York. He was barbequing and we were talking about how to perform the songs at the show. We traded thoughts and I even revealed to him that I someday wished to play him in a movie. He told me all about the new book he was writing. As we exchanged stories and thoughts with one another, I thought to myself, "This is one of the greatest artists the world has ever seen," and I was honored just to share the moments we had as artists and as brothers.

I know Gil Scott-Heron shared his soul in every note, lyric, and song we heard from him. I will always appreciate the influence and impact he had on me and the world. I will forever work to keep his inspiration alive.

(Common is a three-time Grammy winner, including the 2015 award for Best Song Written for Visual Media for "Glory" from the film *Selma*.)

RAVI SHANKAR

LIFETIME ACHIEVEMENT AWARD, 2013

David Redfern/Redferns/Getty Images

Ravi Shankar has arguably done more to bring awareness to what has come to be called world music than any single musician, and he's done it by being an ambassador of Indian music and cross-pollinating it with various forms of Western music.

Shankar spent more than a decade studying Indian classical music and becoming probably the most famous sitar player in India before venturing out for recitals in Europe and the United States. Through the '60s, he not only helped popularize Indian music outside his own country, but he spearheaded its influence on Western classical and popular music through his associations with violinist Yehudi Menuhin and Beatles guitarist George Harrison. (Harrison arguably started the raga rock trend when he added sitar to the Beatles' "Norwegian Wood.")

In 1967 Shankar played the Monterey Pop Festival, a clear indication of not only his growing impact in the West, but his resonance with a young generation of music fans who were gravitating toward Eastern mysticism and its exotic musical counterparts. He won a Grammy that year for his appropriately titled *West Meets East*, his teaming with Menuhin. Shankar also later joined in important collaborations such as the album *Passages* with minimalist American composer Philip Glass.

Shankar died in 2012 after a long, influential career. Not the least of his influence on both Indian and popular music are his daughters, Anoushka Shankar and Norah Jones.

> *When I was a child, my mom realized we couldn't find his Grammy anywhere. And he'd lost it. I guess he left it in a suitcase at a friend's house years ago and didn't know what had happened to it. So we made loads of fun of him for losing a Grammy. And when she called up The Academy to see if she could get a copy made, they said, "Certainly, we can make a copy. Which Grammy is it that you want to get copied?" And she said, "What do you mean, which Grammy?" And it turns out he'd won two, he just didn't know it. That was the kind of musician he was.*
>
> —Anoushka Shankar, daughter, acceptance speech, 2013

RAVI SHANKAR
Tribute by Philip Glass
February 10, 2013

In the mid-'50s, while the academics, pundits, and practitioners of "new music" were debating and legislating the future of their art, a young man from India arrived in the West and, unbidden and unannounced, set into motion a revolution in Western musical language that is today, more than 50 years later, still powerfully shaping our landscape.

That young man was, of course, Ravi Shankar.

He was already famous in India as a leading master of the classical music world and foremost sitar player of the day. He soon became a close friend and collaborator of the great French flutist Jean-Pierre Rampal and the formidable violin virtuoso Yehudi Menuhin.

His appearance at the Monterey Pop Festival in 1967 would lead him to all manner of performances at other festivals as well. He had become a living pied piper of music with a huge following among young musicians, composers, and theater/dance enthusiasts. In fact, Raviji (as he was affectionately known to students and friends alike) was well-known and adored not only by the rich and famous but by the young and passionate as well. In that regard, the Beatles qualified in all four categories. Not surprisingly, he had a long and close friendship with George Harrison and, along the way, made formidable waves in the worlds of popular and commercial music.

He was particularly drawn to young people—both musicians and music lovers. He was an indefatigable teacher. Lessons could begin anytime. On several occasions I saw him lay down the sitar and lecture his audience on the immorality of drug taking, smoking, and drinking. These kinds of sermons were tolerated kindly enough by the young fans who were sitting it out, waiting for that magnificent torrent of music to begin again. In those days, and to the end, he was treated as a superstar. Always gracious and kind, though occasionally not exactly on time, except in his music, when he would be impeccable.

He is no longer with us but his legacy is all around us. Simply, today's music world would not be what it is without him. His companions, students, and friends are everywhere. His brilliance, enthusiasm, and simple love for the life in which he was immersed remain as a wave of energy that continues to animate everything it touches.

I spoke to Raviji just a few days before he died. Sukanya, his wife and longtime companion, arranged the call for me, for which I will always be grateful. It wasn't a long conversation, nor did it need to be. Things were said that had been said before but needed to be said one last time.

Seeing a great man die is like watching a sunset. For me, he was the greatest of the great and the best of the best. At that unbelievable and unknowable event, as with the last tender light of the evening, all the beauty and sadness, joy and terror of life at last come together. Even Death, at that moment, is briefly robbed of its finality.

(Philip Glass has been called one of the most influential composers of the 20th century. He has earned four Grammy nominations. Glass collaborated with Ravi Shankar on the 1990 album *Passages*.)

CHRIS STRACHWITZ

TRUSTEES AWARD, 2016

Record producer, label owner, and preservationist Chris Strachwitz is a walking personification of the universal language of music. Born in Germany and raised in Southern California, he has recorded, released, and helped preserve music including blues, Cajun, folk, zydeco, norteño, klezmer, and other forms of roots music that might otherwise have vanished or never been recorded.

While attending high school near Santa Barbara, California, Strachwitz first discovered jazz, and during a stint at Pomona College he saw his first blues shows featuring Lightnin' Hopkins and Howlin' Wolf. While at UC Berkeley, he booked jazz and blues acts as entertainment for football games. He also began learning how to record music.

In 1960 he recorded his first act, Mance Lipscomb, and his *Texas Songster and Sharecropper* became the first release on Strachwitz's Arhoolie label. Soon he'd record many other artists, including the first dates for acts such as zydeco musician Clifton Chenier. Strachwitz also started licensing forgotten blues works for rerelease.

It was all purely a labor of love until 1966, when Strachwitz recorded Country Joe and the Fish's "I-Feel-Like-I'm-Fixin'-to-Die Rag" in his living room and traded the cost of the session for a piece of the publishing. When the song generated significant royalties from its appearance in the Woodstock festival film and soundtrack, Strachwitz was able to set up shop formally, buying a building in El Cerrito, California, and funding more recordings. Among his most important work from that period included notable releases from Mississippi Fred McDowell, Charlie Musselwhite, Big Mama Thornton, Michael Doucet and his band BeauSoleil, and Flaco Jiménez.

The latter signing reflected Strachwitz's love of Mexican-American music. In fact, through the years, he has amassed what is thought to be the largest private collection of Mexican and Mexican-American recordings—now called the Frontera Collection—which Strachwitz's Arhoolie Foundation is cataloguing and preserving with the help of a grant from The Recording Academy–affiliated Grammy Foundation.

Fittingly, in 1999 he was inducted as a nonperforming member of the Blues Hall of Fame, just one nod to his indefatigable role in celebrating underserved music.

I fell in love with records as a little kid . . . I thought they were just the darnedest, neatest objects I ever encountered. You could put the needle down and out come the most amazing sounds from around the world.

—Chris Strachwitz, acceptance speech, 2016

CHRIS STRACHWITZ
Tribute by Country Joe McDonald
February 15, 2016

In the summer of 1965, having not prepared copy for a magazine I was publishing, it occurred to me that we could make a "talking issue" in the form of a seven-inch EP. One partner in the magazine knew Chris Strachwitz and said we could make the recording at his house. A small group of us went to Chris's living room and gathered around a microphone hanging from a light fixture. This skiffle band recorded a few songs, one of them being "I-Feel-Like-I'm-Fixin'-to-Die Rag." Chris offered to handle the publishing for my song in exchange for the recording. He administered the publishing for 12 years.

The name Country Joe and the Fish was invented for the label of that EP. We sold 100 copies for 50 cents each at a local bookstore. Then four years later, I sang "I-Feel-Like-I'm-Fixin'-to-Die Rag" at the Woodstock festival. It was featured on the record and in the Academy Award–winning documentary *Woodstock*. Chris and I got some large royalties. I used the royalties to purchase a house and Chris bought a building in El Cerrito, California, to house Arhoolie Records. I went on to record hundreds more songs and make 35 albums. He went on to record thousands of songs and hundreds of albums by American roots music artists.

Arhoolie Records brought the sound of American roots music to a national and international audience that never knew this style of music existed. Music recorded by Chris Strachwitz is now the fabric and foundation for American popular music. Chris helped expose artists such as Mance Lipscomb, Charlie Musselwhite, Clifton Chenier, Flaco Jiménez, and Cajun band BeauSoleil. He's been as important to the preservation of authentic American music as Alan Lomax. The money from Arhoolie's releases supported the careers of hundreds of musicians for the next 50 years. It is hard to believe that it all happened just like that and that 50 years have passed.

And now The Recording Academy is presenting Chris Strachwitz with a Trustees Award to acknowledge the pioneering contributions he has made to American music. Congratulations Chris on a job well done.

(Country Joe and the Fish's "I-Feel-Like-I'm-Fixin'-to-Die Rag" became an anthem of Vietnam War protests. Country Joe McDonald continues to write and perform and has become a leading expert on Florence Nightingale, the founder of modern nursing.)

BARBRA STREISAND

LIFETIME ACHIEVEMENT AWARD, 1995

O ne of the most iconic figures in music and pop culture, Barbra Streisand has had a transformative presence in film, music, television, and on the stage. From the beginning she pursued her own muse, probably the only major artist to establish her singing career as a traditional vocalist at the height of the British Invasion rock era.

Streisand's debut album, the Grammy Album of the Year–winning *The Barbra Streisand Album*, was a remarkable reinvention of the traditional pop album, made more remarkable given it was made before her 21st birthday. The song choices were novel, and her brilliant performances defied expectations. One year later, in 1964, she scored her first Top 10 hit and another Grammy Award with "People."

Having conquered the record world with her first couple albums, she took on Broadway with *Funny Girl*, which also became her first movie hit in 1968. In 1971 she reinvented herself as a contemporary pop/rock singer, deftly choosing material alongside pop's premier producer of the time, Richard Perry, resulting in a Top 10 hit with Laura Nyro's "Stoney End."

In 1973 she'd deliver the film, and its hit title track, *The Way We Were*. In 1976 came *A Star Is Born* and its Grammy-winning song "Love Theme from A Star Is Born (Evergreen)." In 1980 she launched arguably her biggest album with another reinvention, *Guilty*, and another Grammy, working with Bee Gee Barry Gibb.

In 1983 she'd assume the director's chair for *Yentl*, and then again in 1991 for *The Prince of Tides*, which earned her an Academy Award nomination, making her among the earliest and few female auteurs in Hollywood.

Her list of awards runs longer than the *Encyclopedia Britannica*. She ranks No. 3 on *Billboard*'s list of the top *Billboard* 200 artists of all time. She's earned the reverence of the operaesque title "La Streisand." And mostly, and most simply, she's recognized as arguably the top diva of her time.

BARBRA STREISAND
Tribute by Linda Richman
March 1, 1995

Long story short: When the Grammys called me on the set of *Saturday Night Live*'s "Coffee Talk" and asked me to write a tribute to Barbra Joan Streisand, I got all able-boodled in the keppy. That I, Linda Richman, should be called upon to pay homage to Barbra, that poor little shayna madel from Brooklyn who soared to the top through God-given talent and sheer chutzpah. It was like the Sunday *Times* crossword, Steve & Eydie, and *Bridget Loves Bernie* all rolled into one.

Naturally, the first thing I did was to call my dear friend, Paul Baldwin (who I'm happy to report is recovering from the relapse of schpilkas in his ganectagzoink). I said, "Paul, talk to me. The Grammys are finally giving Barbra her Lifetime Achievement Award, and they asked me to write about it. Too much good is nichtgut. Hand to God, Paul, I'm dying."

So Paul says to me, "Linda Richman, do not get emotional. It's no big whoop. Who better to toast Barbra than her number one fan? Write it as though you were talking directly to Barbra, and you'll have no problem."

Paul was right. So here it goes:

Hello, gorgeous! I feel as if I'm once again camped out in the front row of the Park Slope Bardavon. A 12-year-old meiskite worshipping you in *Funny Girl* while my traitor sister Judy stayed home to watch the Beatles on Ed Sullivan. The years since have been a medley of Barbra Moments: "People." *The Owl and the Pussycat.* "You Don't Bring Me Flowers." *Yentl. The Prince of Tides.* And, of course, *Back to Broadway.* Every song like buttah. Don't get me started!

Barbra Joan Streisand, tonight is your night. . .

Now I'm getting emotional. I'm a little ferklemt. Talk amongst yourselves. I'll give you a topic: Pearl Jam is neither Pearls nor Jam. Discuss. . .

(Linda Richman talked about coffee, New York, daughters, dogs, and of course, Barbra, as host of "Coffee Talk.")

ALLEN TOUSSAINT

TRUSTEES AWARD, 2009

Allen Toussaint was a singular talent as a producer, arranger, songwriter, and artist who was among a handful of music makers who forged the sound of New Orleans in the early rock and R&B years. He even turned up in some unlikely places under an equally unlikely name.

Toussaint was born in New Orleans in 1938 and had some minor early successes as a sideman, recording artist, and songwriter in the '50s. (It was during this time he cowrote "Java," which New Orleans trumpeter Al Hirt would take to No. 4 on the *Billboard* Hot 100 in 1964.) In 1960 Toussaint was hired to head A&R for Minit Records and began a string of hits as a songwriter and producer, including Ernie K-Doe's "Mother-In-Law," Benny Spellman's "Lipstick Traces (On a Cigarette)," and Lee Dorsey's "Ya Ya," among others. While in the army in 1963, Toussaint wrote "Whipped Cream" under his mother's maiden name, Naomi Neville. The song became a mid-chart hit for Herb Alpert's Tijuana Brass in 1965, but a giant cultural touchstone when it was adopted as the theme for TV's *The Dating Game*.

After starting his own label and freelancing, Toussaint would write more hits—including Lee Dorsey's "Working in the Coal Mine," the Pointer Sisters' "Yes We Can Can," and Glen Campbell's "Southern Nights"—and produce two of the biggest hits in New Orleans' transition from '60s R&B to '70s funk: Dr. John's "Right Place, Wrong Time" and LaBelle's "Lady Marmalade" (Grammy Hall of Fame, 2003).

Toussaint, who died in 2015, would eventually become a revered ambassador of New Orleans music and would work with admirers such as Elvis Costello, Eric Clapton, and Paul McCartney. He was inducted into the Rock and Roll Hall of Fame in 1998.

WireImage.com

ALLEN TOUSSAINT
Tribute by Daniel Lanois
February 8, 2009

The sound of Allen Toussaint was ringing in my ear long before my time living in New Orleans. The groove of "Working in the Coal Mine" made me feel like that was me up at five o'clock in the morning going down, down the coal mining shaft. When the music is gotten right, it transports a listener to a magic place. I believe we can safely say that Allen Toussaint has had his finger on the magic button a good many times. Upon hearing La-Belle singing "Voulez-vous coucher avec moi, ce soir" (on "Lady Marmalade," which Allen produced) my French immediately improved. To this day the recordings that Allen made with Lee Dorsey get under my skin and pique my curiosity—that wonderful blend of innocence and full command of form keeps me sharp about my own skills.

Think of the world without Dr. John or without the Meters—a force of neighborhood music that reached the ears of so many. Sometimes it takes an Allen Toussaint to be the conduit for talent like the Meters' Art Neville, George Porter Jr., Leo Nocentelli, and Zigaboo Modeliste. These fine young men sure had their groove together and under the umbrella of Toussaint were able to have their sound memorialized and catapulted to the rest of the world. The Meters, of course, will be forever remembered as a beacon of American funk.

Allen Toussaint did what we should all do—he paid attention to what was going on in his own neighborhood and found a way to elevate raw talent to a plateau of world recognition. The sound of Allen Toussaint is a magic sound that embraces all that he is. He is a giving and generous man. We should all be thankful for the magic of Allen.

(Seven-time Grammy winner Daniel Lanois lived in New Orleans from 1988 to 2001. His production credits include Bob Dylan, Peter Gabriel, the Neville Brothers, and U2.)

DOC WATSON

 ## LIFETIME ACHIEVEMENT AWARD, 2004

You know you come by your bluegrass and folk roots authentically when you're born and raised in a place called Deep Gap, North Carolina. Maybe only Loretta Lynn's hometown of Butcher Hollow, Kentucky—or Butcher *Holler* in the local parlance—can top it.

Arthel "Doc" Watson came by his renown as a guitar player and performer authentically as well. He wasn't part of a country music royal family and certainly didn't come from means. He busked the streets with his brother and tuned pianos to help make ends meet. He faced the further challenge of having lost his eyesight at an early age due to an illness.

He played locally in his youth and then regionally with bands. He taught himself his signature guitar style by learning to play fiddle music on guitar for square-dance performances.

It wasn't until the early '60s, when Watson was nearing 40 years old, that he was really "discovered." The folk revival was picking up steam in New York, and several events put him and son Merle on the music map: an appearance in Greenwich Village, his part in the recording *Old Time Music at Clarence Ashby's*, and a performance at the Newport Folk Festival.

Soon, he and Merle had a following on the folk circuit that would continue even after the glow of the folk revival dimmed. In 1971 the Nitty Gritty Dirt Band's country-rock breakthrough *Will the Circle be Unbroken* featured Watson prominently, exposing him to more fans.

Watson would win seven Grammy Awards and his self-titled 1964 album and the song "Black Mountain Rag" have both been inducted into the Grammy Hall of Fame.

> *Doc's goal was to take his Appalachian heritage—often disparaged in mainstream culture—and share it with, and thus have it claimed by, the rest of America, and the rest of the world. He found tremendous satisfaction when people who had grown up in very different backgrounds—from Ivy League universities to rural Africa—would respond to and be moved by [his] songs.*
>
> —Mitch Greenhill, coproducer of Doc and Merle Watson's *Pickin' the Blues*, acceptance speech, 2004

DOC WATSON
Tribute by Ricky Skaggs
February 8, 2004

Arthel "Doc" Watson is a true American treasure and one of America's most important musicians. His depth of understanding of old-time mountain music is second to nobody's. He understands the old style of playin' and the old-time style of singin' better than anyone, and for more than four decades he has had a profound influence on folk, traditional acoustic, and bluegrass music.

I don't know any bluegrass musician or lover of traditional old-time music who doesn't admire Doc Watson and what he's done for this music. His unique style and sound have awed and inspired folks for years. He's a true innovator and has transformed guitar playing by his distinctive high-speed style of picking reminiscent of the old mountain fiddle tunes. Although drawing heavily on the influences of guitar greats Maybelle Carter, Riley Puckett, and Merle Travis who had come before him, it was Doc who invented the lightning-fast, flat-picking leads that became the standard in bluegrass and country music.

Doc plays it simple and down-to-earth. His playing says, "I'm from Deep Gap, North Carolina, from the Appalachians, the Blue Ridge Mountains." It's just that pure, simple, traditional mountain sound. And though Doc is physically blind, he is a deeply spiritual man who sees better than most people I know.

Doc has had a deep impact on ensuring that the legacy of traditional American music has survived through the years by honoring these songs, playing them, and keeping them alive and vital for new generations of listeners. Along the way, he's won seven Grammy Awards; he has been honored with such awards as the National Heritage Fellowship and the presidential-appointed National Medal of Arts; and he's transcended styles and eras, becoming one of the focal points of the folk resurgence in the '60s while continuing to influence artists today, from Emmylou Harris to Vince Gill and, of course, myself.

Over the years, I've been lucky enough to team up with Doc a few different times, and I had the distinct honor and privilege of playing with Doc on a very special project called *The Three Pickers* (along with the banjo-playing legend Earl Scruggs). For me as an artist and a lover of old-time music, getting to play with legends like Doc and Earl was a dream come true. Players like these have done so much for American music.

Doc Watson is without a doubt one of the most renowned and influential acoustic flat-picking guitar players of the century and a true American musical master.

(Ricky Skaggs is a 13-time Grammy winner. In 2003 he collaborated with Doc Watson and Earl Scruggs for the album *The Three Pickers*, which garnered a Grammy nomination for Best Traditional Folk Album.)

GEORGE WEIN

TRUSTEES AWARD, 2015

If you're looking for the spiritual godfather of today's ever-growing music festival phenomenon, look no further than George Wein.

Originally the founder of the Newport Jazz Festival, Wein would go on to produce the Newport Folk Festival, the New Orleans Jazz & Heritage Festival, and the Playboy Jazz Festival, all of which continue to be going concerns. Wein was so closely associated with the development of the festival business, he called his company Festival Productions. He not only grew sizable audiences to which he could showcase both established and emerging music talent, he created the template for a lucrative festival industry by pioneering corporate sponsorships, starting with the Schlitz Salute to Jazz and Kool Jazz Festival events.

The Newport Jazz Festival began humbly in 1954 when local Newport, Rhode Island, residents Louis and Elaine Lorillard—heirs to a tobacco dynasty—asked Wein, who had been running a jazz club in Boston, to stage a festival in their town, which they financed. It was reported to be the first outdoor jazz festival, and over the weekend artists such as Dizzy Gillespie and Billie Holiday, and thousands of fans, made history.

History was made again in 1965 when Bob Dylan went electric at Wein's Newport Folk Festival. The festival crowd was displeased, but the reverberations were monumental.

As an impresario, there have been few bigger and more important. He has been honored with numerous awards, including recognition as a Jazz Master by the National Endowment for the Arts and recognition at the White House by Presidents Jimmy Carter and Bill Clinton.

WireImage.com

GEORGE WEIN
Tribute by Mavis Staples
February 8, 2015

I've known George Wein a long time, and I have to say that he's one of my favorite people in the world. He brought my family, the Staple Singers, to the Newport Folk Festival back in 1965, and from our first meeting he was just a jewel. That was the very first folk festival that we had ever seen, and I was so green I didn't know why we were there—as far as I knew, we sang gospel music, not folk music. But George knew we belonged, and I'm so grateful he heard our music and made us a part of his family. He used to call me "the little girl with the big voice."

George is the cofounder and promoter of the Newport Jazz and Folk Festivals, but if you didn't know he was running things you'd never guess it. He's such a good, humble man, and a gentleman. A real sweetheart. He truly loves the music, and he has always wanted to keep his artists happy. He's there in the dressing room to say hello and to make sure you're OK, and he's out there by the stage listening to all the music. It's really *his* show, but he acts like he's just one of the crowd.

I've celebrated three birthdays at the Newport Folk Festival, and last year it was for my 75th. George sang "Happy Birthday" to me and that was a real treat. I really got choked up. George also asked me to close out last year's festival singing "We Shall Overcome," because that's the way Pete Seeger had always closed it. All the artists got together onstage, locked arms, and we sang together just like back in the day. And George was sitting right there looking at us with the biggest smile on his face.

I always look forward to seeing my friend George Wein. I'm so grateful that I've had the opportunity to know him, to work for him, and to smile, laugh, and sing with him. It's an honor for me. He's just a beautiful spirit. Every time I see him I can't help but hug him. And I can't wait to see him at the next festival. I told him, "George, I'll be there even if you don't ask me to be there. After all these years, I know how to get to Newport."

(As a member of the Staple Singers, Mavis Staples was honored in 2005 with a Recording Academy Lifetime Achievement Award. The group have three recordings inducted into the Grammy Hall of Fame, including "Respect Yourself." Staples has won two Grammys as a solo artist, including Best Americana Album for 2010's *You Are Not Alone*.)

BOB WILLS

Charlie Gillett/Redferns/Getty Images

Like Ford and mass production or Apple and the personal computer, Bob Wills and His Texas Playboys have come to be regarded as the face of Western swing. Wills didn't create the concept of fiddle-driven dance bands, but as an answer to the popularity of big bands in the late '30s and early '40s, he innovated their approach in ways that would echo through the years.

Born in Texas in 1905, Wills formed bands in his youth such as the Wills Fiddle Band. When the group scored a regular radio show sponsored by the Burris Mill and Elevator Company (which made Light Crust Flour), they became the Light Crust Doughboys, though Burris' control of the band eventually led Wills and company to leave and form the Playboys.

At KVOO-FM in Tulsa, Oklahoma, the band began to define their sound, adding electric steel guitar and a horn section. In 1936 they recorded "Steel Guitar Rag" (Grammy Hall of Fame, 2011), which has become a standard for the instrument. But it was late in the decade, with competition coming from the enormous popularity of big bands, when Wills assembled a band capable of playing intricate jazzy arrangements and had his first major national hit, "New San Antonio Rose" (Grammy Hall of Fame, 1998).

More hits would follow, with the band working across California during this time, drawing huge dance crowds in Los Angeles, Oakland, and Sacramento. As a result, the Playboys would have a tremendous influence on Buck Owens and Merle Haggard as they were coming of age in Bakersfield, California. Haggard would record a Wills tribute album in 1970, and Ray Benson's Asleep at the Wheel dedicated themselves to keeping the flame of Western swing burning.

Wills and the Playboys would ultimately be inducted into both the Country Music and Rock and Roll halls of fame.

BOB WILLS
Tribute by Ray Benson
February 11, 2007

Bob Wills was a world-renowned bandleader, Western fiddler, songwriter, singer, Western movie star, and cocreator and practitioner of a uniquely American musical genre known as Western swing.

Born near Kosse, Texas, in 1905, Bob Wills began his career while working his family's cotton farm in West Texas. At an early age he began fiddling at ranch dances with his father and uncles. Enamored with the jazz and blues music he heard working the cotton fields with black laborers, he began a musical journey that would meld the fiddlin' music of his family with the blues and jazz that was being played and developed by African-Americans in the Southwest at that time.

After moving to Fort Worth, Texas, and forming a group with legendary vocalist and bandleader Milton Brown, they joined W. Lee O'Daniel's Light Crust Doughboys to promote O'Daniel's flour company. O'Daniel, future governor of Texas, was not happy when Bob left to form the Texas Playboys and used his influence in radio to force Bob Wills to move to Tulsa, Oklahoma, radio station KVOO.

From Tulsa, on KVOO and in Cain's Ballroom, Bob Wills and his Texas Playboys, with featured vocalist Tommy Duncan, forged a sound that was a blend of Southwestern fiddle music, big band swing rhythms, and South Texas Mexican influences. Starting in 1930 he began a recording career that would span more than 40 years. In 1941 "The New San Antonio Rose" was released and became a million seller for Wills and his Playboys. Not only was it a hit for Bob, Bing Crosby recorded it as well, making it a bona fide standard in both genres.

After World War II, Wills relocated to California where his fame and popularity soared. He made dozens of movies in Hollywood, recorded hundreds of records, radio shows, and TV shows, and rivaled the biggest names in show business.

As a member of both the Country Music Hall of Fame *and* the Rock and Roll Hall of Fame, Bob Wills' influence has been felt during the formation of rock and roll and in the sounds of modern country music out of Nashville, California, Oklahoma, and Texas in the past and today.

I met Bob Wills once but never got to talk to him. After 37 years of playing his music and telling his story on our tribute albums and in our musical play about his life called "A Ride with Bob," I hope Bob enjoys all of our efforts and is somewhere where he can holler "Ah ha" one more time.

(A nine-time Grammy winner, Ray Benson formed Asleep at the Wheel in 1970. For more than 45 years the band has helped keep Western swing a vital force in country music.)

FRANK ZAPPA

LIFETIME ACHIEVEMENT AWARD, 1997

Serious, satirical, political, absurdist: Frank Zappa may be the most difficult musician of the rock era to categorize. He was ostensibly a rock artist, but seldom made music that could be called traditional rock. He was an experimental composer and also a satirical jokester. He wasn't so much an icon but rather an iconoclast, truly moving in directions that the popular culture wasn't. It made him widely admired and respected, if not wildly successful.

It was telling that a teenage Zappa was a fan of both R&B and avant-garde classical music. In Los Angeles, he formed the Mothers in 1965, began playing clubs such as Whiskey A Go Go, and was signed by Verve, which changed the band's name to the Mothers of Invention. The band released albums through 1975, including *Burnt Weeny Sandwich* and *We're Only In It for the Money*, titles that revealed Zappa's nose-thumbing spirit.

Zappa's solo career lasted up to his death in 1993, and even beyond, thanks to his wife Gail curating his catalog. His output included albums that ranged from the pop-oriented *Sheik Yerbouti* to an album with the London Symphony and *Guitar*, a virtuoso instrumental record, as well as his biggest hit, 1982's "Valley Girl," on which he and daughter Moon Unit parodied the consumerist vapidity of L.A. teens.

It all added up to a transcendent artist whose reach was astounding. Artists who have professed a debt include Alice Cooper (who was first signed by Zappa to his Bizarre label), Trey Anastasio, Jeff Buckley, Jimi Hendrix, Steve Vai, jazz musicians Bill Frisell and John Zorn, new age pianist George Winston, and fellow parodist "Weird Al" Yankovic.

FRANK ZAPPA
Tribute by Jello Biafra
February 26, 1997

Frank Zappa's first impact on me was in ninth grade. We'd go to a friend's house near school during lunch hour, and roll on the floor laughing at the *Mothermania* LP on Verve. The all-too-true satire in the grooves gave us strength—it wasn't just OK to be a *mutant*, it was damn good fun. Terrorizing normal classmates with my very existence was something to be proud of.

In high school, I joined the radio club that broadcast music into the cafeteria during lunch hour. Crushed when people didn't dig the obscure sounds we were trying to turn them on to, we started playing music designed to make them mad. Big band records dug out of the store room got a reaction, but not as much as the jocks storming the barred studio windows over "Brown Shoes Don't Make It." By then the Zappa fans (we all knew each other) had memorized every word on his albums. For drama class, I directed a stage adaptation of "Billy the Mountain."

Due in no small part to Frank, my musical horizons expanded too: the avant-electronics on *Freak Out*, jazz and fusion on *Hot Rats* and *Weasels Ripped My Flesh*, symphonic forays on *Lumpy Gravy* and *Uncle Meat*, and seamless ventures into funk and progressive by the time of *Roxy and Elsewhere*. All crowned by Frank's fountain of humor. Those album covers! Those titles! When most rock trailblazers were running out of ideas, Frank had more and more. Without touching drugs, no less. In *200 Motels*, he called his work "comedy music," but we knew better.

I didn't truly grasp what a brilliant production wizard Frank was in the studio until Dead Kennedys' drummer D.H. Peligro played "Apostrophe" in the van late one night as we crossed the Canadian Rockies in a snowstorm. Here was Frank changing sound and atmospheres every 30 seconds and somehow making it all work—Phil Spector one minute, Roy Thomas Baker the next. I was floored.

When Tipper Gore and her Religious Right pals sat across from their husbands and lied at the '85 Senate anti-music hearings, I couldn't believe it. No one fought back. When Frank finally took them on with his wit and fire and intelligence, it truly showed how out-of-it and spineless the rest of the commercial music industry is to this day. Everything Frank predicted about half-hearted '60s idealists in "We're Only In It for the Money" had come true.

People thought I was crazy when I said Tipper and the Washington Stepford wives were a Trojan Horse for the religious right and were out to bust people. Within weeks, it happened to me. Frank called my house (not the other way around) offering friendship and some very valuable advice, "Remember: *You* are the victim. When you fight back, do it with *dignity*."

About the only silver lining from Dead Kennedys' *Frankenchrist* album obscenity trial was getting to meet Frank and come to his—well, let's call it a lab. Straight from the "True Cheepnis" monster movies he loved, there were loose wires and bits of equipment in the den, creeping out from under the couch. The Xerox machine was in the shower. A piece of metal collage from the *Burnt Weeny Sandwich* cover hung from a wall.

My generation has not produced anyone the caliber of Frank Zappa. I see no one on the horizon even interested in mastering rock, jazz, classical, studio production, and above all intelligence and humor the way Frank did. Unlike most entertainment icons, he wasn't afraid to keep growing.

When Czechoslovakia's Velvet Revolution came, Frank was energized. When he announced his candidacy for president to wake up our country, no one claimed it was to further his own career. Could he have been our Vaclav Havel? We need something like that in the worst kind of way. More likely it will take all of us, and a few thousand more, if we ever hope to fill Frank's shoes.

(Jello Biafra is the leader and main songwriter for extreme punk pioneers Dead Kennedys.)

PAST SPECIAL MERIT AWARD RECIPIENTS

LIFETIME ACHIEVEMENT AWARD

The Lifetime Achievement Award, established in 1962, is presented by vote of The Recording Academy's National Trustees to performers who, during their lifetimes, have made creative contributions of outstanding artistic significance to the field of recording.

RECIPIENTS (induction year)

Roy Acuff (1987)

The Allman Brothers Band (2012)

Marian Anderson (1991)

Julie Andrews (2011)

Louis Armstrong (1972)

Eddy Arnold (2005)

Fred Astaire (1989)

Chet Atkins (1993)

Gene Autry (2009)

Burt Bacharach (2008)

Joan Baez (2007)

The Band (2008)

Count Basie (2002)

The Beach Boys (2001)

The Beatles (2014)

Bee Gees (2015)

Harry Belafonte (2000)

Tony Bennett (2001)

Irving Berlin (1968)

Leonard Bernstein (1985)

Chuck Berry (1984)

Art Blakey (2005)

Bobby "Blue" Bland (1997)

Blind Boys of Alabama (2009)

Booker T. & the MG's (2007)

Pierre Boulez (2015)

David Bowie (2006)

James Brown (1992)

Ruth Brown (2016)

Dave Brubeck (1996)

Maria Callas (2007)

Cab Calloway (2008)

Glen Campbell (2012)

Benny Carter (1987)

(Original) Carter Family (2005)

Enrico Caruso (1987)

Pablo Casals (1989)

Johnny Cash (1999)

Ray Charles (1987)

Clifton Chenier (2014)

Van Cliburn (2004)

Patsy Cline (1995)

Rosemary Clooney (2002)

Leonard Cohen (2010)

Nat "King" Cole (1990)

Ornette Coleman (2007)

John Coltrane (1992)

Perry Como (2002)

Sam Cooke (1999)

Cream (2006)

Bing Crosby (1963)

Celia Cruz (2016)

Bobby Darin (2010)

Miles Davis (1990)

Sammy Davis Jr. (2001)

Doris Day (2008)

Bo Diddley (1998)

Fats Domino (1987)

The Doors (2007)

Bob Dylan (1991)

Earth, Wind & Fire (2016)

David "Honeyboy" Edwards (2010)

Duke Ellington (1966)
Bill Evans (1994)
The Everly Brothers (1997)
Ella Fitzgerald (1967)
The Four Tops (2009)
Aretha Franklin (1994)
The Funk Brothers (2004)
Judy Garland (1997)
Marvin Gaye (1996)
Dizzy Gillespie (1989)
Benny Goodman (1986)
Glenn Gould (2013)
Morton Gould (2005)
Stephane Grappelli (1997)
Grateful Dead (2007)
Al Green (2002)
Woody Guthrie (2000)
Buddy Guy (2015)
Charlie Haden (2013)
Merle Haggard (2006)
Herbie Hancock (2016)
George Harrison (2015)
Roy Haynes (2011)
Jascha Heifetz (1989)
Jimi Hendrix (1992)
Woody Herman (1987)
Billie Holiday (1987)
Buddy Holly (1997)
John Lee Hooker (2000)
Lightnin' Hopkins (2013)
Lena Horne (1989)
Vladimir Horowitz (1990)
The Isley Brothers (2014)
Mahalia Jackson (1972)
Michael Jackson (2010)
Etta James (2003)
Jefferson Airplane (2016)
Ella Jenkins (2004)
Flaco Jiménez (2015)
Antonio Carlos Jobim (2012)
Robert Johnson (2006)
George Jones (2012)
Hank Jones (2009)

Janis Joplin (2005)
Juilliard String Quartet (2011)
B.B. King (1987)
Carole King (2013)
The Kingston Trio (2011)
Kraftwerk (2014)
Kris Kristofferson (2014)
Led Zeppelin (2005)
Brenda Lee (2009)
Peggy Lee (1995)
John Lennon (1991)
Jerry Lee Lewis (2005)
Little Richard (1993)
Loretta Lynn (2010)
The Louvin Brothers (2015)
Henry Mancini (1995)
Armando Manzanero (2014)
Bob Marley (2001)
Dean Martin (2009)
Johnny Mathis (2003)
Curtis Mayfield (1995)
Paul McCartney (1990)
The Memphis Horns (2012)
Glenn Miller (2003)
Mitch Miller (2000)
The Mills Brothers (1998)
Charles Mingus (1997)
Joni Mitchell (2002)
Thelonious Monk (1993)
Bill Monroe (1993)
Jelly Roll Morton (2005)
Willie Nelson (2000)
Jessye Norman (2006)
Roy Orbison (1998)
Patti Page (2013)
Charlie Parker (1984)
Dolly Parton (2011)
Tom Paxton (2009)
Pinetop Perkins (2005)
Itzhak Perlman (2008)
Oscar Peterson (1997)
Maud Powell (2014)
Elvis Presley (1971)

André Previn (2010)
Leontyne Price (1989)
Richard Pryor (2006)
Tito Puente (2003)
Ramones (2011)
Otis Redding (1999)
Max Roach (2008)
Paul Robeson (1998)
Smokey Robinson (1999)
The Rolling Stones (1986)
Sonny Rollins (2004)
Linda Ronstadt (2016)
Diana Ross (2012)
Artur Rubinstein (1994)
Run DMC (2016)
Gil Scott-Heron (2012)
Earl Scruggs (2008)
Pete Seeger (1993)
Andrés Segovia (1986)
Ravi Shankar (2013)
Artie Shaw (2004)
George Beverly Shea (2011)
Wayne Shorter (2015)
Simon & Garfunkel (2003)

Frank Sinatra (1965)
Bessie Smith (1989)
Georg Solti (1996)
The Staple Singers (2005)
Isaac Stern (1987)
Igor Stravinsky (1987)
Barbra Streisand (1995)
Art Tatum (1989)
The Temptations (2013)
Clark Terry (2010)
Mel Tormé (1999)
Arturo Toscanini (1987)
Sarah Vaughan (1989)
Fats Waller (1993)
Muddy Waters (1992)
Doc Watson (2004)
The Weavers (2006)
Kitty Wells (1991)
The Who (2001)
Hank Williams (1987)
Bob Wills (2007)
Stevie Wonder (1996)
Frank Zappa (1997)

TRUSTEES AWARD

This Special Merit Award is presented by vote of The Recording Academy's National Trustees to individuals who have made significant contributions, other than performance, to the field of recording. The Trustees Award was established in 1967.

RECIPIENTS (induction year)

Chris Albertson (1971)
Herb Alpert and Jerry Moss (1997)
Harold Arlen (1987)
George Avakian (2009)
Clarence Avant (2008)
Estelle Axton (2007)
Burt Bacharach and Hal David (1997)
Dave Bartholomew (2012)
Béla Bartok (1984)
Count Basie (1981)
The Beatles (1972)
Al Bell (2011)

Marilyn and Alan Bergman (2013)
Emile Berliner (1987)
Chris Blackwell (2006)
Harold Bradley (2010)
Owen Bradley (2006)
John Cage (2016)
Hoagy Carmichael (2005)
Elliott Carter (2009)
Leonard and Phil Chess (2013)
Dick Clark (1990)
Aaron Copland (1981)
Don Cornelius (2005)

Pierre Cossette (1995)
Clive Davis (2000)
Walt Disney (1989)
Thomas A. Dorsey (1992)
Tom Dowd (2002)
Thomas A. Edison (1977)
Duke Ellington and Billy Strayhorn
    (1968)
Ahmet Ertegun (1993)
Nesuhi Ertegun (1995)
Christine M. Farnon (1992)
Wilma Cozart Fine (2011)
Fred Foster (2016)
Alan Freed (2002)
Milt Gabler (1991)
Kenneth Gamble and Leon Huff
    (1999)
George Gershwin and Ira Gershwin
    (1986)
Gerry Goffin and Carole King (2004)
Berry Gordy (1991)
Norman Granz (1994)
Florence Greenberg (2010)
Rick Hall (2014)
Oscar Hammerstein II (1992)
John Hammond (1971)
W.C. Handy (1993)
Lorenz Hart (1992)
Larry Hiller (1971)
Brian Holland, Lamont Dozier, and
    Edward Holland (1998)
Jac Holzman (2008)
Steve Jobs (2012)
Eldridge R. Johnson (1985)
Quincy Jones (1989)
Orrin Keepnews (2004)
Jerome Kern (1987)
Alan Jay Lerner and Frederick Loewe
    (1999)
Jerry Leiber and Mike Stoller (1999)

Goddard Lieberson (1979)
Alfred Lion (2005)
Alan Livingston (2013)
Alan Lomax (2003)
Bruce Lundvall (2011)
Barry Mann and Cynthia Weil (2015)
Arif Mardin (2001)
Jim Marshall (2014)
George Martin (1996)
Cosimo Matassa (2007)
Marian McPartland (2004)
Johnny Mercer (1987)
Walter C. Miller (2010)
Willie Mitchell (2008)
Dr. Robert Moog (1970)
Ennio Morricone (2014)
New York Philharmonic (2003)
Les Paul (1983)
Krzysztof Penderecki (1968)
Richard Perry (2015)
Sam Phillips (1991)
Cole Porter (1989)
Frances Preston (1998)
Phil Ramone (2001)
Richard Rodgers (1998)
Al Schmitt (2006)
George T. Simon (1993)
Frank Sinatra (1979)
Georg Solti and John Culshaw (1967)
Stephen Sondheim (2007)
Phil Spector (2000)
Leopold Stokowski (1977)
Chris Strachwitz (2016)
Dr. Billy Taylor (2005)
Allen Toussaint (2009)
Rudy Van Gelder (2012)
George Wein (2015)
Paul Weston (1971)
Jerry Wexler (1996)

TECHNICAL GRAMMY AWARD

Presented by vote of The Recording Academy's National Trustees, the Technical Grammy Award recognizes individuals and companies that have made contributions of outstanding technical significance to the field of recording. The Technical Grammy was first awarded in 1994.

INDIVIDUAL RECIPIENTS (induction year)

Emile Berliner (2014)
Ray Dolby (1995)
Tom Dowd (2006)
John Eargle (2008)
Thomas A. Edison (2010)
Geoff Emerick (2003)
Clarence "Leo" Fender (2009)
Dr. Harvey Fletcher (2016)
Ikutaro Kakehashi and Dave Smith (2013)
Ray Kurzweil (2015)

Roger Linn (2011)
George Massenburg (1998)
Dr. Robert Moog (2002)
Rupert Neve (1997)
Roger Nichols (2012)
Les Paul (2001)
Bill Putnam (2000)
Phil Ramone (2005)
Douglas Sax (2004)
David M. Smith (2007)
Dr. Thomas G. Stockham Jr. (1994)

COMPANY RECIPIENTS (induction year)

AKG Acoustics GmbH (2010)
Ampex Corporation (2008)
AMS Neve plc (2000)
Apple Computer, Inc. (2002)
Bell Labs/Western Electric (2006)
Celemony (2012)
Digidesign (2001)
EMT (2016)
Georg Neumann GmbH (1999)

JBL Professional (2005)
Lexicon (2014)
Royer Labs (2013)
Shure Incorporated (2003)
Solid State Logic, Ltd. (2004)
Sony/Philips (1998)
Universal Audio (2009)
Waves Audio (2011)
Yamaha Corporation (2007)

GRAMMY LEGEND AWARD

This Special Merit Award is presented on occasion by The Recording Academy to individuals or groups for ongoing contributions and influence in the recording field. The Grammy Legend Award was inaugurated in 1990.

RECIPIENTS (induction year)

Bee Gees (2003)
Johnny Cash (1991)
Aretha Franklin (1991)
Michael Jackson (1993)
Billy Joel (1991)
Elton John (1999)
Quincy Jones (1991)
Curtis Mayfield (1994)

Liza Minnelli (1990)
Willie Nelson (1990)
Luciano Pavarotti (1998)
Smokey Robinson (1990)
Frank Sinatra (1994)
Barbra Streisand (1992)
Andrew Lloyd Webber (1990)

MUSIC EDUCATOR AWARD

Launched by The Recording Academy and the Grammy Foundation in 2013, the Music Educator Award recognizes current educators (kindergarten through college, public and private schools) who have made a significant and lasting contribution to the field of music education and who demonstrate a commitment to the broader cause of maintaining music education in their schools. The recipient is approved by The Academy's Board of Trustees.

RECIPIENTS (induction year)

Jared Cassedy (2015)

Kent Knappenberger (2014)

Phillip Riggs (2016)

CREDITS

All tributes were originally printed in the GRAMMY Awards® program book.

The Allman Brothers Band, Lifetime Achievement Award, 2012; Kid Rock; © 2012 Kid Rock; page 9.

The Allman Brothers Band, Lifetime Achievement Award, 2012; Kenny Wayne Shepherd; © 2012 Kenny Wayne Shepherd; page 9.

Julie Andrews, Lifetime Achievement Award, 2011; Carol Burnett; © 2011 Carol Burnett; page 11.

George Avakian, Trustees Award, 2009; Dave Brubeck; © 2009 Dave Brubeck; page 13.

Clarence Avant, Trustees Award, 2008; Kenneth "Babyface" Edmonds; © 2008 Kenneth Edmonds; page 15.

Estelle Axton, Trustees Award, 2007; Isaac Hayes and David Porter; © 2007 Isaac Hayes and David Porter; page 17.

Burt Bacharach, Lifetime Achievement Award, 2008; Jackie DeShannon: © 2008 Jackie DeShannon; page 19.

Dave Bartholomew, Trustees Award, 2012; Dr. John; © 2012 Dr. John; page 21.

The Beatles, Lifetime Achievement Award, 2014; Danger Mouse; © 2014 Danger Mouse; page 23.

Bee Gees, Lifetime Achievement Award, 2015; Russ Titelman; © 2015 Russ Titelman; page 25.

Al Bell, Trustees Award, 2011; Huey Lewis; © 2011 Huey Lewis; page 27.

Marilyn and Alan Bergman, Trustees Award, 2013; Cynthia Weil and Barry Mann; © 2013 Cynthia Weil and Barry Mann; page 29.

Blind Boys of Alabama, Lifetime Achievement Award, 2009; Ben Harper; © 2009 Ben Harper; page 31.

Booker T. & The MG's, Lifetime Achievement Award, 2007; Dan Aykroyd; © 2007 Dan Aykroyd; page 33.

David Bowie, Lifetime Achievement Award, 2006; Win Butler; © 2006 Win Butler; page 35.

Owen Bradley, Trustees Award, 2006; k.d. lang; © 2006 k.d. lang; page 37.

Ruth Brown, Lifetime Achievement Award, 2016; Rep. John Conyers Jr.; © 2016 Rep. John Conyers Jr.; page 39.

John Cage, Trustees Award, 2016; Thurston Moore; © 2016 Thurston Moore; page 41.

Cab Calloway, Lifetime Achievement Award, 2008; John Lithgow; © 2008 John Lithgow; page 43.

Rosemary Clooney, Lifetime Achievement Award, 2002; Diana Krall; © 2002 Diana Krall; page 45.

Leonard Cohen, Lifetime Achievement Award, 2010; Kris Kristofferson; © 2010 Kris Kristofferson; page 47.

Ornette Coleman, Lifetime Achievement Award, 2007; Charlie Haden; © 2007 Charlie Haden; page 49.

Celia Cruz, Lifetime Achievement Award, 2016; Marc Anthony; © 2016 Marc Anthony; page 51.

Doris Day, Lifetime Achievement Award, 2008; Brian May; © 2008 Brian May; page 53.

Tom Dowd, Trustees Award, 2002; Eric Clapton; © 2002 Eric Clapton; page 55.

Earth, Wind & Fire, Lifetime Achievement Award, 2016; Big Boi; © 2016 Big Boi; page 57.

David "Honeyboy" Edwards, Lifetime Achievement Award, 2010; Mick Fleetwood; © 2010 Mick Fleetwood; page 59.

Clarence "Leo" Fender, Technical Grammy Award, 2009; Eric Johnson; © 2009 Eric Johnson; page 61.

Fred Foster, Trustees Award, 2016; Dolly Parton; © 2016 Dolly Parton; page 63.

The Four Tops, Lifetime Achievement Award, 2009; Lamont Dozier; © 2009 Lamont Dozier; page 65.

Glenn Gould, Lifetime Achievement Award, 2013; Lang Lang; © 2013 Lang Lang; page 67.

Grateful Dead, Lifetime Achievement Award, 2007; Sen. Patrick Leahy; © 2007 Sen. Patrick Leahy; page 69.

Florence Greenberg, Trustees Award, 2010; Dionne Warwick; © 2010 Dionne Warwick; page 71.

Buddy Guy, Lifetime Achievement Award, 2015; Jeff Beck; © 2015 Jeff Beck; page 73.

Charlie Haden, Lifetime Achievement Award, 2013; Flea; © 2013 Flea; pages 74–75.

Merle Haggard, Lifetime Achievement Award, 2006; Dwight Yoakam; © 2006 Dwight Yoakam; page 77.

Rick Hall, Trustees Award, 2014; Alicia Keys; © 2014 Alicia Keys; page 79.

Herbie Hancock, Lifetime Achievement Award, 2016; Chick Corea; © 2016 Chick Corea; page 81.

George Harrison, Lifetime Achievement Award, 2015; Tom Petty; © 2015 Tom Petty; page 83.

Roy Haynes, Lifetime Achievement Award, 2011; Page McConnell; © 2011 Page McConnell; page 85.

Buddy Holly, Lifetime Achievement Award, 1997; Marshall Crenshaw; © 1997 Marshall Crenshaw; pages 86-87.

Jac Holzman, Trustees Award, 2008; Judy Collins; © 2008 Judy Collins; page 89.

John Lee Hooker, Lifetime Achievement Award, 2000; Bonnie Raitt and Mary Katherine Aldin; © 2000 Bonnie Raitt and Mary Katherine Aldin; page 91.